ADVANCE PRAISE FOR *REALITY, MAGIC, AND OTHER LIES*

"*Reality, Magic, and Other Lies* is a comprehensive, sophisticated study of how fairy-tale and fantasy films contain more truth than so-called conventional realistic films. But this is not Greenhill's only accomplishment. She is a thoughtful and astute critic who pierces many false notions about magic and wonder, and on the basis of numerous, largely independent fairy-tale films, she demonstrates that their alternative worlds offer hope that we can change the depraved conditions of our present reality. Her book is, indeed, marvelous and opens our eyes to the power of fantasy in all its forms and aspects."
—JACK ZIPES, author of *The Enchanted Screen: The Unknown History of Fairy-Tale Films*

"Greenhill's lively and accessible book provides a pioneering venture into the wonders and truths of fairy-tale cinema. It is an excellent piece of scholarship. Precise interrogation of the films is skillfully matched with a dexterous discussion of broader, overarching themes. I am sure it will quickly become the definitive text in its field."
—LAURA HUBNER, professor of film, University of Winchester, UK

"Greenhill's brilliant close readings invite us to reflect anew on how some fairy-tale media unsettle expectations of reality, truth, wonder, magic, or science; how fairy-tale films do not always take the shape of fantasy; and how, by making "the impossible thinkable," fairy tales on screen can provide visual and narrative alternatives for imagining our bodies, communities, and futures. A must-read not only in fairy-tale studies but in film and media studies as well as in studies of the fantastic, *Reality, Magic, and Other Lies: Fairy-Tale Film Truths* promises to spark lively discussion within and across these fields."
—CRISTINA BACCHILEGA, University of Hawai'i at Mānoa

REALITY, MAGIC, AND OTHER LIES

SERIES IN FAIRY-TALE STUDIES

Series Editor
DON HAASE, Wayne State University

A complete listing of the advisory editors and the books in this series can be found online at wsupress.wayne.edu.

Reality, Magic, and Other Lies

FAIRY-TALE FILM TRUTHS

PAULINE GREENHILL

WAYNE STATE UNIVERSITY PRESS
Detroit

Copyright © 2020 by Wayne State University Press, Detroit, Michigan, 48201. All rights reserved. No part of this book may be reproduced without formal permission.

ISBN (paperback): 978-0-8143-4222-0
ISBN (hardcover): 978-0-8143-4782-9
ISBN (ebook): 978-0-8143-4223-7

LIBRARY OF CONGRESS CONTROL NUMBER: 2020935120

Published with the assistance of a fund established by Thelma Gray James of Wayne State University for the publication of folklore and English studies.

Wayne State University Press
Leonard N. Simons Building
4809 Woodward Avenue
Detroit, Michigan 48201–1309

Visit us online at wsupress.wayne.edu

CONTENTS

Acknowledgments   7

INTRODUCTION

1. Reality, Magic, and Other Lies: Fairy-Tale Film Truths   13

STUDIO, DIRECTOR, AND WRITER OEUVRES

2. Stop-Motion Animation and the Uncanny Real: LAIKA's *Coraline*, *ParaNorman*, *The Boxtrolls*, and *Kubo and the Two Strings*   33

3. Camera Obscura, Zoetrope, and Flying Monkey Drone: Science and Magic in Transcultural Fairy-Tale Media   66

4. Ça existe vraiment (It really exists)! *Babine*, *Ésimésac*, and Ostension at Saint-Élie-de-Caxton   94

THEMES AND ISSUES FROM THREE FAIRY TALES

5. "Hansel and Gretel" Films: Queer Death, Queer Failure, Family Horror, and Science Fiction   127

6. Witches, Mothers, a Vampire, and a Babadook: Women Coping with Crimes and Harms in "The Juniper Tree" Films   163

7. Transforming Cinderellas and Cinderfellas: Intersectional Perspectives   191

MOVING FORWARD?

8. Final Thoughts: To Overcome the Real   229

Filmography   233
References Cited   239
Index   259

ACKNOWLEDGMENTS

OVER THE YEARS THAT THIS BOOK HAS BEEN IN THE WORKS, LOTS OF people have helped make it possible. In many cases, folks helped in multiple areas, but I've chosen to thank them in only one location.

I hope the first two anonymous reviewers for Wayne State University Press will forgive my liberal use of their words, which succinctly address matters I had long-windedly grasped at and incisively state common issues and links I had less clearly identified.

Interviewees and filmmakers to whom I'm indebted include Annie Bédard, Josée Bédard, Kellie Benz, Matthew Bright, Danishka Esterhazy, Sean Garrity, Rebecca Gibson, Mary Harron, Ashley Hirt, David Kaplan, and Annika Pampel.

I received invaluable advice, support, and wisdom from Nyala Ali, Jaimz Asmundson, Sonia Bookman, Andrea Braithwaite, Jane Burns, Chris Carton, Andrew Loo Hong Chuang, Allison Craven, Roewan Crowe, Anne E. Duggan, Bill Ellis, Angela Failler, Paul-André Garceau, Parvin Ghorayshi, Fiona Green, Don Haase, Naomi Hamer, Laura Hubner, Nabila Huq, Vanessa Joosen, Anne Kustritz, Kirstian Lezubski, Sidney Eve Matrix, Jodi McDavid, Glenn Moulaison, Sadhana Naithani, Emma Nelson, Michelle Owen, Monique Raimbault, John Rieder, Liliane Rodriguez, Sharanpal Ruprai, Trish Salah, Cy-Thea Sand, Claudia Schwabe, Susanne Schwibs, Amanda Slack-Smith, Andrew Teverson, Catherine Tosenberger, Emily Toth, Francisco Vaz da Silva, Brittany Warman, Emma Whatman, and Ida Yoshinaga.

I thank coauthors and coconspirators Leah Claire Allen, Anita Best, Anne Brydon, Steven Kohm, Heidi Kosonen, Martin Lovelace, Sidney Eve Matrix, Vanessa Nunes, Jill Terry Rudy, Kay Turner, and Diane Tye, plus book-naming fairy godmother Marcie Fehr.

Research assistance came from Lauren Bosc, Alexandria van Dyck, Baden Gaeke Franz, Bryce Gallant, Jennifer Hammond Sebring, Yaoyao Liu, Kendra Magnus-Johnston, Allison Norris, Grace Paizen, Marie Raynard, Iryna Stepaniak, Evan Wicklund, and Jude Yallowega.

For support in getting this book ready for publication, I thank Wayne State University Press's editorial team, superhero copyeditor Anne Taylor, and indexer Kristy S. Gilbert of Looseleaf Editorial & Production.

Research fairy godmother Jennifer Cleary constantly came through with support, advice, and funding magic. Research for the book was funded by two Social Sciences and Humanities Research Council of Canada (SSHRC) grants, on which I am principal investigator—Standard Research Grant 410-2011-29, Fairy Tale Films: Exploring Ethnographic Perspectives; and Partnership Development Grant, 890-2013-17, Fairy Tale Cultures and Media Today, which also in part funded the International Fairy-Tale Filmography, iftf.uwinnipeg.ca, an invaluable resource for searching the films I discuss—and by Insight Grant 435-2016-1078, Frozen Justice: A Century of Crime in Canadian Film, on which Steven Kohm is principal investigator. I am thankful for SSHRC, as well as for support from the Office of Research, University of Winnipeg; Research Manitoba; and the Institute for Women's and Gender Studies.

To Tarsem, Ajit Singh, and Linda Lichter, I extend my gratitude for allowing and arranging for our use of the wonderful cover image from Tarsem's *The Fall*. I can't believe my luck!

This book owes what I trust is an obvious intellectual debt to two sterling fairy-tale media scholars, Cristina Bacchilega and Jack Zipes. But I am also fortunate to count Cristina and Jack as mentors and friends, for which I am eternally grateful. And, of course, I'm indebted to John and Neko.

Thanks to the following publishers for permission to use excerpts of my work originally published elsewhere:

Utah State University Press/University Press of Colorado
With coauthor Anne Brydon. 2010. "Mourning Mothers and Seeing Siblings: Feminism and Place in *The Juniper Tree*." In *Fairy Tale Films: Visions of Ambiguity*, edited by Pauline Greenhill and Sidney Eve Matrix, 116–36. Logan: Utah State University Press.

Wayne State University Press
2014. "*Le piège d'Issoudun*: Motherhood in Crisis." *Narrative Culture* 1 (1): 49–70.
2019. "Camera Obscura and Zoetrope: Tarsem and Magic/Reality in Transcultural Fairy Tale Film." *Narrative Culture* 6 (2): 119–39.

Fernwood Publishing
2017. "*Le piège d'Issoudun*: Fairy-Tale Murder." In *Screening Justice: Canadian Crime Films, Culture and Society*, edited by Steven A. Kohm, Sonia Bookman, and Pauline Greenhill, 218–39. Winnipeg: Fernwood.

Oxford University Press
2017. "Fairy-Tale Films." In *Oxford Research Encyclopedia of Literature*, edited by Paula Rabinowitz. Oxford: Oxford University Press. http://literature.oxfordre.com/view/10.1093/acrefore/9780190201098.001.0001/acrefore-9780190201098-e-83

Routledge
With coauthor Steven Kohm. 2016. "Fairy-Tale Films in Canada/Canadian Fairy-Tale Films." In *Fairy-Tale Films Beyond Disney: International Perspectives*, edited by Jack Zipes, Pauline Greenhill, and Kendra Magnus-Johnston, 246–16. New York: Routledge.

2019. "Sexes, Sexualities, and Gender in Cinematic North and South American Fairy Tales." In *The Fairy Tale World*, edited by Andrew Teverson, 248–59. London: Routledge.

ABC-CLIO
With coauthor Kay Turner. 2016. "Queer and Transgender Theory." In *Folktales and Fairy Tales: Traditions and Texts from Around the World,* edited by Anne E. Duggan and Donald Haase, 843–46. Copyright © 2016 by ABC-CLIO, LLC. All rights reserved. Reproduced with permission of ABC-CLIO, LLC, Santa Barbara, CA.

INTRODUCTION

1

Reality, Magic, and Other Lies

Fairy-Tale Film Truths

"NOW SIR, IF THAT'S NOT AS GOOD A LIE AS ANY MAN CAN TELL . . . I think that's as good a lie, now . . . as ever you heard" (quoted in Best, Lovelace, and Greenhill 2019, 223). After relating the traditional fairy tale he called "The Suit the Colour of the Clouds," storyteller Pius Power made the above comment to visiting folklorist Kenneth S. Goldstein.[1] Lies have a bad reputation these days, while stories, fairy tales, and folklore have retained interest or become even more popular in a multitude of media. And yet in English, the words "story," "fairy tale," and "folklore" can be used as synonyms for "lie." Indeed, many results from a search of "fairy tale reality" on the global library catalog WorldCat not only use "fairy tale" to mean "lie" but also reference deliberately misleading falsehoods. Searches for "Trump fairy tales" on Google include a number of the latter, as well as some play with the metaphor to ironic effect (see, e.g., Petri 2016; Allsop 2017), including the *Washington Post*'s biting "Pinocchio" rating system (see Kessler 2018), applied to false and/or misleading political claims. Of course, fairy tales as

---

1 "The Suit the Colour of the Clouds" combines tale types ATU 301 "The Three Stolen Princesses" and ATU 314 "Goldener." Power (1912–93) was born in Clattice Harbour, Placentia Bay, Newfoundland.

traditional and literary forms aren't actual lies, because though they're not strictly speaking truthful, they lack the falsehood's intention to deceive. Even a duplicitous narrative like the tall tale, which initially seeks credibility, stops being deceptive at its conclusion when the happenings described go far beyond believability.

To underline both connections and discontinuities between lies and truths in fairy-tale film, this work periodically breaks the academic frame to directly address the current politics of fairy tale and reality. The linkages within what Cristina Bacchilega calls "the politics of wonder" (2013)—the ways that fairy tales and fairy-tale media remain a propos to contemporary life, sometimes in resisting hegemony, sometimes in maintaining it—are a hallmark not only of her work but also of other fairy-tale scholars, mentors, and colleagues, including Jack Zipes. As the first section of this book—"Studio, Director, and Writer Oeuvres" (chapters 2, 3, and 4)—indicates, sometimes fairy-tale films engage with and challenge scientific or factual approaches to truth and reality. My examples show different modes for doing so, coming from the animation company LAIKA Entertainment; from the independent filmmaker Tarsem; and from the storyteller Fred Pellerin, looking at their creation, tropes, and ostension.[2] But as I show in the second section—"Themes and Issues from Three Fairy Tales" (chapters 5, 6, and 7)—fairy-tale film magic also explores real-life issues and experiences. Of course, all forms of fiction concern reality in some way, but I deal here with how specific stories—"Hansel and Gretel" (ATU 327A), "The Juniper Tree" (ATU 720), and "Cinderella" (ATU 510A)[3]—become unexpected (at least beyond the interdiscipline of fairy-tale studies) locations for shifting subjects and concerns of representation. These chapters address queer, feminist, and intersectional theoretical concerns.

Though broadly indicative of the ways fairy tales and films intersect, these specific examples frankly reflect my personal enthusiasms in the area of fairy-tale film studies. I'm not proposing a scientific system for analyzing such works in general. However, I note that having three takes on two areas

---

2 I discuss ostension, wherein stories—in any medium or form—engender events (rather than the more conventional opposite that events engender stories), in chapter 4.
3 The numbers from the Aarne-Thompson-Uther (ATU) series order tale types according to plot; they come from *The Types of International Folktales: A Classification and Bibliography*, an index by Hans-Jörg Uther published in 2004 based on earlier work by Antti Aarne and Stith Thompson.

echoes magical numbers from all sorts of traditions. And I hope that looking at less well-known films, including many from outside North America, helps to further discussion on the international scope of fairy-tale media, beyond the usual suspects.

Lutz Röhrich argues, "Every folktale is somehow connected to reality" (1991, 3)—which would include fairy tales. Even so, few consider fairy tales as literally true, as direct historical accounts of actual events (see, e.g., Tatar 1987, 39–57). The relationship between magic and science, between wonder and reality, has long been fraught.[4] Enlightenment thought would have magic and wonder exclusively the realm of the fanciful, thus of fairy tales, and would have science and reality decided a priori, by definition, as objective and true. But the skepticism associated with postmodern thought and critiques from diverse perspectives—including but not limited to anti-racist, decolonial, disability, and feminist theorizing—renders an easy distinction questionable. Further, the precise content of magic and science—which phenomena and ideas can be considered one and which the other—has shifted through history and across location.

For example, First Nations' sacred narratives, once dismissed by settler colonial scholarship as inherently fictional, metaphorical, and irrelevant, have recently been acknowledged as containing accounts confirming events also recognized by empirical Euro–North American science. Further, Indigenous knowledge simultaneously offers not just corroborating facts but also alternative perspectives and modes for contesting exploitative capitalist renderings of the earth as little more than a consumable resource (Cruikshank 2014). And so, in this book, I proffer the idea that fairy tales often address just those kinds of distinctions, making magic real and sometimes rendering science their proper realm. I suggest this idea applies not only to those traditional wonder stories canonically enumerated in the ATU series as 300–745, "Tales of Magic," but also to the literary and filmic creations of authors like

---

4   I define science, magic, reality, and wonder in conventional senses, though I understand all as contested. Science is the result of processes of explaining phenomena by prediction, testing, and explanation of physical causes. Magic includes practices and effects usually described in terms of supernatural forces and causes often associated with the fictional. Reality exists or appears to exist beyond the mind, usually but not always observable and comprehensible, in contrast to idea(l)s and concepts that remain as thoughts. Wonder relates to the miraculous and astonishing. Magic and wonder have affinities to one another, as do science and reality.

Fred Pellerin and auteurs[5] like Tarsem, particularly but not exclusively in their mediated versions. I thus consider some ways in which fairy tales in all their mediated forms deconstruct the world and sometimes offer alternative views for peaceful, appropriate, intersectionally multifaceted[6] encounters with humans, nonhuman animals, and the rest of the environment.

While fairy tales can be oral (told by people in different geographical locations and at various historical times up to the present) and/or literary (written by known authors), they concern the fantastic, the magical, the dark, the dreamy, the wishful, and the wonderful (IFTF 2014–).[7] Yet, as I argue here, not all events in fairy tales and fairy-tale media are beyond reality or realism. Indeed, it's their manifest connection to current experience (as indicated, for example, by "Trump fairy tales") that makes these apparently fictional texts in all media sometimes controversial. I contend that their precise relationships to the realities of their creators and potential hearers, readers, and viewers are worth exploring, as I do here, even if no single perspective results. Fairy tales and fairy-tale media can reflect a reality that's already out there, and/or they can seek to influence the creation of a better world.

Often the express aim of fairy tales and fairy-tale media is to encourage their audiences to believe in, and sometimes to reproduce, the relationships and world they depict, even when that communicated domain is fictional. Think, for example, of Nicole Kassell's 2004 film *The Woodsman*, which uses "Little Red Riding Hood" (ATU 333) to present "an alternative and inclusive approach to managing sex offenders in the community" (Bennett 2008, 363;

---

5   Auteur theory, developed in the 1950s, not only makes a film director the equivalent to an author for a written work but refers in particular to directors whose oeuvre suggests a unified point of view (see Stam 2000, 83–88). Later work did not entirely dispense with that perspective but usefully critiqued, for example, the notion of a single primary responsibility within what is always a collaborative creative work (see, e.g., Sayad 2014). Note that the idea of authorship itself came under criticism especially from Michel Foucault's influential article "What Is an Author," originally published in 1969 (reprinted 1980, 113–38).
6   Intersectionality, famously coined by feminist legal scholar Kimberlé Williams Crenshaw and used to refer to the ways that race and sex/gender intertwine as vectors of oppression (1991), is now used by feminists to describe how a multitude of identity aspects—adding, for example, class, ability, and sexual orientation—complexly interact in the development of social inequality (see, e.g., Chávez and Griffin 2012).
7   For more information about definitions and distinctions, see "About Filmography" n.d.

see also Kohm and Greenhill 2014). C. Lewis Holton suggests that fairy tales could be used therapeutically in correctional environments, even arguing that to reach "any goal that seeks to engender positive change . . . we must be prepared to work magic to provide the resources necessary to reconcile such ideals with reality. But have magic and reality ever been compatible? Certainly; *once upon a time* . . ." (1995, 220; emphasis and ellipsis in original). Fairy tales in all media play with and through reality and fiction, sometimes offering alternatives to the conventional and expected in the relationships and spheres they depict.

Just before the turn of the millennium, Jack Zipes famously said in his first pronouncement on defining fairy-tale films:

> Just as we know, almost intuitively, that a particular narrative is a fairy tale when we read it, it seems we know immediately that a particular film is a fairy tale when we see it. . . . It is almost as though it were natural that there be fairy-tale films since fairy tales are so much part of our cultural heritage as oral and literary tales. (1996, 1)

I have to agree that on some level fairy-tale film is in the eye of the beholder—and I'm sure some beholders (or readers) will have difficulty taking as fairy tale many of the movies I work with here. But I continually return to Kevin Paul Smith's useful structural exploration of the ways that fairy-tale parts, wholes, and diegetic contexts make their way into all kinds of media (2007). The diversity of modes that Smith identifies for quoting and including fairy tales means that the ways they can be used are multifold. The inclusion of fairy tales in media varies from the direct employment of a full narrative to the quotation of a story element.

Using Smith's classification for literary fairy tales, fairy-tale media intertexts can draw on their hypotexts[8] by including explicit reference in the title—for example, Duane Journey's film *Hansel & Gretel Get Baked* (2013, discussed in chapter 5); using implicit reference in the title—for example, Tale of Tales' video game *The Path*, alluding to Red Riding Hood's dangerous

---

8 Gérard Genette defines that "hypertextuality refers to any relationship uniting a text B (which I shall call the hypertext) to an earlier text A (I shall, of course, call it the hypotext), upon which it is grafted in a manner that is not that of commentary" (1997, 5). Intertextuality is a contested term, but it is used here to refer to texts in any media that refer to other texts (Allen 2011), in this case, specifically fairy-tale versions.

trail through the woods; involving explicit incorporation into the text—such as Micheline Lanctôt's film *Le piège d'Issoudun* (2003, discussed in chapter 6), which presents alongside its realist narrative of a mother murdering her children a theatrical play of "The Juniper Tree"; containing implicit incorporation into the text—as when Steven Spielberg's *A.I.: Artificial Intelligence* (2001, discussed in chapter 5) has the mechanical child David's human mother abandon him in the woods, as do Hansel and Gretel's parents; discussing fairy tales—as in the "Once Upon a Crime" episode of the American television show *Castle* (2009–16), when the writer and police dispute what fairy tales *really* mean; and invoking fairy-tale chronotopes (settings and/or environments)—as in the portions of Tarsem's *The Fall* (2006, discussed in chapter 3) co-narrated by the two main characters, located in the realm of magical encounters but actually filmed in a range of diverse, international locations. Alternatively, creators may revision a story, sometimes with a new spin, as when Danishka Esterhazy relocates "Hansel and Gretel" to millennial Winnipeg, Canada, with two underclass children trying to find their way home in *H & G* (2013); or filmmakers may create an entirely new tale—like *El laberinto del fauno* (*Pan's Labyrinth*, directed by Guillermo del Toro, 2006), which is not directly based on any specific previous literary or traditional story (see, e.g., Hubner 2018, 159–90).

Not all audiences will necessarily recognize the presence of fairy tales in a film they are watching—and it need not matter whether viewers actually identify general or specific hypotexts. But these stories can provide another level for appreciation and analysis. For example, the creators of *Hard Candy* (2005), including director David Slade, claim that the film's links to "Little Red Riding Hood" were unconscious decisions, afterthoughts, and/or coincidences. Yet mapping the two primary characters, Hayley (played by Ellen Page) and Jeff (played by Patrick Wilson), as alternating Reds and wolves considerably nuances explorations of the range of harms and crimes the film addresses, their effects, and the appropriate and inappropriate consequences. The characters' ambivalence—both Red and the wolf can be victims and victimizers—reflects back not only on the well-known traditional narrative but also on other filmed versions (discussed in Kohm and Greenhill 2014, 275–76).

And, of course, the uses of fairy tales don't always easily and simply fit into Smith's structures; many (including the examples above) don't reflect only one mode; nor are they always absolutely clearly identifiable. For example, the title *H & G* is potentially an explicit reference to Hansel and Gretel or an implicit one to the parallel names of the two main child characters, Harley (played by Annika Elyse Irving) and Gemma (played by Breazy Diduck-Wilson). In any case, I count all such uses as legitimate versions of fairy tales and thus possible subjects for my discussion in this book. And chapter by chapter I seek to explore the different ways that understanding fairy-tale intertexts can contribute to cinematic texts, performances, and contexts, including such areas as audience expectations, narrative structures, visual elements, and themes.

Real Fairy-Tale Origins

Even beyond fairy-tale revisions of magic and science and their uses, the concept that these traditional stories themselves have a single, potentially identifiable source—that they're not works primarily (re)created in the crucible of oral tradition—links to the idea of fairy-tale reality. Long part of folkloristic and fairy-tale scholarship, historic-geographic studies sought to specify times and locations of sources for traditional narratives. Yet that theoretical perspective nevertheless presumed that approximate dates and locations would be the most accurate descriptions possible. When the basics behind that point of view are reprised by recent scholars like Ruth Bottigheimer (2009) and Willem de Blécourt (2012), the origin of traditional narratives locates within elite cultures and with particular literary figures. This idea has met with considerable resistance, both empirical and ideological, from a variety of academics concerned with traditional culture (e.g., Ben-Amos 2010a, 2010b; Vaz da Silva 2010; Ziolkowski 2010; Zipes 2012, 158–70).

The notion that fairy-tale origins can be detailed—perhaps even scientifically rescued from oral tradition's vague, even magical, associations with intangible transmission by way of the spoken word from one memory to another—has also made its way into popular culture, as Vanessa Joosen's work (2011) might predict. It's not only "historians [who] have looked for connections beyond ordinary conditions, to identify actual events and known individuals at the root of a certain fairy tale," says Marina Warner (2014, 85)—so have literary scholars and folklorists. But Warner joins the skeptics resistant to the idea of single elite sources, warning that "the thirst for stable genealogies . . . can never be appeased" (88).

Thus, in a meta-swerve into the historicized fictionalization of a real search for documented, specified origins—the truth behind the fairy tale—a recent series of murder mystery novels by Maia Chance, entitled "Fairy Tale

Fatal," features a nineteenth-century scholar who seeks to authenticate a variety of objects and people as traditional narrative forebears. They include the discovery of "the suspected remains of Snow White's cottage, along with a disturbing dwarf skeleton," as well as a victim "poisoned by an apple" in *Snow White Red-Handed* (2014); a woman supposed to have a direct kinship to Cinderella in *Cinderella Six Feet Under* (2015); evidence of a preternatural animal with characteristics of human and boar in *Beauty, Beast, and Belladonna* (2016); and a woman "trapped in a morbid lethargy from which she cannot be woken and which—so her parents insist—was caused by the prick of an enchanted spindle" in *Sleeping Beauty, Borrowed Time* (2017) (quotations from "Fairy Tale Fatal" n.d.).

Other media abound with similar examples, fictions within which fairy tales have their magic excised and replaced with purported historical truths. A well-known example is Andy Tennant's 1998 film *Ever After: A Cinderella Story*, with its divestment of supernatural elements and the frame narration as history by a French woman to the Brothers Grimm of her ancestor's story as that of the real Cinderella. Terry Gilliam's (2005) *The Brothers Grimm* is more equivocal, beginning with the Grimms as bunkum artists who discover that some of the mysteries they encounter are actually linked with the supernatural. More recent examples include the television series *Grimm* (2011–17), with the premise that the famous brothers were in a long line of hunters of the supernatural creatures described in their own and others' collections, and director Eli Roth's *The House with a Clock in Its Walls* (2018), where the wise but troubled witch Florence Zimmerman (played by Cate Blanchett) describes the Black Forest as "the place where the Grimms wrote their histories." When young Lewis Barnavelt (played by Owen Vaccaro) responds, "You mean their fairy tales?" she gives him a pitying look, by which she conveys the sense that he and others have long been duped into thinking those narratives mere fantasy.

And yet, beyond fictional media, it's easy to recognize the truth in fairy tales on a metaphorical or symbolic level, but their imaginary nature is unquestionable—or is it? Take this narrative, for instance:

> Once a man and his wife were sitting by the entrance to their house. They had a roasted chicken in front of them and were about to eat it when the man saw his father coming toward them. So the man quickly grabbed the chicken and hid it because he did not want to give him any. The old man came, had a drink, and went away. As the son reached to put the roasted

chicken back on the table, he found that it had turned into a toad, which then sprang onto his face, sat there, and would not leave him. If anyone tried to take it off, the toad would look at the person viciously as if it wanted to spring right into his face too. So nobody dared touch it. And the ungrateful son had to feed the toad every day; otherwise it would have eaten away part of his face. Thus the son wandered about the world without a moment of rest.

However much this story might provide a scenario for a horror film, offer a magic realist narrative, or represent a dream screaming for Freudian analysis, it's a folktale in the Brothers Grimm's *Children's and Household Tales* (1857 edition, Zipes 2003, 457). Like many other stories therein, it falls outside the classic fairy-tale canon of "Tales of Magic" (Uther 2004, 1:7–15). And it's no conventional Disneyfied fairy tale, lacking an innocent persecuted heroine, a rescuing prince, and a heterosexual happy ever after. Somewhat bizarrely, the ATU index categorizes this narrative under "Realistic Tales" (ATU 980D). It hardly fits most notions of realism; few people expect their dinner to wreak vengeance for their miserliness by turning into an amphibian that attaches itself to their face. But the practice of failing to provide for aged parents is, sadly, all too accurate. Thus stories like this one hold simultaneously true and not true aspects. Indeed, just about any of their features can be understood as factual or counterfactual, on different levels of understanding and analysis.

Fairy-Tale Truth: Metaphor, Fact, Science?

Warner indicates that fairy-tale truth relates to the stories' evocation of problems that are all too real—"poverty, scarcity, hunger, anxiety, lust, greed, envy, cruelty, and all of the grinding consequences in the domestic scene and larger picture. . . . The wishful thinking and the happy ending are rooted in sheer misery" (2014, 74). She contends that "fairy tales, while being utterly fantastical in presentation, are forthright in their realism as to what happens and can happen" (78). But she also questions, "do [fairy tales] interact with reality and shape it?" (81). Thus, Warner joins fairy-tale scholars who see the form's truth more in its address to realistic problems than in its reference to specific empirical fact.

Skepticism about the necessary unreality of phenomena that now count as magic and wonder, however, may be relatively recent. As Suzanne

Magnanini discusses, the fairy-tale collections of Giovan Francesco Straparola in the sixteenth century, of Giambattista Basile in the mid-seventeenth century, and of other sources from the beginning of the Enlightenment (1600s to the end of the 1700s) include not only "valiant lads [who] slay dragons and hydras" but also "women [who] give birth to animals, a young girl [who] sprouts a penis, and an ogre [who] believes that his flatulence possesses reproductive powers" (2008, 3). Though these might now been seen as literal impossibilities, Magnanini argues that "the literary fairy tale was born at a time when marvels were not relegated to fantastic fictions, but swirled around the courts, academies, churches, and public squares of Europe" (4). She argues that "the first literary fairy tales" were linked "to scientific description of five types of monstrous generation: spontaneous female-to-male sex change . . . ; the power of the maternal imagination to deform the fetus *in utero* . . . ; the birth of animal-human hybrids . . . ; the manufacture of artificial monsters . . . ; and the power of the wind to impregnate animals and plants" (7). She concludes that "from its origins the literary fairy tale functioned as a locus for the contestation or affirmation of scientific theory and practice" (7). In an epilogue, Magnanini notes the gendered ways that this exploration manifested.

Similarly, Kathryn A. Hoffman discusses how monkey girls, hog-faced gentlewomen, and other apparently hybrid creatures served as "marvel[s] that live[d] in the spaces of connection among fairy tales, fairgrounds, cabinets of curiosities, and medical literature" (2005, 67) in early modern Europe. Some of the phenomena she discusses, recalling the semi-fictitious Brothers Grimm's ostensive marvels at the beginning of Gilliam's film about them, are fabrications in the sense of being created to deceive, but also in the sense of being created as mimetic physical objects; others, like women whose bodies are hairy beyond an expected norm, clearly exist. Hoffman ultimately argues that "within that mix of threads . . . anomalous bodies became tellable, collectible, and commercial" (82). I would go even further and assert that the telling not only of anomalous bodies but also of a variety of "impossibles" (events, bodies, and so forth that cannot be created or actualized) in the context of fairy tales and other traditional forms renders those seeming impossibles thinkable.[9] Thus, flying on carpets may prefigure flying in airplanes, and the magical sex change in "The Shift of Sex" intellectually anticipates present-day transpeople who actualize their senses of themselves in

---

9   See, for example, Greenhill (1997) on impossibles in traditional folksongs.

somatic transfiguration (see, e.g., Greenhill and Anderson-Grégoire 2014). Of Magnanini's inventory, then, female-to-male sex change (but also male-to-female), the creation of animal-human hybrids, and the manufacture of artificial creatures have clearly existed in the world for some time (see Haraway 1997; Jörg 2003).

In a move similarly connecting fairy tales to significant aspects of daily life, Dorothy Noyes compares them to the social science of economics, in particular, microeconomic game theory, suggesting that both are "exercises in modeling the behavior of individuals . . . with how individuals in competition with other individuals decide among their options" (2015, 3). She concludes that "the oral tales collected in the nineteenth century constitute . . . a space of analysis and debate among poor people evaluating their life options. Later mass-produced fairy tales, though highly diverse in surface decor and variably appropriated, often urge their audience to choose what has been chosen for it" (4). As I discuss below, however, examples from non-mainstream media—but also, sometimes, from Hollywood and the mainstream—can offer more than just encouragements to accept and conform; they can be critical, providing possibilities for resistant, alternative worlds.

In this book, then, I explore several examples of the rendering of fairy-tale magic in terms of metaphor, fact, and science. Most of my cases come from fairy-tale cinema (that is, films intended for theatrical release), but I occasionally draw on materials created for television (where I find compelling reasons, such as when work is produced by the same director) and on materials perhaps more fantasy and/or magical realism than fairy tale per se, which draw on similar processes and progressive ideas.

Film Truth: Material and Immaterial Realities

David Butler approvingly discusses "fantasy's presence at the heart of human creativity. . . . The basic principle of fantasy, *imagining a world different to the one we know*, is at work in the act of speculation" (2009, 4; my emphasis).[10] His examples of fantasy include a number of films that most fairy-tale scholars

---

10 See also Claudia Schwabe's (2014, esp. 294–300) discussion of different forms of what she calls "magic realism" especially as it is used on television: one world without threshold (e.g., *Grimm*); one world with threshold (e.g., the Harry Potter series); two worlds with threshold (e.g., *Once Upon a Time*); and neo-magical realism, in which two worlds are linked through the main protagonist (e.g., *Pan's Labyrinth*).

would include in their area (and that also fit Smith's classifications above), including del Toro's *Pan's Labyrinth,* in which magic and reality coincide, and Gilliam's Alice in Wonderland–themed *Tideland* (2005), in which "fantasy is a means of making sense of and surviving in [the] world" (8).

Fantasy is a popularly accepted film genre (including, for example, on the Internet Movie Database, or IMDb), but fairy tale is not. Given Smith's inventory of the variety of fairy-tale references in creative works, that absence is not surprising, and I prefer to call fairy-tale media a form not a genre. Academics generally reject fantasy as a genre for movies because "it embraces too many types of film" (18); their idea of genre films comprises "those commercial feature films which, through repetition and variation, tell familiar stories with familiar characters in familiar situations" (Grant 2012, xviii).[11] Fairy-tale films as I discuss them don't fit the latter description, including as they do works as diverse as *Kubo and the Two Strings* (directed by Travis Knight, 2016, discussed in chapter 2)—an animated reflection on community; *The Babadook* (directed by Jennifer Kent, 2014, discussed in chapter 6)—a supernatural horror depiction of motherhood; and *Dancehall Queen* (directed by Don Letts and Rick Elgood, 1997, discussed in chapter 7)—a "Cinderella" story set in Jamaican street culture. Butler discusses fairy-tale films as a (sub)type of fantasy (2009, 48–58). But he includes in separate sections Arabian nights films (58–70)—which would by my definition fit into fairy-tale film; and the "'film blanc' or supernatural rom-com" (45–48) and sword and sorcery (70–76) film—some examples of which would overlap with my definition. As I'll discuss in chapter 5, however, the familiar film genres of horror and science fiction often take fairy-tale form.

Butler further rejects the idea of fantasy as pure escapism while affirming that escape is not "necessarily a bad or irresponsible thing" (96) and concomitantly that "naturalism is no guarantor of truth (however we define that concept)" (97). Fantasy, like fairy tale, can be used to "perpetuate dominant beliefs and the status quo" (99) or encourage a more critical perspective.

---

11 Because of the great complexity of the concept, as well as the fact that I do not consider the fairy tale or fairy-tale film as genres, I do not address genre theory in any detail. John Frow (2006) provides a valuable introduction to the idea of genre as both productive and reproductive. And specifically for film, see, for example, Silvia Dibeltulo and Ciara Barrett (2018), Raphaëlle Moine (2008), James Monaco (2000), Lúcia Nagib and Anne Jerslev (2014), Roy Stafford (2014), and Robert Stam (2000), as well as a multitude of works on specific film genres, including material on horror and science fiction, as discussed in chapter 5.

While not assuming that all escape is useful, says Butler, "the dissatisfaction with the real world or acknowledgement of its failings is something that fantasy has often dealt with in a subversive form" that seems "superficially harmless because [it is] assumed to be not real, assumed to be mere fantasy or child's play" (102). He points out that "genuine subversion in film fantasy . . . is more likely to be found in the work of independent filmmakers with considerable creative control than big-budget mainstream productions" (103). Not surprisingly, then, the majority of works I examine here in detail come from independent cinema and from smaller production houses. The bigger the budget, and the closer the film to Hollywood and the mainstream, the greater the likelihood that any subversion creators put into their work will be deeply buried and profoundly coded.[12] The greater also is the likelihood that alternatives to the status quo are presented as unreal or unrealistic, perhaps even alternative precisely *because* they are unreal or unrealistic.

But what makes a film fantasy in the first place? Tzvetan Todorov sees the fantastic as the "inexplicable centre-ground between" the marvelous—"clearly supernatural and genuine magic"—and the uncanny—wherein a "natural explanation can be offered in which all strangeness is generated by unconscious forces (our own psyche)" (Butler 2009, 25). Todorov looks at specific types of texts that have fantasy, magical, and/or fairy-tale elements, drawing on the uncanny as the hesitation between what is (or might be) real and what is (or might be) imagined. He distinguishes the fantastic tale from the marvelous, wherein characters accept the magical universe but so do readers, recognizing the tale's universe as imaginary, and thus magic as normal within it.

Thus, for my examples above, *Pan's Labyrinth* invokes the marvelous—the magic of the faun (played by Doug Jones) affects the real world—and *Tideland* brings the uncanny—Jeliza-Rose (played by Jodelle Ferland) is the sole conduit for magical happenings, which appear in her mind alone. The fantastic always involves hesitancy "between a natural and supernatural

---

12 Coding comes in "a set of signals—words, forms, behaviours, signifiers of some kind—that protect the creator from the consequences of openly expressing particular messages" (Radner and Lanser 1993, 3). In particular, with implicit coding, the message's meaning, and even whether or not coding is present, remains arguable. Filmmakers may intend to present a subversive viewpoint, but since directly expressing that message can bring dangers (including being socially or economically unwise), "performance is meant to pass for an uncoded activity" (7).

explanation of the events described" (Todorov 1970, 33). Butler points out that mainstream cinema "is geared toward a strong sense of narrative closure and clarification of any unresolved issues, leaving the inexplicable and uncertain nature of Todorov's fantastic at odds with dominant filmmaking traditions" (2009, 26). Thus, many independent and alternative fairy-tale films implicate the uncanny,

> concerned with the strange, weird and mysterious, with a flickering sense (but not conviction) of something supernatural. The uncanny involves feelings of uncertainty, in particular the reality of who one is and what is being experienced. . . . It is a crisis of the natural, touching upon everything that one might have thought was "part of nature": one's own nature, human nature, the nature of reality and the world . . . something familiar unexpectedly arising in a strange and unfamiliar context, or . . . something strange and unfamiliar unexpectedly arising in a familiar context. (Royle 2003, 1)[13]

Many fairy-tale films obviously offer the marvelous, the fantastic, and the uncanny. Though as I've delineated them (following Smith), many develop an apparently fictional world that's nevertheless intended to be understood as realistic, the cinematic form makes them inherently uncanny. I recall while channel surfing on television many years ago unexpectedly coming across a lecture by a friend who had been killed less than a week before in a terrible accident. While there was an obviously mundane, rational explanation for my dead friend's sudden appearance in my living room, the sense of manifest doubling, of his simultaneous presence and absence, was palpable. Even in the most apparently prosaic, realist documentary film, there's the "reality" behind it, what actually happened in the world as a scene was being produced. But that actuality is inevitably very different from what appears on the screen. Of course, all films have multiple layers. For example, the reality of the production of the sound and/or extra-diegetic music can be spatially and temporally separate from the final product, and the editing of scenes that may have been shot on different days and/or in different locations turns them into a single seamless event.

---

13 I sketch out some basic ideas relating to fantasy. Readers seeking to sort out the specifics of each discussed theorist's perspective will need to examine their work.

These relate to cinema as itself magic, not just to any narrative it recounts and its connection or lack thereof to reality. As Rosemary Jackson notes:

> The fantastic problematizes vision (is it possible to trust the seeing eye?) and language (is it possible to trust the recording, speaking "I"?). . . . In . . . cinema, these problems are re-focused around the vision of the camera "eye" which can produce similar conflation of "objective" or documentary recording and an implication of "subjective" vision. . . . Or there can be a presentation of "unreal" combinations of objects and events as "real" through the camera eye itself—in this sense, the cinematic process itself could be called "fantastic." (2003, 30–31)

Jessica Tiffin offers a parallel analysis, indicating that

> while apparently offering the real, [film] is a fertile ground for trickery, in which apparently real objects may disappear, reappear, change size or orientation, change shape. . . . The authority of the camera is such that the impossible takes on the same status as the realistic, which is . . . a good working definition of magic. . . . Film powerfully realizes the transcendence over reality with which magical narrative is intrinsically concerned. (2009, 181)

Tiffin echoes commonly held concerns that "a visual medium can be crippling to . . . imaginative exercise" (182) or that films can "supplant all other versions" (183) of fairy tales—trepidations I do not share. Film requires a *different* kind of "imaginative exercise" than hearing or reading a tale; and while Disney in particular maintains hegemony over many fairy tales, resistance is possible even to the most conventional texts.[14] Tiffin usefully points out how different viewing contexts—in cinemas or at home—relate to diverse experiences. But linking them to folk culture, she invokes by implication notions of authenticity or lack thereof of film versions of fairy tales, again, as suggested above, a perspective I do not share.

---

14   I think, for example, of the ways that transchildren, especially transgirls, relate to "The Little Mermaid" or, more accurately, to Disney's *The Little Mermaid* (directed by John Musker and Ron Clements, 1989), as a girl whose embodiment, like theirs, doesn't match their self-concept (see, e.g., Hurley 2014; Spencer 2014).

And, so, I offer here six possible alternatives to the canonical separation of fairy tales as magic and wonder from fairy tales as reality and science. In the next chapter, I explore how one company that produces fairy-tale-inflected feature films using stop-motion animation—LAIKA Entertainment—incorporates play (and work) with the interactions between their films' creation and content. Particularly in their distinctive closing credit sequences, the real world becomes part of the fantastic, and fantasy is expressed by invoking the real world—which also intervenes when their films' audiences raise concerns about casting choices or reflect upon the philosophical issues implicated.

Next, I look at live-action works by the auteur Tarsem. Two of his films and one of his television productions present diegetic real worlds that require fantasy as the solution to their problems and use specific tools to render apparent magic and wonder as what turn out to be scientifically conventional productions. For Tarsem, rather than contrasting, science and magic coexist, working in the same contexts—sometimes at cross-purposes and sometimes in harmony. Then I consider two Canadian magic realist/fairy-tale films, *Babine* (2008) and *Ésimésac* (2012), by Quebec director Luc Picard based on the original stories of oral/written teller Fred Pellerin, that link to an actual location. Saint-Élie-de-Caxton (where Pellerin was born and currently lives) appears within the films' diegesis, and many of their characters are based on actual residents. But Pellerin's stories and the films so resonate for Quebecois that they recreate aspects of them at crucial points in their lives. Further, Saint-Élie-de-Caxton has become a tourist attraction, which calls on the real and fictional aspects alike of Pellerin's stories and the films.

Next are three chapters that discuss different takes on traditional tales. "Hansel and Gretel" films with supernatural or science fiction content offer reflections on individual and collective human survival. Two are explicitly apocalyptic, involving conclusions in which *Homo sapiens* has been eliminated completely. All implicate concepts of queer families and what theorists have called the queer death drive and queer failure; they offer, then, opportunities for criticisms of mainstream culture's dismissal of queer as apocalyptic.

I next turn to four films by women directors riffing on "The Juniper Tree," which use the metaphor of vision to explore what is real within their diegesis. Using witchlike figures who themselves work at the cusp of magic and reality, the films offer views of justice, often in the realm of the preternatural or supernatural. But these movies also consider the value of witnessing, disclosing, and explaining the origins of crimes and harms against children, often in terms of coping with them.

My discussion of generally non-mainstream "Cinderella" films explores the ways in which their title characters are not the (female, White, heterosexual, European) people whom Euro–North American audiences may expect to find. In particular, they more accurately represent the actual international diversity of races/ethnicities, genders, sexes, sexualities, and languages—and the need for just and fair access to privileges simply assumed by White middle- and upper-class Euro–North Americans.

I discuss several crucial scenes in the films, especially in terms of their visuals. Although proverbially seeing is believing, these works deconstruct the notion of relying on one's senses to know what is real and what is not. In film, as already indicated, the audience must use its judgment to decide whether or not, or more crucially, precisely how, reality is being represented. As Warner puts it, "fantasy often exercises a stronger pull than reality" (2014, 91). Noyes contends that "the fairy-tale plot must . . . catch up with the changing horizon of the low-resourced liberal individual: the disappearance of life-long employment and social safety nets, the rise of debt and difficulty of a living wage, an environment pushed beyond its carrying capacity, and a body politic collapsing under its own weight" (2015, 20). In dystopian times, magic, the extraordinary, and wonder can be as necessary as science, the ordinary, and reality.

STUDIO, DIRECTOR, AND WRITER OEUVRES

2

Stop-Motion Animation and the Uncanny Real

LAIKA's *Coraline, ParaNorman, The Boxtrolls*, and *Kubo and the Two Strings*

I FELL IN LOVE WITH STOP-MOTION ANIMATION WHEN I SAW NICK Park and Peter Lord's *Chicken Run* (2000). The film's combination of a variety of fascinating female characters; the unsentimental—indeed sometimes brutal—representation of animals as thinking, feeling beings oppressed by humans; and Julia Sawalka's voicing of courageous protagonist Ginger makes it a favorite despite my usual preference for live action. In *Chicken Run*, the visuals support the ideology: among other manifestations, chickens have an innate sense of justice; they have literal, but also figurative, teeth; though ostensibly unpromising as heroes, they act as such; they build amazing mechanical contraptions; and they literally, but also figuratively, outshine their dreary context (as discussed in Halberstam 2011, 27–52). *Chicken Run* is produced by the British Aardman Animations, famous for both short and feature-length films that may be accessible to children but are also compelling for adults. Aardman movies tend to be set in a present-time, realistic mode, even if they feature magical creatures like loquacious chickens, a were-rabbit, or Santa Claus. These movies' representation of talking nonhuman creatures, however, is their primary feature shared with fairy tales.

In contrast, the American studio LAIKA Entertainment has (as of 2018) produced four feature films, all incorporating fairy-tale content. *ParaNorman* (directed by Chris Butler, 2012) includes "Sleeping Beauty" (ATU 410) as a bedtime story for a ghost; *Coraline* (directed by Henry Selick, 2009), based on Neil Gaiman's novella (2002), employs a recent literary fairy tale, as does *The Boxtrolls* (directed by Graham Annable and Anthony Stacchi, 2014), based on Alan Snow's novel *Here Be Monsters!* (2005); and the Japanese culture–themed *Kubo and the Two Strings* (directed by Travis Knight, 2016) creates an original wonder tale.[1] According to the IMDb, LAIKA's first appearance was in their participation in the Tim Burton and Mike Johnson co-creation *Corpse Bride* and in making the short *Moongirl* (both 2005).[2] (The latter was directed by Selick, director of another Burton fairy-tale vehicle, *The Nightmare Before Christmas*, 1993.) In this chapter I focus on the concluding moments of LAIKA's four feature productions. In these closing segments, animators deconstruct the stop-motion animation used in the film to display its uncanny nature. These are flashes when revelation of the science/reality behind the magic/fiction renders their processes in terms of, and in service of, one another: fairy-tale magical reality.

LAIKA and Uncanny Real Animation

Animation, as described by Paul Wells, is "a cross-disciplinary and interdisciplinary art and craft, embracing drawing, sculpture, model-making, performance, dance, computer science, social science and much more. It has a distinctive language that enables it to create the art of the impossible" (2006, 6–7). Stop motion, sometimes called 3-D stop motion since other forms like hand-drawn animation also take advantage of the illusion that individual shots displayed in sequence produce what appears as movement, uses "figures with wire skeletons [that] can be moved and fixed into different positions. The movements are filmed frame by frame.... In stop-motion the

---

1   Knight also directed *Bumblebee* (2018), and IMDb lists LAIKA Entertainment as an uncredited production company for that film.
2   Joanne Clarke Dillman critiques *Corpse Bride*'s incorporation of the violent murder of its title figure (2014, 44–53) in the context of a discussion of other women dead by violence in films.

object is moved in small increments between individually photographed frames" (Pikkov 2010, 21). Wells discusses how in animation, bodies, animal as well as human (and other), "become *forms* subject to manipulation, exaggeration and reconfiguration" (1998, 188) in six ways. A body can be:

> *malleable*—it may be stretched over long distances, be compressed or extended, take the shape of another form, fit into incompatible spaces, etc... [;] *fragmentary*—it can be broken into parts, reassembled and conjoined with other objects and materials ... [;] a *contextual space*— ... a physical environment in itself, which may be entered into and used as if it were ostensibly hollow ... [;] a *mechanism*—it may be represented as if it was a machine. ... [It can have] *impossible abilities* (i.e., it can fly, lift heavy objects, experience violence without pain, etc.). ... [It can] directly express *explicit emotions* (i.e., it fragments in surprise, contorts in terror etc.). (188–89)

All those processes apply equally to stop motion. The results can include that "Bodies of humans/animals/creatures which are apparently incompatible are rendered equable in size, strength, ability, etc." and that "Bodies may redetermine the physical orthodoxies of gender and species" (189).

Stop motion, then, combines movement of actual figures with the illusion resulting from sequential recording of that uncanny process. The uncanny is "indissociably bound up with a sense of repetition or 'coming back'—the return of the repressed, the constant or eternal recurrence of the same thing, a compulsion to repeat. ... At the same time, the uncanny is never far from something comic: humour, irony and laughter" (Royle 2003, 2). As in the IMDb-termed "comedy, fantasy, romance"[3] live-action *Groundhog Day*

---

3   Here and below I use the IMDb designations to help indicate the tone and perspective of films, in case readers are unfamiliar with them. These labels are, of course, a bit of a blunt instrument, perhaps more helpful as evocations rather than strict descriptions. Of course, mistakes can happen, but IMDb classifications remain useful. The designations are given by registered users of IMDb, who may submit new material and edit entries, checked for accuracy by employees of the company. Those working in the entertainment industry and/or having an IMDb page add material via IMDb PRO. Filmmaker Rebecca Gibson notes: "The content creators assign the genres—I've done that in the past for shows" (email communication, February 12, 2019). Filmmaker Danishka Esterhazy, who has also submitted work, commented that "the page options are very deep and complex so I often ignore a large chunk of their form." She added, "But

(directed by Harold Ramis, 1993), in which main character Phil (played by Bill Murray) must live the same day over and over until he gets it right, repetition, sometimes with slight difference, makes the uncanny. That very repetition-with-difference is also the concept behind animation.

Like animation and fairy tales, films are uncanny. "Cinema's obsession with special effects aspires to create a technological optical simulacrum torn between realistic appearance and believability and uncanny effects" (Gunning 2008, 86). As discussed in chapter 1, what actually happened in the world during production differs from what appears in the final creation. Viewers may not always have a strong sense of disjuncture between those two realities. Yet documentaries, like other film forms, usually conceal most if not all motivating work—questions asked by interviewers, setup of particular locations and events, elements outside the camera's view, and so on.

Some documentaries, however, break genre, including using the superficially unrealistic form of animation. Of course, animated sequences have always appeared in documentaries to "explain, clarify and illustrate" (Roe 2017, 274), "commonly in the form of animated diagrams and maps" (273). But more recently, usually in photorealist style, animation serves as "connective tissue," for example "to reconstruct historical scenes for which no original filmed material exists" (280). Or, often in "cartoony aesthetic" (277) style, animation forms a "disruptive interjection," drawing attention to itself, often in "films that have . . . political or activist messages" (283). Such interjections "contribute to the arguments being made by each film" (283) in that "the sudden and unannounced change in visual register metaphorically shouts at us, 'this is important'" (284). And despite the popular association of animation with children's entertainment, the serious "drawn documentary" has a longer history than might commonly be known and is by no means restricted to the Oscar-nominated *Waltz with Bashir* (directed by Ari Folman, 2008) (see Murray 2017). Indeed, animation as an art form has few boundaries (see Faber and Walters 2003, 6–9).

Yet if documentaries generally obscure how they render a world they seek to extract for the viewer as simply real, in the fantastical LAIKA films

---

I do know that broadcasters (like CBC) and streaming services (like Netflix and Amazon) assign genres without filmmaker input. They choose the genre that they think will be most popular. Hence, Amazon classified my film *Black Field* ["history" on IMDb] as a western, which surprised me, but which actually attracted a lot of eyeballs" (email communication, February 12, 2019).

I discuss here, the intention is not to suggest that the audiovisual result reflects something that is actually out there in the world—except for the closing segments. The latter marked scenes reflect the idea that "many of the 'tricks' associated with a sense of the uncanny . . . convey the sense of an ordinary world rendered extraordinary through perfectly ordinary mechanisms" (Jervis 2008, 28). As already indicated, film scenes may have been shot on different days and/or in different locations, but their final product usually seeks to cover the editing and other work that produces a seamless event.

The LAIKA closing sequences, in contrast, make that labor part of the magic of their fairy-tale films; "the slumbering uncanny power of cinema, its ability to animate the inert, to make the impossible occur before our eyes and, like so many modern optical devices, to summon up fantasies of a mode of vision beyond ordinary sight" (Gunning 2008, 87). But further, as Wells and Johnny Hardstaff aver, "the pictorial realms of the imagination, the parameters of surreal fantasy, and the visual signifiers of spontaneity, are increasingly controlled, measured and authenticated as if they were real. . . . [A]ccepted knowledge . . . is challenged by using animation" (2008, 164). Working through the *understanding* of animation, LAIKA's fairy-tale films, particularly in their disjunctive closing segments, offer background and alternatives, along with frequent homage to their stop-motion animation hero Ray Harryhausen (e.g., Chris Butler quoted in Haynes 2016, 51; Knight quoted in Haynes 2016, 99).

LAIKA's website describes the company as founded in 2005 and

> occupy[ing] a unique and distinctive place in American cinema by continuously expanding the boundaries of the 120-year-old technique of stop motion animation. We are a community of storytellers, artists, inventors, technicians, and craftspeople from around the world, committed to fusing filmmaking's state-of-the-art technologies with a handmade animation tradition as old as film itself. ("About" n.d.)

Producer Travis Knight underlines the importance of LAIKA's freedom from the constraints that too often come with working in the Hollywood mainstream. He comments that "we're an outlier. We work in an industry that is dominated by franchises and sequels and prequels and remakes and reboots, but we're devoted to telling new and original stories" (quoted in Watercutter 2015, 3). Knight also notes:

> We *are* an independent animation house. We're not a part of some international media conglomerate. There are great things that come with that—freedom, the ability to tell these kinds of stories. At the same time, we've got to be very sensible.... We've got to keep our budgets low. Overall, our independence is one of our greatest strengths. (quoted in Tallerico 2016, 3)

Indeed, Knight sees LAIKA's work as being "to shelter the art from the obligatory and unavoidable assaults of commerce" (quoted in Watercutter 2015, 6).

At LAIKA, the stop-motion "animators endow the film with vitality... [and] the gratification can be transformative" (Brotherton 2014, 157). Indeed, "each LAIKA animator is encouraged to filter his character through his or her own imagination and life experiences" (158). And yet LAIKA films each have a "unique look, often centering on the line quality in the designs." *Coraline* depended on illustrator Tadahiro Uesugi (1966–); *ParaNorman* on a look that was "sketchy, rough-hewn confident"; *Boxtolls* on German Expressionism; and *Kubo* on the woodblock prints of Kyoshi Saitō (1907–97) (Haynes 2016, 10).

On one level, as the closing segments indicate, stop motion is real, in the sense that at least part of its complex visuality results from a direct camera record of something that actually took place in the world. As director Burton notes with respect to *Corpse Bride*, stop motion gives "the feeling [of] being there." Producer Allison Abbate concurs: "Stop motion's charm is in it's not being too slick and not feeling like it's made in a computer.... Keeping it real and keeping it live, 'cause I think that's what makes it very accessible and appealing" (both quoted in "Animators" 2005). With the process,

> Every shot has to be meticulously planned and choreographed. Every frame of every camera move must be programmed and translated to mechanized motion control rigs. Every gesture of every puppet is calculated, but it all needs to feel spontaneous. That it's alive. It's a testament to the collective ingenuity and toil of the story team, rigging department, camera and lighting crew, VFX artists, and the animators. (Knight quoted in Haynes 2016, 116)

Nevertheless, in LAIKA films, complex scenes may also include added computer-generated imagery (CGI). Yet the creators do not mix stop motion and CGI in a single character; for example, in *Boxtrolls*, primary characters and scenes are puppets and builds, but background characters and scenes are often CGI ("Making" 2015).

Throughout, however, "we always try to veer from realism. . . . We're always exploring how we can translate the art into a three-dimensional object that will look like the thing that you're trying to represent, but not be photorealistic" (Brotherton quoted in Haynes 2016, 123). The play of real and fantasy forms part of LAIKA's aesthetic but also part of their mode of working. They frequently discuss their method paratextually (see Gray 2010) in interviews and represent it on media; they produce books explaining and detailing their feature films from *ParaNorman* on, including the presentation of behind-the-scenes material that further illuminates their work, with contributions from many of those involved. Meta-filmicly further playing with the viewer's sense of reality, LAIKA films' ending sequences uncover aspects of the stop-motion animation process. In the three later films, preternaturally fast-moving humans render the animation realistic and the animators as caricatures (Renée 2016). But in their first film, *Coraline*, the end sequence reveals only the machinery—wires and rigging holding up the figures.

Coraline (Henry Selick, 2008)

This "eerie, atmospheric fairy-tale-styled fantasy" (Brotherton 2014, 13) is termed "animation, family, fantasy" by IMDb. Like Gaiman's novella, it concerns a girl who discovers a parallel realm behind a door in her new home, wherein her parents and neighbors have counterparts with button eyes. Though the doppelgängers of her parents, and in particular her mother (see Chang-Kredl 2015), at first seem preferable to their equivalents in the real world, as distinctions between the two worlds begin to break down, the experience becomes a nightmare, with clear elements of horror (see Myers 2012, 250–55). Some of the film's acclaim comes from its technical aspects; one DVD edition includes a 3-D version, meant to be watched with (headache-inducing) pink and green lenses mounted in cardboard. Scott Higgins notes that *Coraline* is "a historically significant aesthetic solution to the 3D conundrum" (2012, 196) of being "caught between novelty and norm" (207), mainly because "stop motion makes a strength of 3D's difficulty with representing scale" (200).

Given my work's interest in ways that reality is (and is not) included in fairy-tale films, it's worth considering that Selick's aesthetic for the film, including the 3-D, required not maintaining an illusion of similitude but drawing attention to the artificial. He "sought to impress viewers with the artifice of his craft; authenticity is to be found in subtle imperfection" (Higgins 2012, 200). Much of the commentary Selick provides on the DVD is about working with 3-D. On the one hand, the process offers an illusion of greater reality, given most humans' capacity for stereoscopic vision to view their world. On the other hand, in context, conventional ideas of what cinema looks like include its presentation in two dimensions. Thus, it is important that "despite its creative investment in 3D, *Coraline* is perfectly legible in its 2D version" (206).

The closing animation of circling mice recalls a brief shot early in the film. As Coraline (voiced by Dakota Fanning) sleeps, the scene dissolves to the opening of the small door the girl recently located. When her mother (voiced by Teri Hatcher) unlocked it earlier, the space behind was bricked up. But now in the center of the bricked-up entrance, first one, then two, then four two-dimensional mouse figures appear, and they swirl around tail-first in a clockwise motion—the image reprised at the film's end (see figure 2.1). In an abrupt cut, a three-dimensional, squeaking kangaroo mouse wakes Coraline and leads her to the door, which now has an expanding blue and purple tunnel behind it. The girl's first encounter with the alternate realm follows. Because the sequence below has the mice moving forward, not backward as in the previous scene, it appears the two mouse passages are, indeed, not identical, though they are similar.

FIGURE 2.1. Circling mice on the wall

The final segment (see figure 2.2), immediately following the credits, begins with the mundane; on a blue screen background, four unrecognizable objects, reminiscent of television antennae, divide the bottom half of the screen. The central, tallest one has what at first appears to be a light bulb on top. Behind-the-scenes/studio reality changes to also reference the figurative/fantasy, however, when the seeming light extends into swirling lines that first become a mouse with a long tail. Images of both the everyday and fantasy continue as further unidentifiable rigging objects appear, and the mouse/light object becomes two mice, in a slightly wider shot showing more rigging and with the filaments holding the mice object more visible. As more rigging appears, the two become four mice circling one another, clockwise and headfirst, and the camera begins to pull out (see figure 2.3). But the segment closes on a non-referential studio focus when the mice merge into a

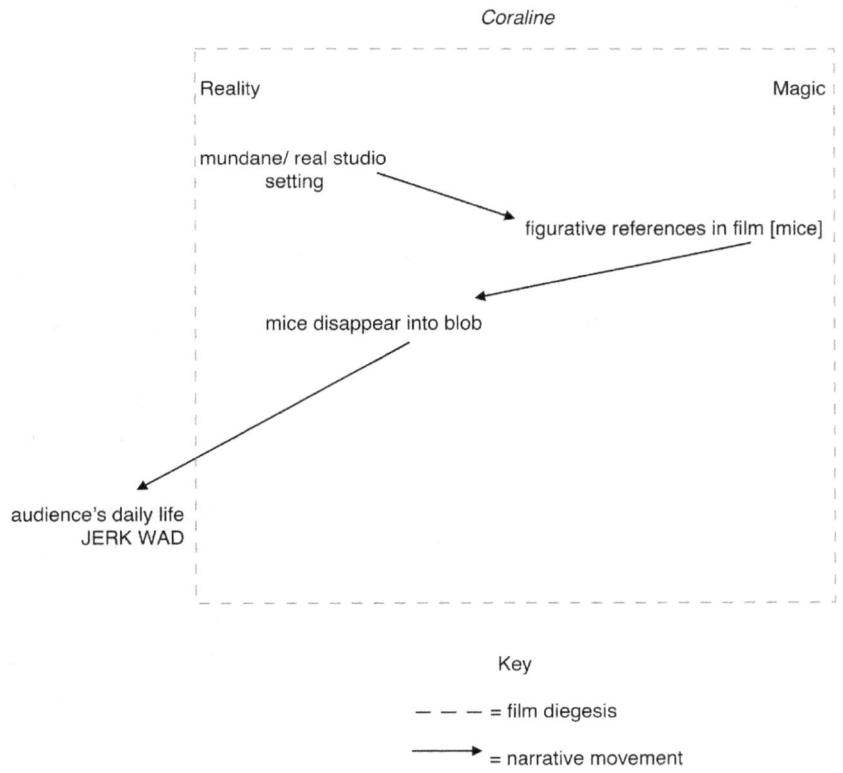

FIGURE 2.2. Relation of reality and magic in *Coraline* credits

STOP-MOTION ANIMATION AND THE UNCANNY REAL * 41

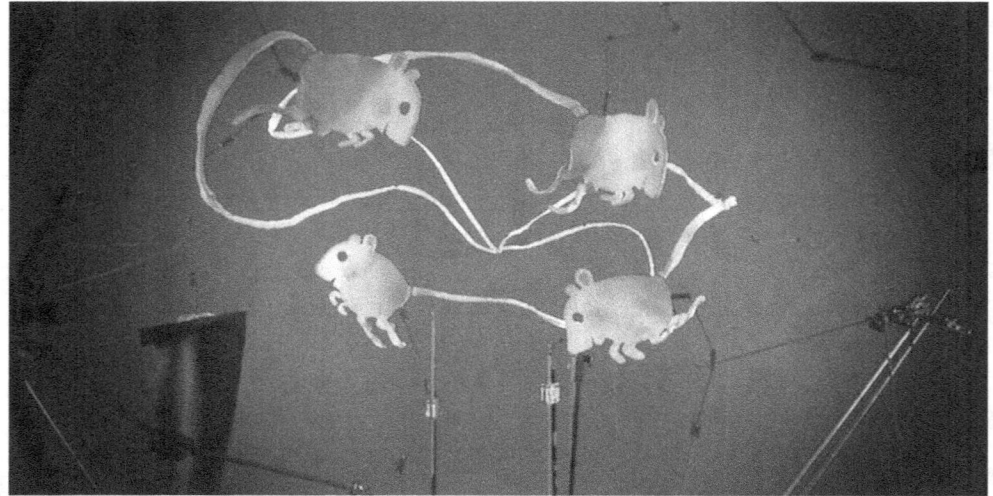

FIGURE 2.3. Circling mice behind the scenes

single blob, as a larger rigging structure, composed of two large poles holding a dark circular form, becomes visible.

The music that accompanies the final credits, written by Bruno Coulais, has a tinkling celesta-like sound[4] as background accompaniment to a children's choir. But as the final text disappears, the children's chorus sounds cease, and the instrumental music remains. The move further draws attention that something different from the rest of the credits, and indeed the rest of the film, is taking place. The celesta continues through the animation sequence and into an abrupt cut to LAIKA's logo, then to that of film production and distribution company Focus Features, and then to the words "For those in the know: JERK WAD," "a clue that could be used on the *Coraline* website in order to get an entry in a contest that ran during the movie's US theatrical run" ("Crazy Credits" n.d.). Arguably, this takes the audience back into their daily lives, their reality outside the film-watching experience.

The DVD accompaniment indicates that "The string mice floating out of the wall was originally a dream sequence that Coraline has, but it was edited down for the sake of pacing. Selick included the animation at the very end of

---

4 The celesta, which resembles a piano, produces a bell-like sound and was most famously used in Pyotr Ilyich Tchaikovsky's "Dance of the Sugar Plum Fairy" in his fairy-tale ballet *The Nutcracker*.

the end credits so the sequence could be seen in its entirety" (Carr 2014). For a nonspecialist in animation techniques like myself, however, the actual process is difficult to decode. Despite the section showing both the mundane and the fantasy, the movement of mice and the studio rigging alike remain magical in appearance, even if the sequence shows the machinery behind it, which would normally be removed in postproduction, more directly. Hands and/or computers must be moving the rigging, but the viewer does not see them. The sequence nevertheless draws attention to the fact that constructing effects requires technique and that movement emerges from an artisanal, specialized process.

This segment offers a brief allusion to stop motion and the mechanical creation of special effects. However, in the context of the film as a whole, the scene to which it refers is not central. As described by Selick, the sequence above was simply an interesting outlier. In LAIKA's later films, however, the play with reality, animation, and fiction relates more centrally to significant characters and events in the film; their semantic content reflects on that of the films.

ParaNorman (Chris Butler and Sam Fell, 2012)

This "zany, zombie-filled homage to eighties teen movies" (Brotherton 2014, 13) is labeled "animation, adventure, comedy" on IMDb (unlike *Coraline*, not family and, surprisingly, given the references in both, not horror). Primary character Norman (voiced by Kodi Smit-McPhee), a young boy who sees and speaks with the dead, encounters several terrifying ghosts who threaten his small Massachusetts town. In part by reading her "Sleeping Beauty," but mainly with his compassionate personality and actions, Norman delivers the town from the ghost of young Aggie (voiced by Jodelle Ferland), a child burned during the witch trials because of her own powers as a medium. The film deals in both direct and coded modes with the real-life problems of bullying and homophobia (see Gordon 2016).

The uncovering sequence in this film, as in *Coraline*, appears after the credits. It takes the Norman puppet through a process of construction. The feature commentary, with directors Chris Butler and Sam Fell, continues simultaneously:

> BUTLER: So yes, starting with Jeremy Spake's armature drawing. I can't keep up with it.

FELL: Yeah. Ah, it's great to see isn't it. I just love this. Well [unclear], because even despite you've seen behind the curtain when [Norman] gets up and walks off, it's still magic. I guess it's even more magic cause it's just all those old bits.

BUTLER: Yeah with one of our studio mugs there, "tragic and ironic."

[On the mug, only "and ironic" is visible.]

Fell laughs as the LAIKA logo appears.

Onscreen, various hands move at lightning speed, beginning with a graph paper drawing of Norman's basic shape, then the construction of the metal armature, then molding, and then removal of the figure and painting and dressing it, ending with the construction of Norman's head and face (see figure 2.4).[5] This portion begins at approximately 1:31:24 and ends at about 1:31:43; it is much too fast to detail. The realities of actual creators (hands) and fantasy creation (puppet) manifest together, although the construction of the puppet has marginally more verisimilitude than the representation of the humans who move at preternatural speed; the reality appears fantastic.

Then the sequence cuts to a shot looking down on the final Norman puppet lying on a surface with various objects around him. The scene continues without any indication of the hands that formerly showed his construction, although as the camera pulls back various objects appear and disappear. The reference throughout is to the studio context; the reality of a puppet build becomes more magical, itself animated as if part of the fantasy. Finally, the scene becomes even more explicitly magical, though still situated in the studio reality, when the completed Norman, surrounded by tools and equipment, pulls his arms and legs inward and then stretches. As he stands up, the camera moves down from the overhead shot to one facing him at an

---

5   The trope of directly showing the animator's relation to the character they create has long been an element of film animations, as in Walter R. Booth's (1906) *The Hand of the Artist*, Dave Fleischer's (1921) *Invisible Ink*, and Jiří Trnka's (1965) *Ruka* (The Hand). In the latter examples, the hand acts as a character within the diegesis (see Faber and Walters 2003, 158–59), arguably unlike the LAIKA animations, wherein humans mainly (but not exclusively) serve to demonstrate the construction of puppets and other processes. Similarly, humans interacting with animated inanimate objects appear, for example, in the stop-motion work of Norman McLaren (e.g., *A Chairy Tale*, codirected in 1957 with Claude Jutra, or *Neighbours*, from 1952) (see also Shadbolt 2013). The latter works, however, are more about the display of the preternatural than about the representation of the metafilmic, as in the LAIKA segments.

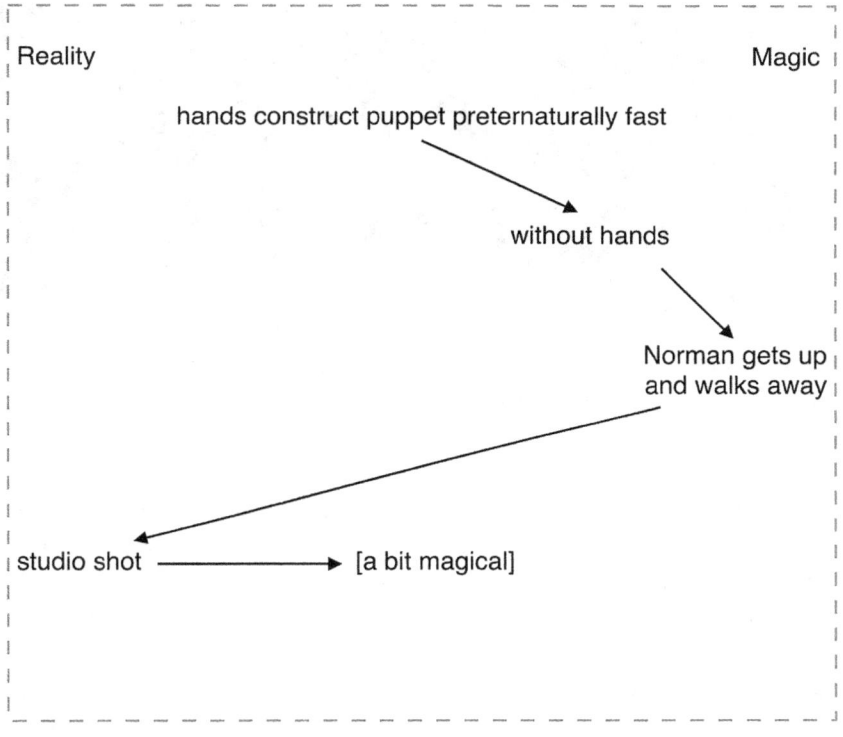

FIGURE 2.4. Relation of reality and magic in *ParaNorman* credits

approximately 90-degree angle, as Norman dusts himself off and walks to the viewer's right out of frame (see figure 2.5). Abruptly, a mundane realism returns. Once he is gone, there is a brief pause on the set, the production context in which the puppet found himself—and from which he has just exited. Yet this realistic location has been transformed by the animated Norman puppet's moving through it; it is now a magical setting as much as a realistic one.

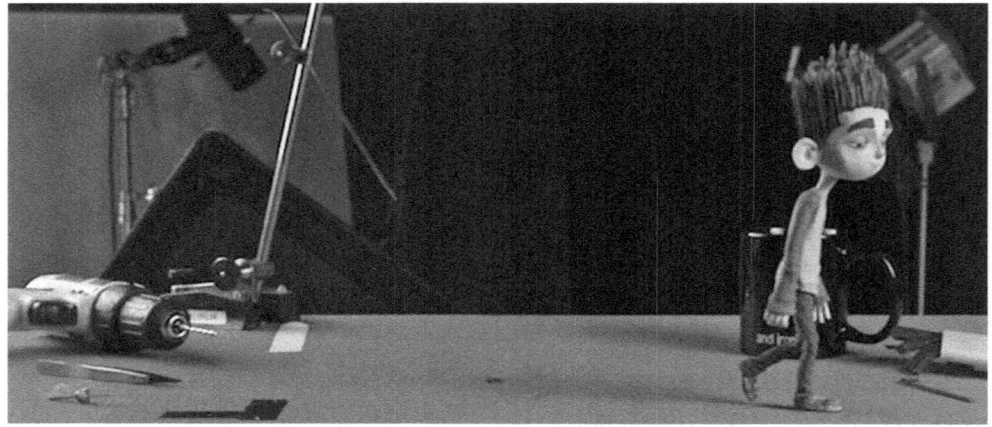

FIGURE 2.5. Norman walks off the set

Though this sequence shows a bit more behind the scenes than does *Coraline*'s, as Fell's "even more magic" comment above indicates, once Norman's puppet moves, the sequence returns to the fantastic; he moves on his own, without the human hands who would actually be manipulating his constructed figure. Nevertheless, the opening sequence plays with the notion that the construction of the puppet is the reality, whereas the preternaturally fast-moving hands offer less realism. The reality is the figure's *construction*, not his *movement*; the latter remains in the realm of magic and illusion. The audience intuits that there must be hands behind Norman's action, as there were in his creation, but they are literally not in the picture.

Thematically, this segment playfully echoes one of *ParaNorman*'s main concepts, the conventional American idea that each person must follow their own lights, be independent, and trust their own instincts. And yet *ParaNorman* goes well beyond such a simplistic idea; it ultimately and overwhelmingly advocates community and kindness. Such an independent Norman puppet is not entirely a good thing; after all, he walks off the set! The science behind the puppet develops a character who, like other fairy-tale characters, saves his town because he believes in himself, but not to the extent of rejecting his relatives, friends, and community. In fact, only by drawing support from other outsiders does Norman, like the unpromising fairy-tale hero, prevail.

The Boxtrolls (Graham Annable and Anthony Stacchi, 2014)

Both *Coraline* and *ParaNorman* offer "distinctly modern stories set in American towns featuring dark and supernatural characters" (Brotherton 2014, 13), but *Boxtrolls* ("animation, adventure, comedy" on IMDb) contrasts as "a period piece of sorts, set in a strange world, in another time . . . populated by charmingly ugly but undeniably harmless characters" (13). (The Boxtrolls may be charming and harmless, but many of the humans are appalling villains.) Like the previous two films, *Boxtrolls* has elements that recall horror. The story focuses on the young boy, Eggs (voiced by Isaac Hempstead Wright), who has been raised by trash-gathering Boxtrolls dwelling beneath the pre-twentieth-century English fictional town of Cheesebridge. The creatures are harassed, captured, and killed by human residents, who fear them. With his human friend Winnie (voiced by Dakota Fanning) and other helpers, Eggs ultimately ensures that the carnage stops and the above- and below-ground beings coexist in peace.[6]

In *Boxtrolls*, stop motion is combined with compositing:

> If the physical set ended at the edge of a road, for example, the camera department could drop in a green screen so that the visual effects (VFX) department could add buildings or a vista later as a postproduction effect. By taking this uncompromising, hybrid approach, LAIKA refuses to let the limitations of the stop-motion format inhibit the . . . production values of its films. (Brotherton 2014, 40)

Most *Boxtrolls* trailers, like others of their ilk, present a teaser of the narrative's content, but one ("'The Boxtrolls' Trailer 2" 2014) instead purports to show aspects of the animation process from behind the scenes. It begins with a fantasy/reality combination as a large human hand comes down from the top right and puts the arm of a tiny record player down on a miniature spinning record (see figure 2.6). After the distinctive sound of the needle's placement and pre-track scratchy noise, the song "They've Got the Whole World in Their Hands" begins. This small action plays with the idea of diegetic music—actually intended to be understood as created within the scene. Immediately, the illusion of movie magic manifests: the human hand manipulates the tiny set element, implying that it is the actual recording of the

---

6 See Odrowaz-Coates (2016) for a discussion of the film's use in critical pedagogy.

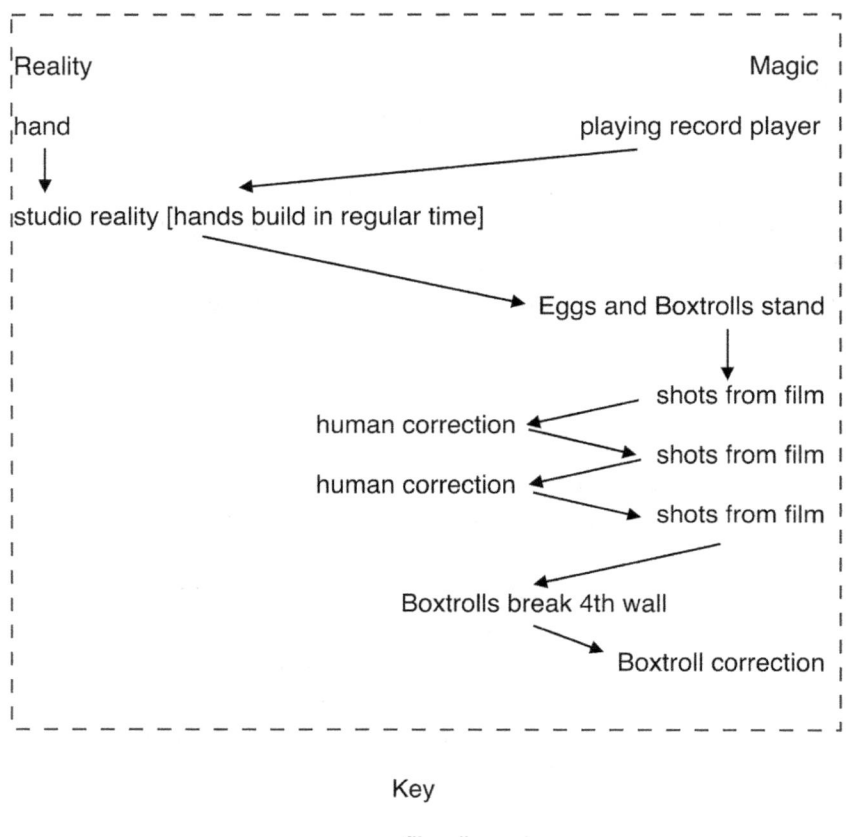

FIGURE 2.6. Relation of reality and magic in *Boxtrolls* trailer

background song. What momentarily appears to be a revelation of behind-the-scenes how-to in fact melds almost immediately into the real world (the hand) intersecting with the fantasy magical (a purportedly, impossibly functioning prop).

The background song choice, a version of the traditional spiritual made popular in the North American folk revival, "He's Got the Whole World in

His Hands," raises implications that, as I'll suggest, are followed in the end sequence—and parodied at the trailer's conclusion. The hands holding the original song's "whole world" are by implication God's; the human hands at LAIKA as contextualized and narrated in the song become godlike, then, in their creation and manipulation of the Boxtrolls' realm, though unlike elsewhere they move at a realistic speed and are not transparent. This notion directs a sequence of extreme close-ups that follows, with the song as nondiegetic background, further indicating the interaction of humans with the set—with studio reality—once again: actual hands rigging, drawing, building, sewing, and manipulating the puppets from the film. Shots follow of the many puppet face masks that allow the characters' expressions and then of hands manipulating and moving tiny objects on the film's sets. This portion recalls the fabrication sections of both *Coraline*'s and *ParaNorman*'s end sequences.

Just short of one minute in, though, an abruptly introduced, much wider shot shows scenery, rigging, and a computer screen as a man moves forward, and then a closer view offers hands setting up a Boxtroll in situ as the camera moves back out to show that puppet in a scene. Rigging drops the Eggs puppet down from the top left into a set. Then the scene moves to the studio magical; with a close-up that obscures his rigging, Eggs stands up as two Boxtrolls beside him emerge from their boxes. The trailer turns next to a sequence of actual shots from the film, sans rigging and hands; it represents the film's fantasy world, not the studio fantasy world that opened it.

Abruptly follow the words "from the hands that mad" as a human hand moves in from the bottom right to add the final "e" to produce "made." This image, repeated, recalls the beginning section's combination of the studio magical and real, though the reality in this case is in direct address to the audience. More scenes from the film (diegetic fantasy) and then another quick cut to the words "Coraline and araNorman" as a human hand moves in from the left with tweezers, to add the "P" to render "ParaNorman." More scenes from the film and then suddenly the title, "The Boxtrolls," is followed by two Boxtroll boxes flying and rolling into the scene from the bottom right. The sequence implies that they are moving in from the previous scene from the film, in which they slid down the tunnel into their underground territory—yet the two Boxtrolls break the fourth wall, also known in film as "direct address," when "characters in movie fictions . . . appear to acknowledge our presence as spectators; they seem to look at us" (Brown 2012, x). Just below the word "Box," the Boxtrolls' heads, legs, and arms emerge from their boxes, and they turn to face and look into the camera; chuckling, with broadly smiling faces, they pat their boxes with their hands as if in self-congratulation.

In theatrical and other audiovisual performance conventions, the fourth wall refers to situations wherein "dramatic conventions governing the separation of real and fictional worlds are deliberately violated so that, for example, a character comments on story events in an aside to the audience or an omniscient narrator reports story events directly to the audience" (Thomson-Jones 2007, 92). Fourth-wall breakers may look at the camera/audience and may even directly address them, as the two Boxtrolls do here, kinesically—their unspoken gesture conveys specific meaning. Tom Brown discusses the "clumsiness and imprecision of the phrase 'direct address'" (2012, x), pointing out that neither is the address direct, since it is always mediated through the camera and screen, nor does it fulfill the implications of address as verbal.[7]

Breaking the fourth wall is a complex mode in which theater and film draw attention to the interactions between the apparent reality of the diegesis and the reality of the watching audience. Peter W. Rea and David K. Irving argue that breaking the fourth wall, "because this can be disturbing for the audience . . . is done for dramatic or comic effect only" (2001, 159). However, the strategy is used in multiple ways in animation. Malcolm Cook discusses a 1920s British example of performance "plurality"—a cartoon set on a stage, thus invoking in its direct address "both the extra-diegetic fictional theatre audience and the extra-filmic cinematic spectators." It involves the main character "turning to the audience, and winking or mugging, breaking the fourth wall and evoking the 'knowingness' typical of music-hall" (2018, 222). Research shows that audiences can find such breaks particularly engaging (Auter and Davis 1991), specifically in terms of encouraging intimacy to boost "sympathy or some other kind of special connection with a character" (Brown 2012, 13). It enhances the audience's sense of a character's power and position of special knowledge as well as their truthfulness (13–16).

All these effects certainly come into play in the brief address of the *Boxtrolls* trailer. But the purposes in *Boxtrolls* may have more to do with further

---

7   Brown also unpacks problems with the notion of the camera, particularly the actor's relationships to that physical object. He ultimately decides, as I do, to "risk the apparent naivety of describing actors or characters looking 'at us' in order to evoke the effect sought rather than labouring at each point the complex ontological status of a look that is, in fact, materially impossible" (2012, xi–xii).

troubling connections between reality and fantasy, augmenting "present-ness" and "present tense-ness" (16). When the two Boxtrolls face their audience, emanating such joy, they may remind viewers—as they did me, watching the trailer *after* seeing the movie—that these oppressed creatures remain nonviolent throughout, in the face of extreme violence against them. For those who have not seen the film, the trailer may reassure them that, despite a horror aesthetic of dark, even gloomy colors and potentially scary-looking puppets, the film offers a happy—and engaging—experience. Since film, in particular animation, requires an extensive suspension of disbelief, a process of hailing the audience, as do the two Boxtrolls, forces a disjuncture. The gesture interpellates the audience in a manner that positively recognizes them as good, friendly humans who will help and support these creatures.

Following this semantically complex move, and supporting its meaning by underlining that both humans and Boxtrolls can fix the world, is an abrupt cut to the release date, "9.26.14," with the LAIKA and Focus Features logos. But the "4" in "14" is slightly askew, and this time not a human hand but a Boxtroll hand comes from the bottom right and straightens it (see figure 2.7), as the "real D 3D" logo and the web address "theboxtrolls.com" appear. In this move to magic and fiction, then, the godlike hands of the LAIKA animators are not in fact holding "the whole world in their hands"; the Boxtrolls themselves have power and control. Thus the trailer ultimately returns to the fully

FIGURE 2.7. Boxtroll reaches in to correct an error.

animated and magical studio topos that began it, changed this time to make the fantasy creatures their own creations, not those of humans.

This trailer in part works to underline the literally handmade aspect of much of the film—as in the *ParaNorman* credit sequence. Human hands manipulate the puppets and objects; "hands" is repeated many times in the song that plays throughout the trailer; and the titles repeat "from the hands that made." The final twist, of course, is the playful notion that at some point the Boxtrolls themselves take over as active characters (as they do in the portions of the trailer that come from the actual film but also as Norman did in the *ParaNorman* closing animation) in the process of making the trailer, even to the point of manipulating and correcting it.

Jonathan Gray (2010) considers trailers and their effects as paratexts commenting on (invariably to promote) a film, as well as their existence as freestanding objects. He examines how parody trailers can signal different genres than their ostensible subjects, such as Stanley Kubrick's 1980 horror *The Shining* as a "feel-good father-son bonding film" (63) or Jerome Robbins and Robert Wise's 1961 *West Side Story* as a "zombie horror flick, reframing dance sequences as zombie attacks" (64). But Gray also details how actual trailers can be created to aim at different notions of national cultures—contrasting the Canadian and American versions of the trailer for Canadian Atom Egoyan's 1997 fairy-tale-inflected *The Sweet Hereafter* (65–70). Gray's insights about presumed audiences for trailers suggest that LAIKA understands that one significant audience for their films is fans of animation, in particular, *hand*made and stop-motion forms.

Similar play with what is real (actual human bodies and human-made objects) and what is magic (the final animated characters) also appears in *Boxtrolls*'s mid-credit sequence—fictional, but not from the film. Yet the DVD commentary from directors Graham Annable and Anthony Stacchi during that scene asserts its linkages to previous examples:

STACCHI: This is a bit of a tradition at LAIKA.

ANNABLE: Yeah.

STACCHI: That there's a behind-the-curtain sequence that comes at the end of every film. It started on *Coraline*, there was a beautiful sequence that had been animated but cut from the film and then the director Henry Selick absolutely wanted it to be shown so it was put in at the end of the credits. And then on *ParaNorman* there was another sequence that showed a puppet being built from the tiniest screws up till the complete Norman puppet and then he walked away. So all the way through this film [producer] Travis [Knight] told us to keep your eyes open.

ANNABLE: We knew we had to figure out something we were going to do at the end of this.

STACCHI: Keep your eyes open for a moment to do it. And we had so many great recordings of [actors] Nick Frost and Richard Ayoade where they played with the tiniest things and they went on and on that we couldn't use in the film because otherwise the film would have been twice as long. And we thought their philosophical discussions were great and we kept thinking there must be a way to use that.

ANNABLE: Yeah.

STACCHI: As our special.

ANNABLE: Just it felt like the perfect way to fit you know within the character arcs we had of them in the story, and yet do that wonderful reveal of pulling back the curtain. I think you know I hope when you watch the film you obviously get lost in the story and the world of Cheesebridge and the Boxtrolls. And then when you get that little button at the end it kind of brings it back to the realization.

STACCHI: Yeah.

ANNABLE: That oh wow wait a minute I mean there were hands all the way through.

STACCHI: Sends your mind reeling back through all the rest of it and you think how did they do that battle sequence and you can imagine somebody standing on all those sets and doing all that stuff.

ANNABLE: Yeah.

STACCHI: After having seen that little treat.

ANNABLE: Yeah I think it's kind of neat the way that works.

The scenes behind the first set of rolling credits are rendered in drawn animation, not stop motion. Following the naming of the character designer and character sculptor, the screen goes black and then opens to an outside scene in the film's set, showing comic relief henchman humans Mr. Trout (voiced by Nick Frost) and Mr. Pickles (voiced by Richard Ayoade) (see figure 2.8). They stand facing the camera, leaning on brooms. As in the main film diegesis, the setting and characters invoke fiction:

PICKLES: Hmm.
TROUT: Just keeping the streets clean.
PICKLES: Free from evil.
TROUT: Yep.
PICKLES: You ever think about the universe, Mr. Trout? What if our world is just like a tiny speck?

Then the segment moves from diegetic fiction to studio reality, and ghostlike human hands appear, moving preternaturally fast to manipulate both figures; the hands become slightly more visible.

TROUT: A tiny little speck.
PICKLES: And there are giants looking down on us?

The reference shifts from a theoretical world to the studio reality. The camera moves out.

TROUT: And every time we move . . .
PICKLES: It's actually them moving us.

As the camera continues to move out, the head and torso of the man manipulating the puppets become visible (see figure 2.9). The result moves from the viewer's sense of a human operator within the fictional location to an apprehension of a human operator in a studio. As this takes place, the actors' commentary also addresses the latter action.

TROUT: Seems a bit tedious.

The camera continues to move out, and the human figure becomes more visible. He stands in a cut into the set. To the left are lights and the open case of different facial expression masks.

PICKLES: Like that, just there, me blinking. That would've taken them a day.
TROUT: Me moving my arm, 500 men!

The camera continues to pull back, showing more lights, a screen, and six cases of face masks on the left, with more lights and rigging on the right.

> PICKLES: I mean, none of them are going home. They're having to do this bit. [He dances.] And now this bit. And this bit [balancing shakily on one leg]. I mean, this should stop.

On "stop," the man disappears. Cut to black, and the credit portion resumes, with drawings superimposed on a black screen. The dialogue continues.

> TROUT: I think it throws up notions of free will.
> PICKLES: It's too much. And then they would have had to have done me talking about the blink, and it never ends. I think they make a meal of it, to be honest. I don't know how they get the time. [The credit naming resumes.] They've got to have other jobs. It's more like a hobby. You know, like stamp collecting, something you do in your free time.

The credits continue rolling, as does the background with drawings of the sets. Like the trailer, the sequence operates on multiple levels. Most obviously, the fictitious characters of Pickles and Trout philosophically comment on the process of animation while further developing their movie personas as (sometimes unintentionally) witty, insightful commentators in the narrative. These roles link to the actors who voice them; Frost's mainly stodgy realist Trout and Ayoade's wackily philosophical Pickles echo the roles that make them familiar to those who watch Britcoms. Frost's slightly dull Trout recalls, for example, some of his protagonists as movie sidekick to Simon Pegg, and Ayoade's sardonic Pickles invokes his character Moss on *The IT Crowd* (2006–13).

Reflecting simultaneously on the outside world as much as on the present filmic context, Ayoade's dismissal of the human work of animating stop motion puppets as "more like a hobby . . . something you do in your free time" surely finds an echo in all of us who do jobs not conventionally understood as labor by most people. (In a moment of synchronicity, one morning while I was working on this chapter, I returned a phone call from a student who immediately expressed great surprise that I was working on a Saturday. In fact, it would be more of a surprise were I *not* working on a Saturday.)

Ayoade's dialogue offers a reverse on the expectation that creators would comment on their characters (which often appears in DVD extras), not vice versa (more akin to postmodern novels and films). And, of course, on some levels it's accurate to say that the characters control the people who

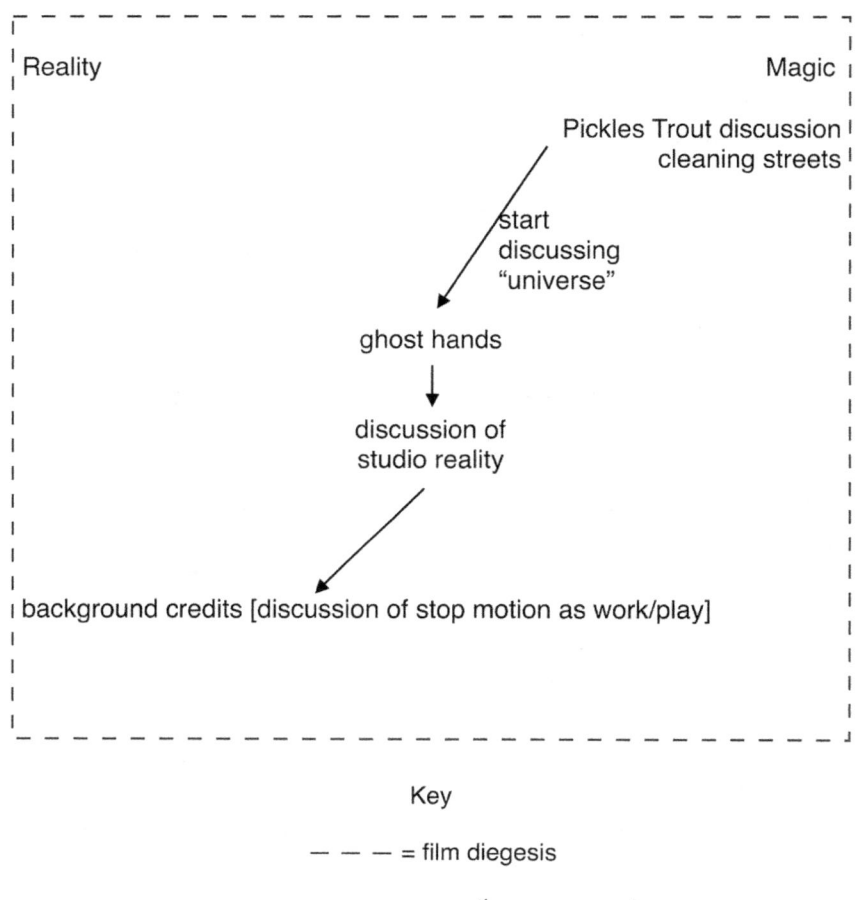

FIGURE 2.8. Relation of reality and magic in *Boxtrolls* credits.

manipulate their puppets, at the very least in terms of requiring consistency in interpretation and presentation. The level of dedication needed to spend a week on a few seconds of film is truly extraordinary; I suspect that Frost and Ayoade, if not Trout and Pickles, actually are impressed. The puppets both literally control their creators (in the sense of taking up their lives) and figuratively do so (in the sense that the actions these fictitious characters

FIGURE 2.9. Animator with Trout and Pickles puppets.

choose—moving their arms or dancing—affect how their creators must manipulate them).

But Frost/Trout's and Ayoade/Pickles's dialogue is also a sardonic refutation of the presumption that people who sweep the streets would never have discussions of the nature of the universe or notions of free will. As one of the lessons of *Boxtrolls* is to look behind appearances and to avoid negative or dismissive presuppositions about both human and nonhuman characters, their commentary resounds with the liberal principle of fundamental equality, at the same time as it goes beyond it by locating that idea in the personae of actually inanimate stop-motion puppets.

As in the reveal portions of *ParaNorman*'s closing sequence, the ghostly human hands move preternaturally fast, and the animated puppets appear with solid, realistic humanlike characteristics. Like the other LAIKA ending portions, these are metacommentaries, filmed representations of the filming process, as well as verbal discussions about it. As in the final walk-off of *ParaNorman*'s puppet, the audience should understand that even a behind-the-scenes segment ultimately represents the puppets as really real, not only within the context of their film but also in the context of their creation. That this is on at least some level true—the puppets actually exist as physical if normally inanimate beings—makes their comment on the human actions particularly poignant. The puppets are real, and the humans are ghostly, unreal, perhaps even magical. And the question of who, indeed, has the whole world of stop-motion animation in their hands is raised again in the final sequence of the fourth LAIKA feature.

Kubo and the Two Strings (Travis Knight, 2016)

Kubo and the Two Strings ("animation, action, adventure" on IMDb) comes from an original story idea from character designer Shannon Tindle and developed by writers Marc Haines and Chris Butler (Knight 2016, 7). Its visuals are inspired by Japanese woodblock prints but also by processes like origami, Kabuki, and Japanese opera and by objects like netsuke[8] and kimonos. The film's one-eyed Kubo (voiced by Art Parkinson) plays a magical shamisen—a three-stringed traditional instrument. His mother (voiced by Charlize Theron) warns him that her sisters want to steal his other eye, and so with his Japanese macaque netsuke magically come to life, and with the help of a cursed samurai turned into a rhinoceros beetle (voiced by Matthew McConaughey), he looks for his father Hansu's protective armor. Ultimately, with the assistance of Kubo's living and dead community, his quest succeeds, and he returns the world to its proper form.

Though the film was generally well received, some critics including the group Media Action Network for Asian Americans noted the absence of Japanese actors as the voices of the main characters (though Asian actors have secondary parts) (see Pedersen 2016). Director Knight's justifications for this choice, that casting was based on merit, appeal to the stereotyping self-reproducing argumentation used too often in Hollywood, which given LAIKA's argument that it is beyond Hollywood, seems disingenuous (see also discussions of casting in chapter 3). Knight repeats that talent, not race, is his prime consideration. The DVD commentary indicates that the character Kubo was cast using voice recordings only, which Knight terms "a true meritocracy"—not entirely factual, as aspects of voice quality and accent may betray ethnicity, language, and gender among other identity markers.

But even if I might grant a simple meritocracy argument in the case of the auditions for Kubo, the same cannot be said for casting stars McConaughey as Beetle and Theron as Monkey; they were sought specifically for those roles.

---

8   Netsuke are small representational carved ornaments used as decorative toggles to secure pockets on kimonos.

Knight's DVD commentary also periodically betrays the extent to which visuals are influenced by what the actors look like and how they move. The process of animation crucially includes filming the actors' faces as they pronounce their lines, indicating that facial contours are by no means epiphenomenal. Knight also describes the importance of having George Takei (the highest-profile actor of color in the work) playing the ideal father figure Hosato:

> Being able to work with George was a dream come true. I'm a lifelong *Star Trek* fan and I absolutely adore George for not only his iconic film and TV characters but for his tireless and selfless activism for a better world.... We wanted the actor playing this role to embody the best aspects of what it means to be human, the best aspects of what it means to be a father. Someone who carries wisdom and understanding and passion and warmth and mercy even in their voice. And when I think of actors that embody that for me, I think of George Takei. He's a beautiful soul and an inspiration. (DVD commentary)

Manifestly, all that makes up actor Takei's persona is vastly important to Knight. He also talks about Theron's and McConaughey's interest in the film and the quality of their performances as being related to their positions as parents. Again, it's not just the voice that influenced Knight's choices or uses of actors.

Though Knight declares that "we honestly were trying to do what we thought was the best interest in this movie, to bring this film to life in the best way" (quoted in Cheng 2016), this simplistic allegedly color-blind presumption depends on the circular logic of systemic discrimination that works against actors of color. They tend to be less familiar than White-identified actors because they get less work; they get less work because they have had less experience; so they get less exposure and are thus less familiar. Further, film distributors tend to be convinced by their own circular, self-fulfilling arguments that what has worked before will work again. Though commendable, the casting of Ayoade, Ben Kingsley, and Tracy Morgan as White-identified characters in *The Boxtrolls* doesn't let LAIKA off the hook.

Indeed, some of LAIKA's previous work shows that while animation doesn't require the actor voicing a character to look the part, there is a tendency to match the two. For example, initially the two sisters in *Coraline* were cast on the basis of their physical resemblance to voice actors Jennifer Saunders and Dawn French; when the roles were reversed, the players and director were much happier with the results (DVD commentary). And the clear matching of Frost and Ayoade with their characters' heights and sizes, though not with race, as Trout and Pickles are White identified and Ayoade is Norwegian/Nigerian, and the use of their personas in creating and enhancing their on-screen figures do suggest that voice casting is a complex mix, not a simple reflection of talent. As Sophie Lucido Johnson puts it, trenchantly:

> "Kubo" should be brought to the forefront of discussion because it's a tremendous anomaly. On the one hand, it is hands-down the most breathtakingly animated film of the past several years. On the other, its casting choices were, despite Knight's supposed good intentions, racist. This is a great movie with fundamental problems. How do we, as viewers, balance these heavy extremes? What are the ethical lines when it comes to painstaking, money-siphoning art? And finally, how do we reward a beautiful film without letting it off the hook for its director's bad decisions? (2016)

In the creation of this manifestly fictitious, fairy-tale-like story, significant issues of whitewashing and Asian erasure intervene. Perhaps it is not coincidental that LAIKA's next work, *Missing Link* (directed by Chris Butler, 2019), has actors of color (all women) Zoe Saldana, Ching Valdez-Aran, and Amrita Acharia in main roles, along with White-identified stars Hugh Jackman, Timothy Olyphant, and Emma Thompson.

Like *Boxtrolls*, *Kubo* included hybrid forms of animation (see Roper 2016), essential to creating its specific look in part imitating two-dimensional Japanese woodblock prints:

> First, the art department designed the various magical effects. The puppet department and model shop then built the corresponding physical puppets and props. The camera team lit them on set for reference, and VFX [visual effects] brought it all together. Having all departments in one place ensures that we have a unified look. (Nelson Lowry quoted in Haynes 2016, 67)[9]

Many effects in the film draw on Japanese woodblock prints. Crucially recalled in *Kubo*'s closing scene is a monstrous skeleton that has menaced

---

9   Stop motion remains crucial, though. For example, "Get Into Film" (2016) shows Monkey being flipped by her human operator.

Kubo, based on the triptych "Takiyasha the Witch and the Skeleton Spectre" by Utagawa Kuniyoshi (ca. 1844) (see "Takiyasha" n.d.; Haynes 2016, 100). The puppet behind the monster is huge. "At first we looked for different ways to cheat the scale.... But ... [w]e had to bite the bullet and build it. He stands sixteen feet tall and his arm span is seventeen feet. So the skeleton is almost one hundred feet tall in relation to Kubo" (Oliver Jones quoted in Haynes 2016, 102). The closing sequence focuses upon this monster. Commentary by director Phil Knight begins when the skull becomes visible:

> Every movie that we've done at LAIKA going back to the first one, going back to *Coraline*, during the end credits we always peel back the curtain to show the audience how this thing was done. You know you hope that over the course of the film that people get immersed in the story and the characters that they forget that they're looking at these little tiny objects that have been brought to life by the hands and the will of the animators. But at the end of it, it's always to see just a tiny little glimpse of how this was done. And that's what we have here. You get a sense of the scale of this creature that we have in the film and you see ... it's probably the first time ever that the puppet has been bigger than the animator. So it's always a nice little nod to the craft that we like to show at the end of the movie.

The sequence takes off from images of the figures of Kubo (center), his mother (left), and his father (right), rendered in drawn animation, compressing into bright lines that become the ropes of actual rigging, a quick transition from fantasy to reality (see figure 2.10). The camera moves down to display more of the rigging with hooks attached to two ropes, but it recedes as the foreground shows an origami samurai figure wielding his sword on a curved brown surface with several sticks in it and the hilt and part of the blade of a much larger sword penetrating the same surface. Reality-as-fantasy, the now-familiar ghostly hands and implements appear as the camera moves down and back to reveal more swords piercing the surface. The camera continues to pull down and back, revealing hands placing more swords on the surface of what the audience now recognizes as the skull. The scale of the hands to the skull indicates that it is, indeed, much more than life size.

The hands place lights in the skull's eye sockets as the camera pans toward screen left revealing the skeleton's giant arm, suspended on rigging. The fast-moving ghostly human hands place finger bones in the skeleton's right hand,

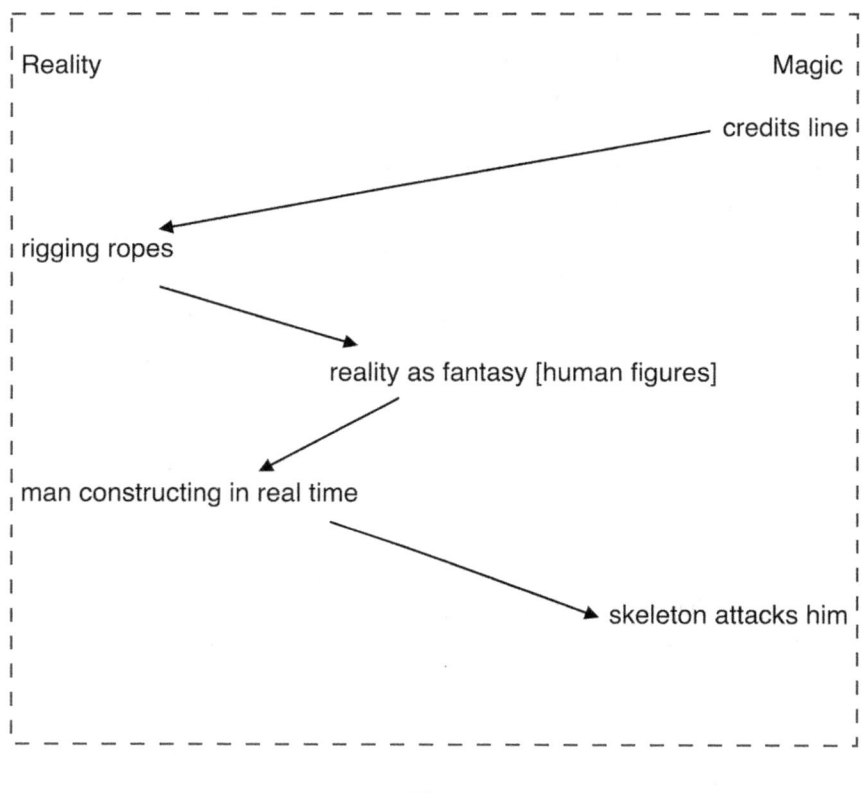

FIGURE 2.10. Relation of reality and magic in *Kubo and the Two Strings* credits.

and then the camera follows a small blue object that appears to be some kind of remote, also suspended from rigging moving to screen right. As it moves out of the frame on the right-hand side, a keyboard and computer screen on a trolley are revealed screen right. The head and partial torso of the human technician who has apparently been constructing the skeleton are joined screen right by another ghostly human figure who seems to discuss and direct (it is, indeed, the film's director) as the camera moves toward screen left again, and we see two and then three ghostly humans building the skeleton.

As the camera pulls out, the human figures appear and disappear, and the skeleton torso rotates forward. The not-ghostly figure of the director reappears screen left. Finally, with a total of four computer screens visible, one ghost human waves goodbye to the director, who walks out into the middle of the frame. With a move to more conventional reality, the final man—now substantial instead of ghostly—is left alone standing at the first computer screen. But then the unfolding narrative returns to fantasy when, absent any manipulation, the skeleton's eyes light up, it turns toward the final man (probably lead skeleton animator Charles Greenfield), and raises its arms menacingly as curtains close (see figure 2.11). The scene dissolves to a continuation of the credits.

For the first time, LAIKA offers a literal rendition of the "behind the curtain" metaphor, to which their commentaries frequently refer, though only at the end. The sequence also plays with the horror and threat that recur in LAIKA films, in *Kubo* in particular with three monsters who threaten its main hero characters, the second of which is the giant skeleton. Arguably, we return here, quite literally, to the idea originally broached in the Frost/Ayoade commentary on *Boxtrolls*, that the puppets are taking over the animators.[10] Again, the question returns of who controls whom. Are the animators in charge of the puppets or the puppets guiding the animators? Who are the gods who hold the whole world? And as in *Boxtrolls*, the sequence answers that, at some point, fantasy literally controls reality, not vice versa. As Knight explains during the DVD commentary: "Stop motion puppets are like little vampires; they suck the life out of the artists who touch them. . . . These artists really do give part of themselves to the film." The end sequence skeleton may not be a vampire, but like Frankenstein's monster turning on his creator, it menaces its animator.

This sequence also fits with conventionalized endings of horror and science fiction films (discussed with respect to "Hansel and Gretel" films in chapter 5), wherein an apparently dead, disappeared, or otherwise vanquished monster reappears, with an implicit or explicit threat to the film's characters and/or all humans. Thematically, this idea fits less well with the

---

10 Fleischer's *Invisible Ink* similarly uses the idea of an animated figure (in this case, drawn animation) that can't be controlled by its creator.

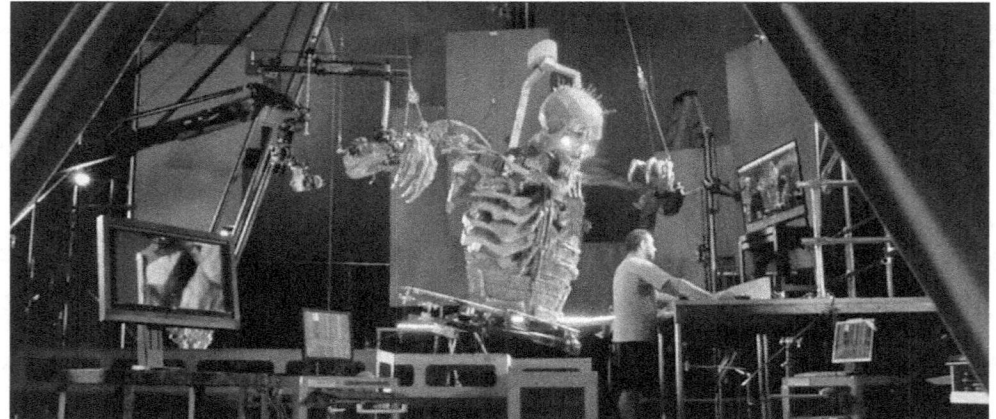

FIGURE 2.11. Skeleton attacks.

overall premise of *Kubo*. When science or magic portends evil results, as does the monster's attack on the technician in the credits, the film elsewhere suggests that love and goodness will prevail.

Human versus Animated Bodies

What does it mean to represent reality as fantasy and fantasy as reality in fairy-tale films, as LAIKA does in these excerpts? Clearly these closing sequences play with the uncanny real aspects of stop-motion animation in particular. They uncover, but also make fantastic, not only the construction behind figures in the films but also the methods of actually animating them. When I first saw LAIKA credits in theatrical releases, watching the films for my own enjoyment, I glossed the processes in my mind as rendering the creation of animation as magical and the results of that process as real. I did, indeed, come to anticipate the enjoyment of the credits' inventiveness. Though I nuance the analysis, my initial impression remains.

But some film theorists worry that animation in the form of "the digital seems almost to be stalking the real, revealing its presence and power only in certain circumstances, and suggesting ultimately an apparently common postmodern fear that the real itself might simply disappear, collapse, or prove an illusion" (Telotte 2010, 231). The *Boxtrolls* trailer and the *Kubo* final sequence seem to be literal instantiations of that process—the former offering a humorous view of fictitious creatures correcting what the viewer assumes are human errors and the latter showing the horror of a magical monster threatening a murderous takeover. But the linking of animation with reality also thematically connects it to real-world concepts—how films instantiate hegemonic or anti-hegemonic viewpoints, and sometimes both—and in particular recent moves to make critical, social activist, even utopian animations—or partial animations—for both children and adults.

For example, Jack (Judith) Halberstam notes how the animation house Pixar imagined turn-of-the-millennium alternatives to the conventional American individualist ethos of most American children's films, replacing it with "stories of collective action, anti-capitalist critique, group bonding and alternative imaginings of community, space, embodiment and responsibility" (2008, 271). Those comments equally apply in general to the LAIKA films, wherein fairy tale and fantasy can draw audiences' attention but technical, even industrial, marvels encourage a critical turn toward real-world parallels. Audience critiques of *Kubo*, linking its content to pressing current issues, seem very much in keeping with the films' critical stances.

Drawing together these concepts and ideals, I turn now to live-action works by fairy-tale film auteur Tarsem. Two of his films and one of his television productions render diegetic real worlds that require fantasy as the solution to their problems and that also use specific tools to render magic and wonder as what turn out to be scientifically conventional productions. He presents ideal worlds in which, as in the LAIKA films on a literal level, at best, science works in the service of magic; the two must coexist and, in balance, the wondrous is the better option.

3

Camera Obscura, Zoetrope, and Flying Monkey Drone

Science and Magic in Transcultural Fairy-Tale Media

THE ROLE OF MAGIC IN FAIRY TALES VARIES BUT OFTEN INVOLVES, like the stories themselves, transcending time and space. Think, for example, of those helpers who can eat a banquet in a trice or boots that cover seven leagues in one step. The forces these characters and objects draw on respectively compress what's physically possible in time (things get done faster than expected—reduced interval) and/or extend what's physically possible in space (distances get covered without ordinary exertion—reduced effort). Films, recalling fairy-tale magic, also transcend time and space. Though created in particular sequences and locations, films' wondrous effect fashions an account developing over a relatively short time of what may actually take weeks, months, or even years to produce. Movies also compress physically diverse spaces, via processes like compositing (such as green screen) and editing, to create apparently seamless places of the imagination, often represented as being within the real world. As Jessica Tiffin notes, "cinema has always been the site of magic" (2009, 181).

Thus films, like fairy tales, play with their audience's sense of (un)reality and (im)possibility. The role of magic in fairy tales similarly varies—

sometimes remarkable, sometimes simply possible—but it's not the only vehicle for audience interest. Tiffin declares, "Not only the creation of the marvelous causes pleasure. . . . the repetition of familiar patterns and structures is itself pleasurable" (2009, 19). Those enjoyable repeated magical structures and tropes include transforming things or people, like hedgehog to human; conjuring objects, like food from a sack; or linking together the unlikely, as when a cat not only speaks human language but does so with remarkable persuasiveness and style. From the earliest days of cinema, live-action films could render such wonders using techniques like stop motion and dubbing, as do the previous chapter's LAIKA animations. And, of course, magic's representation in animation can be even less restrictive than in live action, theoretically limited mainly by the animator's imagination and the two-dimensional audiovisual medium. But films and fairy tales offer more than just pleasure. Trickery and transcending reality have implications for politics, as they do in *Coraline*, *ParaNorman*, *The Boxtrolls*, and *Kubo and the Two Strings*. In particular, as I'll continue to argue in this chapter, sometimes progressive viewpoints can be found in the apparently unlikely locations of fairy-tale films.

In director Tarsem's[1] live-action fairy-tale films *The Fall* (2006) and *Mirror Mirror* (2012), the magic (but also realistic) compressions and extensions of time and space offer overlaps between heterospatiality (using multiple, diverse spaces) and heterotemporality (using multiple, diverse times). Filmed in twenty-four countries over a four-and-a-half-year time span (Wise 2008) and invoking the fairy-tale fantastic, *The Fall* often collapses, expands, and generally fictionalizes *space*; *Mirror Mirror*, drawing on "Snow White" (ATU 709), generally collapses, expands, and fictionalizes *time*, juxtaposing sixteenth- to nineteenth-century-inspired costumes with twenty-first-century slang and closing with a Bollywood musical number. In both works, Tarsem puts filmic magic and science—historical and current—to postmodern and implicitly resistant uses. He does the same in his television series, *Emerald City* (2017), which plays quite freely with time and space, often moving between scenes set in Kansas, now, and in Oz, out of any conventional time frame. And the connections to the present-day United States, and by implication to US politics, are difficult to miss.

In *The Fall*, magic works through the multiple filmed locations that embrace a transcultural approach, at the same time that the co-created and

---

1   The director uses Tarsem, Tarsem Singh, and Tarsem Singh Dhandwar.

conflicted plots in the embedded story critique its own visually lavish escape by pointing to the real conflicts, limitations, and coalitions of its exploited characters. In *Mirror Mirror,* the juxtapositions of time planes and the fear of aging and mortality permeate the film, finally giving its Snow White and Dwarfs a new possible future, even while the director eschews any simplistic sense of continuity. Thus, both movies draw on and reference fairy-tale magic/reality to create transcendent possibilities. The films further draw attention early in their expositions to filmmaking magic/reality by showing two pre-cinematic image-manipulation devices: a camera obscura (*The Fall*)[2] and a zoetrope (*Mirror Mirror*).[3] *Emerald City* combines the magical and the mechanical; in particular, the Wizard's flying monkeys resemble simian-shaped drones, which record but also project images they document. All work to present, and sometimes to conflate, multiple times and spaces.

Heterospatiality and Heterotemporality

According to Brian L. Price, heterotemporality "allows for the simultaneous coexistence of a variety of meaningfully organized historical periods within the confined visual space of the camera's gaze. This heterotemporality creates a productive tension in which the illusion of temporal stability is interrupted and the audience can perceive thematic parallels between the past and the present" (2012, 260). He later comments that heterotemporality results in "the productive tension between what viewers expect to see in chronological setting and what they actually and sometimes unconsciously see. The visual field takes in more than what is consciously registered and, though embedded within the background, just slightly out of the audience's conscious gaze or ... hidden in plain sight" (274). "Hetero*spatiality*" as I use

---

2   The camera obscura, first recorded in China circa 400 BCE (Renner 2009, 8), takes advantage of the optical phenomenon wherein an image projected through a small hole appears on a surface in a dark room or container opposite, with the resulting copy reversed and inverted—thus, manipulating space.

3   The zoetrope, an animation machine invented in 1834 (Pikkov 2010, 181), produces the impression of motion by quickly displaying a sequence of drawings or photographs of progressive phases of an event—thus, manipulating time. As in other forms of animation, in Estonian filmmaker Ülo Pikkov's terms, "the illusion of motion is located inside the viewers' minds and not in outside reality. . . . The human eye is capable of retaining an after-image for a fraction of a second, which allows for a perception of motion if a sequence of slightly different pictures is shown at a certain rate" (14).

it (recasting Price) refers to the coexistence of a variety of meaningfully organized spatial locations within the confined visual setting of the camera's gaze. This heterospatiality creates a productive tension in which the illusion of spatial homogeneity is interrupted and the audience can perceive thematic parallels between here and there.[4] The creative play between the expected and the actual can result in a new consciousness of the possible.[5]

Both films and fairy tales offer heterospatiality as they invoke but also obscure their multiple locations and places of creation and transmission. Fairy tales often display the residue of the places they have traveled to become one instantiated text. Any oral telling manifests in a single particular sociocultural and performance context, declaimed by a performer to an audience (who may or may not be involved in the narrations) in a specific location. And yet the story may refer to places and times beyond the experience or knowledge of anyone involved in the interaction. In the case of fairy-tale films, locations in the world often serve to represent fictional, even wondrous places.

Of course, the story needn't narrate the location in which its telling is physically set, or magical and imagined locales would be impossible. Katharine Galloway Young calls "a realm of events not present to the storytelling occasion at all but conjured up for the occasion by the story" the Taleworld (1987, 211). Fairy tales usher in the presence of the Taleworld by using well-recognized framing formulae like "once upon a time" to open, and they signal departure from the Taleworld with "and they lived happily ever after" to close. Openings can be simply "There was once . . . ," while closings can include "They remained happy and content / While we still don't have a cent"; "They remained rich and consoled, and we're just sitting here and getting old"; "And those who tell this tale and whoever caused it to be told / Will not die a terrible death whenever they grow old"; and many more (Zipes 2013, 75, 238, 511).

---

4 In contrast, Glen S. Elder (2003) uses heterospatiality to describe heterosexually and heteronormatively organized geographical locations.
5 Using Francis Ford Coppola's *Bram Stoker's Dracula* (1992) as case study, Thomas Elsaesser suggests that recent filmmaking relies, in ways that are arguably partially similar to heterospatiality and heterotemporaily, on palimpsest, bricolage, and pastiche—multiple references to previous films, artworks, visual puns, double entendres, and so on (1998).

But the presence of such formulae and of particular kinds of (often repeated) structures, characters, situations, and acts indicates what Young calls a Storyrealm. That is, the listeners understand that whatever the other circumstances of the performance context may be, what's being narrated is a *story*—rather than another genre of speech like a lecture, a sermon, or a conversation. The Storyrealm sets up a series of discursive expectations about who speaks and who listens and, in the case of fairy tales, that the narration is fiction, not (for example) a lie. The time of the Storyrealm is often the here and now, when the story's being told. The Taleworld could be the present (and it often is in fairy-tale films), but it needn't be, and it's always in some sense radically other than the Storyrealm.

Film heterospatiality includes analogues to the Taleworld in the world being represented on screen, but it also calls up a Storyrealm in its use of non-diegetic devices—those that aren't intended to be taken as a literal part of the world represented in the movie—like voice-overs, dramatic sound effects, or mood music. Such sounds, though profoundly meaningful, shouldn't be understood as actually being heard by characters in the film, for example; they take place in a specific location that's phenomenologically between the actual theater or other place where the viewer is watching the film and its Taleworld. Further, as already discussed, the physical locations in which the film is created—whether a sound stage, a back lot, or a place more conventionally inhabited and traversed in the everyday—can be multiple. Of course, as film scholars Gerald Mast and Bruce F. Kawin point out, the latter places, called "locations," needn't be the "place[s] where the film's fictional events are set" (2006, 734).

Similarly, fairy tales are heterotemporal—they invoke the time of their telling or publication but also the (imaginary) time of their narratives. Films, too, begin in particular moments, are often created in multiple locations and over a brief or more extended period, while their finished product (also displayed in specific time that may be continuous or discontinuous) calls on another narrative time, often—but not always—sequential. Their *heterotemporal* dimensions can make fairy-tale films the location not only for the modern (as film theorist Kristian Moen [2012] argues for early fairy-tale film) but also for *postmodern* skepticism, irony, and distrust of grand narratives. Their *heterospatial* aspects can manifest not only the (trans)national but also the *transcultural*, contradicting and complicating unilateral views of intercultural contact, exchange, and change (Hill 2007, 89), not simply as "acquiring another culture" (Ortiz 1995, 102) but how forces like Indigeneity, colonization, slavery, and immigration lead cultures to "exerting an influence and being influenced in turn" (98). *All* cultures in contact change, and "new cultural phenomena" emerge (103).

The Fall: Heterospatiality

The Fall addresses the magic and science of filmmaking. Highly metacinematic, a film about films and filmmaking, it's also about the magic and science of storytelling, including oral telling, and the spinning of narrative wonders of various kinds as fairy-tale magic, often understood in terms of its characters' creative dreams and imaginations, but also their needs and wants. In early twentieth-century Los Angeles, stuntman Roy Walker (played by Lee Pace) paralyzed after a film accident, meets Alexandria (played by Catinca Untaru), a young patient in the same hospital recovering from a broken arm. Attempting to trick her into stealing morphine so he can commit suicide, Roy narrates an epic tale, into which Alexandria inserts herself and others she knows. After being badly injured in another fall trying to get the morphine for Roy, Alexandria insists on hearing the end of the story. Though it first appears the conclusion will not be happy, the heroes ultimately prevail, and it seems both Roy and Alexandria will recover from their injuries, psychological as well as physiological.

Visual illusions and multiple perspectives abound. *The Fall* offers homage to an array of filmmakers, again across time and space, from Andrei Tarkovsky to Roman Polanski, with the story based on Bulgarian director Zako Heskija's *Yo ho ho* (1981). *The Fall*'s singular conditions of production are themselves postmodern and transcultural—even to the background of its director. Tarsem was born in India, grew up in Iran, and attended film school in California. His first feature, *The Cell* (2000), offers the stunning visuals, including over-the-top costuming, also seen in his two fairy-tale features.[6]

Tarsem does not emulate conventional European and North American filmmaking, commenting:

> Anybody in Europe who tries to compete directly with Hollywood will die . . . because they'll just spend more money on it. But things like Hindi

---

6   His *Immortals* (2011) depicts a conflict between mythological figures Theseus and Hyperion. *Self/less* (2015), like *The Cell*, is a science-fiction work based in the concept of individuals entering others' minds.

> cinema have evolved from a different angle, and they've survived because of it. In the west, for example, you don't mix opera and film. If someone is 44 he won't play himself as a 12 or 14-year-old, but he will in a Hindi movie. If he's fat and ugly, people will still call him beautiful. In opera you'd accept that, but you don't accept it in cinema. In the middle of a really serious situation, a dog can have a flashback in a Hindi movie. It is still played seriously, but in the west you wouldn't. (quoted in Wise 2008)

With transcultural influences from Bollywood to European opera, and an eclectic and open aesthetic, Tarsem's work as director of commercials and music videos facilitated *The Fall*'s extreme example of heterospatiality. Hae Jean Chung comments:

> As Tarsem explains in various interviews and in his director's commentary, his career helped finance *The Fall* and enabled him to travel around the world to scout for locations and to find an actress for the main character. His professional travels also proved fruitful once production began, as he saved time and money by flying the actors to the location of a commercial shoot and using the same crew to shoot his film. In fact, he reportedly chose his commercial projects on the basis of whether the geographic location might also be used for his film. (2012, 93)

This assemblage method of creation diverges from conventional mainstream epics, and even from most independent movies, as much as does the film's ethos. Though privilege and wealth are needed to make such a film, the result nevertheless reflects its distance from a Hollywood perspective.

Yet early Hollywood offers part of *The Fall*'s motivating action and one of three narratively crucial falls. The movie opens with a sepia-and-white-toned, slow-motion, multiple-cut sequence of what the audience later learns represents the aftermath of an unsuccessful movie stunt from the early twentieth-century days of cinema, in which a horse dies and the stunt performer is seriously injured. There's no diegetic sound; the somber A minor second movement from Ludwig van Beethoven's Seventh Symphony provides the musical backdrop. The metacinematic levels are multiple. Though the invisibility of the primary creator of the illusion—that is, the absence of a visible camera—can usually be taken for granted in films, even in documentaries that purport to present reality, the filming of a stunt presents illusion upon illusion. That is, generally a stunt player stands in for an actor, and safety apparatus is obscured using camera angles or removed in postproduction.

Thus, at the very least, this complex scene from *The Fall* represents an illusion of another place and time than that of the filming location (its own status as fiction signaled by the smooth extra-diegetic music and staccato images of panic in reaction to the ostensible accident), of the representation of a diegetic reality (the accidental fall), conducted in the service of an illusion (the stunt as performed by the stunt player), which itself sought to convey part of another fictional narrative (the jump from a bridge onto a horse). The exact content of the diegetic film story turns out to be irrelevant to *The Fall*'s plot, though the results of its circumstances are momentous.

In this opening, even without directly entering the realm of fairy tale, director Tarsem immediately begins playing with notions of fiction and nonfiction, illusion and authenticity, and wonder and reality. When Moen says early film fairy tales "negotiated the modern world," rendering modernism and modernity through "highlighting the marvels of technology, the enchantments of consumer culture, the transformative potentials of social mobility and other apparently wondrous facets of modern life" in "instability and spectacular wonder" (2013, xii–xiv), he could have been talking about *The Fall*, though he actually referenced the much earlier, also live-action Georges Méliès *Cinderella* (1899), Maurice Tourneur *The Blue Bird* (1918), and Raoul Walsh *The Thief of Bagdad* (1924), among others. *The Fall* goes beyond the acts Moen outlines, representing postmodernism's criticism, deconstruction, and fragmentation, not only of fairy tales and their contents but also of their associated societies and cultures.

Tarsem repeatedly draws attention to filmmaking magic and the illusions of the visual, beginning early in the film by showing a camera obscura image, through the eyes of the primary child character, Alexandria. The audience first sees the upside-down image of a horse and cart as if created by light passing through a door's keyhole (see figure 3.1), then the same image right-side up framed by the door, and then its shadow on a wall. These images draw the audience's attention to a very literal multiple representation of a physical object in different (hetero)spatial manifestations. They remind the viewer that a single space/event/object can be seen in a variety of ways—diverse but all real. Thus, not only magic allows multiple realities. The real world has individual physical spaces that could be rendered differently—not only by (a film showing) camera obscura, reflection, and direct image but also by different characters.

FIGURE 3.1. Alexandria and the camera obscura view.

Tarsem often shows scenes that explicitly emerge from Alexandria's own perspective (as opposed to that of the ostensibly absent, omniscient, voyeur camera): the child looking at a photograph first with one eye, then the other, demonstrating slightly different images of the same picture; looking through curtains or windows; or doing hand shadows on the wall of the Los Angeles hospital where she's recovering from a broken arm sustained in another of the three falls, while laboring as an orange picker. The primary adult character, Roy, the stunt player paralyzed in the first scene's fall, is for most of the movie fixed in space, while others revolve around him both literally and figuratively. He's bedridden until the very end, when he sits in a wheelchair. Only in Alexandria's imagination does he move. He begins his storytelling by instructing the child to close her eyes. He asks her what she sees, and when she says she sees nothing, he tells her to rub them so she will see stars, and the image dissolves into the sparkling night sky over the first scene of the story within the film.

Underlining that the camera's view of that evolving story is Alexandria's standpoint, the director shows Roy's "Indian" character (played by Jeetu Verma)—who for the teller signifies native North American, as indicated, for example, by his use of the term "squaw"—as instead South Asian (see Stevens 2010). Since the child has come to California from Europe and worked with other immigrants, including South Asians, she decodes Roy's Indian other/wise than he intended; she sees instead a turbaned warrior. This heterospatial doubling, of course, recalls the origin of naming First Nations folks "Indian," in Christopher Columbus's error.

Similarly, Alexandria's image of the scary soldiers who work for her story's despotic villain, the evil Governor Odious (played by Daniel Caltagirone), makes their armor resemble the protection worn by the technicians who perform X-rays at the hospital, whom she fears. When a speaker in the story sneezes because Alexandria sneezes, Tarsem shows that both Roy and Alexandria craft the narrative. But the director also plays with her perspective, often continuing to show images from the story Roy has been telling, even when the dialogue suggests that he has moved on, especially when Alexandria does not want him to halt his narration.

At times, arguably, this Alexandria eye view breaks down; it's unlikely that a child of her age and background, a refugee who has fled Eastern Europe with her mother after her father is shot by marauders, laboring in the California orange groves, would call up images of the pyramids at Giza, the Eiffel Tower, or the Great Wall of China (among the many international locations Tarsem visually quotes). And, indeed, it's improbable that most locations in which he shoots would have been visited by the film's audience, even if they can identify them. But they are nevertheless meaningful. Chung notes:

> He deployed traditional editing techniques instead of visual effects. Indeed, the fast, fluid editing that weaves together numerous shots of visually stunning locations reinforces his point that geographic mobility is the real impetus propelling the story forward. Tarsem also stresses that no digital visual effects were used. Instead, he relied on the combination of shooting in remote locales and carefully positioned camera angles to make the setting look exotic and unfamiliar, and in some cases, almost otherworldly. (2012, 94)

Tarsem also worked hard during filming to maintain the illusion for six-year-old Untaru (Wise 2008), playing Alexandria, that then little-known actor Pace, playing Roy, could not walk, deceiving the crew as well as the girl. The director filmed many scenes between Pace and Untaru through a hole in the curtain that surrounded Roy's bed, seeking to get more spontaneity in their interactions. But deception is also narratively central to the diegesis, since as indicated, Roy tells Alexandria the epic, continuing story in episodes over several days, not for its intrinsic value or for her sake but instead to trick her into stealing morphine for him. Desperate at what he fears is a permanently disabled state, and having lost his girlfriend, he hopes to commit suicide.

One mode for film magic used extensively in *The Fall* is the doubling of actors in two diegetic roles. In Tarsem's film several actors play two roles, one in each Taleworld. Nevertheless, the protagonists overlap semantically: evil characters in the story are also evil in the film's real world; good characters are also good. They never appear together within the same frame, yet the result is heterospatial, offering images suggesting the same person is in two discrete locations. For example, the actor who plays Alexandria's father (Emil Hostina) is the first Masked Bandit, until the child begins imagining Roy as this primary hero character. Robin Smith, who plays the one-legged actor trying to persuade Roy that having a disability can be an advantage, as it has been for him, also plays Luigi, the explosives expert from the Masked Bandit's band. Another fellow Odious hater, Otta Benga, is played by Marcus Wesley, also the hospital's kindly ice delivery worker. And Roy's own nemesis, the lead actor Sinclair, who steals his girlfriend, is Governor Odious.

The Fall likewise incorporates fairy-tale wonder, magic, and multiple personae via fictitious versions of real individuals like Charles Darwin (played by Leo Bill) and Wallace—in the film an uncannily brilliant monkey who's the actual source of all of the diegetic Darwin's ideas, ironically mirroring the historical Alfred Russel Wallace, codiscoverer of evolution. And Ota Benga (1883–1916) was a Congolese Mbuti pygmy man notoriously exhibited at the Bronx Zoo (Bradford and Blume 1992). These characters have a triple aspect, linking actual people with the fictional ones represented in the two Taleworlds. Viewers needn't know the allusions to appreciate the film any more than they must be capable of identifying the many shooting locations. But these then/now, here/there references draw attention to Tarsem's heterotemporal, heterospatial, transcultural, postmodern approach.

His strategies also manifest in Alexandria's part as co-creator and visualizer. When Roy's story veers in directions she does not approve of, she enters the story, wearing a miniature Masked Bandit outfit, to rescue him and his fellow bandits/helpers from capture. Thus Alexandria has four aspects: not only herself but also a Masked Bandit, and thus her father, and then Roy. As this multiply implicated character, she moves between positions as focalizer, as co-narrator, and as intervening actor within the magical Taleworld. Yet at crucial moments, Roy remains in charge. When his story begins to kill off the beloved helper figures, Alexandria accuses him, "You're making this up."

But she takes a different tack when Roy seems bent on destroying his own character, the Masked Bandit. Beside Roy's hospital bed, she begs, "Let him live," but even within the other Taleworld, she cries, "*Roy*, get up and fight." When Roy argues, "He has to die," she counters, "I don't believe you." Here the character doubling intersects the Storyrealms and Taleworlds; when the Masked Bandit finds the strength to live, so does the frame story's Roy—or vice versa (see figure 3.2).

Alexandria seems socially and culturally disempowered as a working-class child, sometimes struggling with English, while Roy as a relatively privileged adult seeks to control her. His manipulations hurt her; when she tries to get him morphine, she tumbles from the chair she is using to reach it—the third fall—and is seriously injured. When Roy places her in the position of fairy-tale helper, not fairy-tale hero, he cuts himself off from her. When he gives in and lets her direct her fairy-tale happy ending of good's triumph over evil, not only does he cease to be merely self-regarding, but he literally begins to heal. In the final conflict between the Masked Bandit and

The Fall

Context		Narrative
Storyrealm		Taleworld
theatrical presentation, home viewing, etc.		film, TV, *The Fall*
early twentieth C LA		encounter between Roy and Alexandria
real world characters	doubled character link	fantasy character
Roy's hospital bed		Masked Bandit Story
	Roy's view	
	Alexandria's view (camera obscura)	
(real world locations)		(magical place)

FIGURE 3.2. Storyrealms and Taleworlds in *The Fall*.

Odious, Roy learns from Alexandria's refusal to give up; he is not only his own character and the Masked Bandit but also Alexandria and her manifestations. So the film concludes with another story within a story, with the main characters watching a film, apparently at the hospital. This is the silent era, so a violinist plays riffs from Richard Wagner's "Ride of the Valkyries." Roy sits up in a wheelchair, suggesting that his mobility is improving; and Alexandria's voice-over indicates that he later returns to stunt work. She visualizes him in every stunt she sees.

On the one hand, the illusion of Roy and Alexandria's co-constructed story as a single narrative is, in part, undermined by its heterospatial geographical spread. Viewers are simultaneously reminded that fairy-tale magic is illusive and elusive and that filmmaking magic collapses space. Sequences that move seamlessly across geographically dispersed locations mimic the mind's abilities to make connections, even unlikely ones, but also create an illusion of all places as equally proximate. The film's domain is presented as if it were an instantiation of the alleged democratization, seamlessness, effortlessness, borderlessness, and frictionlessness that comes from the Internet and other new media (see Chung 2012, esp. 92–97). Any space can be here; though huge and diverse, the world is collapsing into a small, local community.

On the other hand, Tarsem underlines that Roy's and Alexandria's spheres are very different. Sometimes they literally do not understand or they actively misinterpret one another; sometimes their views appear the same but are actually different (as in their concepts of who's an Indian). Like Roy and Alexandria, who meet because of a combination of the transnational forces of refugee dislocation and the individual misadventures of their falls, Tarsem's film combines the contingent with the creative. Stories as a weapon of the weak in political struggle require that teller and audience imagine themselves in another's place; they advocate this form of heterospatiality, not unlike the triple aspect of camera obscura, reflection, and direct view.

Mirror Mirror: Heterotemporality

Mirror Mirror shows Tarsem's postmodern filmmaking's implications for heterotemporality. A widowed king (played by Sean Bean) who marries a beautiful woman (played by Julia Roberts) goes to battle but does not return, leaving his daughter Snow White (played by Lily Collins) with the Queen.

She taxes the kingdom, plots against Snow White, and tries to marry Prince Alcott (played by Armie Hammer). She instructs her servant Brighton (played by Nathan Lane) to abandon Snow White in the woods, where the Beast lives. Instead, the girl meets the Seven Dwarfs, reduced to robbing. The Queen convinces the Prince that Snow White is dead, but before he can marry her, the Queen's evil is revealed, and all ends well for Snow White, the Prince, and the Dwarfs.

Though the film has a less than stellar 45 percent audience approval rate on Rotten Tomatoes,[7] it shows considerably more inventiveness than the 75 percent audience approval rate for *Snow White and the Huntsman* (directed by Rupert Sanders), which came out the same year, based on the same tale type. Tarsem's film shows its director's independent filmmaking roots. Sanders cast the Dwarf roles using familiar British actors like Ian McShane, Bob Hoskins, Nick Frost, and Eddie Marsan, who were rendered smaller with CGI (see Child 2012). The issue of excluding little people actors from such roles echoes concerns discussed around whitewashing in chapter 2. Not only did Tarsem choose little people actors (the generally White-identified Jordan Prentice, Mark Povinelli, Joe Gnoffo, Danny Woodburn, Sebastian Saraceno, and Martin Klebba and the Korean Ronald Lee Clark) to play the Dwarf roles, but he also had them as robbers, with the semantic play of initially attacking their victims on stilts so they would resemble giants.[8]

Roberts (age forty-five at the time) joined a series of forty-something big-name actors who play Snow White's wicked stepmother in American (co) productions: Vanessa Redgrave (forty-seven in Peter Medak's *Snow White and the Seven Dwarfs*, 1984), Diana Rigg (forty-nine in Michael Berz's *Snow White*, 1987), Sigourney Weaver (forty-eight in Michael Cohn's *Snow White: A Tale of Terror*, 1997), and Miranda Richardson (forty-three in Caroline Thompson's *Snow White: The Fairest of Them All*, 2001); Charlize Theron, in

---

7   While Rotten Tomatoes is not an empirically verified measure of audience support, or lack thereof, it helpfully suggests user reactions. As described on its website,

> The Audience Score, denoted by a popcorn bucket, is the percentage of all users who have rated the movie or TV Show positively. When at least 60% of users give a movie or TV show a star rating of 3.5 or higher, a full popcorn bucket is displayed to indicate its Fresh status. When less than 60% of users give a movie or TV show a star rating of 3.5 or higher, a tipped over popcorn bucket is displayed to indicate its Rotten status. ("About Rotten Tomatoes" n.d.)

8   See Allison Craven (2017, 193–204) for a trenchant reflection upon postfeminism in the gender roles displayed in *Mirror Mirror* and *Huntsman*.

FIGURE 3.3. Queen and zoetrope in *Mirror Mirror*.

contrast, was thirty-seven when *Snow White and the Huntsman* came out in 2012. Roberts had to work with a script that made a joke of her character (and by implication of the actor herself) as an allegedly aged woman, with resulting broad comedy.

In *The Fall*, Tarsem avoided digital effects almost completely (with the exception of Alexandria's dream sequence during her operation). In *Mirror Mirror*, by contrast, animations play crucial roles, including the zoetrope, which appears in two scenes. The film opens with Roberts removing the zoetrope's cover and then winding up the machine to display an image of a rose blooming and then dying, repeatedly projected inside a crystal egg (see figure 3.3). Roberts's voice-over intones in a bad English accent: "Once upon a time, in a kingdom far, far away . . ." The camera moves inside the zoetrope, to show multiple reflections of the rose images, and then zooms directly into the blooming rose. Cut to a continuation of the narrative, presented in stylized animation, while Roberts proceeds with the backstory leading up to the present (later revealed as Snow White's eighteenth birthday). The camera moves up through a representation of woods to a CGI castle, perched on the edge of an outcropping over a lake surrounded by trees. As Roberts's narration closes, the camera zooms in on the building to reveal an opening window and Snow White herself standing in it.

The zoetrope's second appearance begins with Roberts's voice-over on a view of the battle between Snow White and the Beast (actually the King, enchanted by the Queen). The Queen reprises the closing portion of her narrative from the first zoetrope sequence—"A dark magic invaded the land...."—with a view of Snow White, on the ground, in her Dwarf-created fighting gear, her head and torso partly turned toward the camera and filling the right side of the frame, backing away from the Beast. With a cut to the zoetrope, the same backing-up action by Snow White, this time frontally from the Beast's perspective in three-quarters close-up, appears in the crystal egg that earlier showed the rose (see figure 3.4). Unlike in the first scene, there's no evidence of the zoetrope's functioning or the images used to create the repeating sequence. The zoetrope is running on its own, presumably by magic. The image changes to a rose as the Queen enters screen right and the camera moves to center her chair directly behind the machine. As she sits, the egg obscuring her image, another cut to the Queen shows her seated on her chair, centered, in full view.

The repetition (without variation) of the same voice-over narrative at different times, in different contexts, and with different images conjures heterotemporality. Both tellings are associated with a zoetrope, as well as with the Queen's obsession with remaining beautiful—a process that her mirror image links directly with aging and time: "I suggest you marry someone rich. Quickly. Because one day soon, you will ask me who the fairest of them all is, and you won't like the answer." The dying rose of the first zoetrope sequence is the Queen's metaphor. Like its view of time itself, the film shows the Queen's efforts to remain beautiful in terms of artifice. Recalling the zoetrope, the procedure is not magical but mechanical (a device for cinching her waist) and cosmetic (application of various disgusting substances)—both relying on illusion. The second image, of Snow White trying to escape, heterotemporally links the Queen's evil deed of transforming her husband into the Beast with its effect on the young woman; she fears a violent attacking creature who, unbeknownst to her (and to him), was once her father. They were separated by the Queen, who announced that the King had died, but his reconciliation with Snow White nears.

The film's costumes signally invoke heterotemporality; designer Eiko Ishioka describes her work as "hybrid classic... from 16th century to 19th century. And plus Eiko's 'Art Nouveau'" ("Looking Through the Mirror" 2012). In contrast, Ishioka's designs for *The Fall* (and indeed for Tarsem's earlier film *The Cell* [2000], with equally spectacular outfits) draw few specific links with the

FIGURE 3.4. Snow White and zoetrope in *Mirror Mirror*.

past. The ball costumes in addition draw on animal metaphors: Snow White's has a swan headdress with a subtly colored beak and wings over an otherwise relatively conventional white gown. (Conveniently shedding the headdress and wings, the young woman flees into the forest wearing that gown.) The Prince has rabbit ears, and the Queen's dress references a peacock.

The time allusions are mixed, but together they summon a feeling of pastness, without specifically using any particular historical period; the Storyrealms and Taleworlds are relatively uncomplicated (see figure 3.5). "Renowned costume designer Eiko Ishioka created an aesthetic for *Mirror Mirror* that combines elements of court fashion from the Elizabethan era and the French ancien régime, with allusions to Versailles" (Goodall 2016). The film's language is, in that context, somewhat jarring. Juxtaposed with the historicized clothing, colloquialisms like "pinky swear," "I just need to process," "Let's agree to disagree," going to one's "happy place," and calling an idea "focus-grouped" offer disjuncture and attention to the film's artifice. *Mirror Mirror*, as the language suggests, is now, though it refers to then, creating the fairy-tale chronotope that is, in fact, no-where, and no-when.

Unlike *The Fall*, which places actors of color in significant roles, *Mirror Mirror* includes them in crowd scenes, but other than Dwarf Chuckles (Clark), all main characters are White identified. Yet the film's soundscape,

Mirror Mirror

Context	Narrative
Storyrealm	Taleworld
theatrical presentation, home viewing, etc.	film, TV, *Mirror Mirror*
storytelling context	Queen's voiceover narration
studio	
temporal mixed	Snow White ATU 709
CGI	
	rose dying and reborn
zoetrope	Snow White backing up

FIGURE 3.5. Storyrealms and Taleworlds in *Mirror Mirror*.

especially Collins's singing "I Believe in Love," which provides the background for the credits, offers another time (and place) in the Bollywood musical. Before the credits begin rolling, however, a "where are they now" sequence in sepia tones updates the Dwarfs, with images mimicking nineteenth-century photography, concluding with "Grimm wrote a book of fairy tales" and "Half Pint found love" and ending in a heart wipe. This sequence takes the movie's fictive present into a fictive future, where the Dwarfs (if not some other characters) apparently live happily ever after. And it addresses the fate of helper figures too often simply left out of all those fairy-tale conclusions.

Once the latter sequence is done, an image of Snow White appears in a mirror frame, slightly to the left, with the credits appearing to the right; as they roll, she sings and dances. Reflecting Tarsem's expertise, this segment reads as a music video. The up-to-date allusion, like the use of slang, belies the costumes' apparent past or other time, but it also removes the film's location far from the simulated White European primary narrative. The implication is that Snow White is singing and dancing at her wedding, yet Collins's performance contradicts the historicized costumes and setting. With Bollywood hand gestures and images from above the twirling actor, the scene shows Snow White's enjoyment and appreciation—and moves her into the start of what may be her happy ever after.

Collins is obviously in her element, and the Seven Dwarfs actors do admirable work as backup dancers. The other actors (especially Bean, who clearly did his level best elsewhere in the film) look uncomfortable. Their discomfiture further separates viewers from the presented event's flow and from the no-when, no-where of the fairy-tale setting into a consciousness of the real time of filming (not unlike the effect of deleted scenes and humorous outtakes that sometimes accompany DVD releases). For the conclusion of the song, the image suggests the wedding party is moving outside and cuts to a full-screen shot above the castle. The camera circles nearly 360 degrees and then moves out till, with a sound of water, it appears to dive down into the lake, and the image ends in black.

Tarsem decolonizes the musical associations of Disney animated feature fairy-tale films (later to be reprised in live-action works like *Beauty and the Beast*, directed by Bill Condon, 2017). Undermining its other/wise, no-where, fairy-tale chronotope, the "I Believe In Love" sequence eschews CGI and (more like *The Fall*) uses creative camera and editing work. And specifically locating the sound and dance moves in India, rather than in courtly Europe, turns conventional ideas of fairy tales on their heads. Just as Sadhana Naithani's (2006, 2010) work, in particular, shows how Indian fairy-tale scholarship offered resistance to British imperialism, Tarsem makes an un-American "Snow White." Even more revolutionary, however, is his un-American "Wizard of Oz."

Emerald City: Science and/versus Magic

Tarsem's uses of science and mechanical machines to render wonder in his two fairy-tale films become directly thematic in *Emerald City* (premiered 2017). This television series narratively and visually pits science against magic. Updating and recasting L. Frank Baum's Wizard of Oz series (1973), the ten episodes call more upon Baum's books than on the famous film, including characters not in the 1939 Victor Fleming work, like Tip/Ozma (played by Jordan Loughran), Ojo (played by Ólafur Darri Ólafsson), and Langwidere (played by Stefanie Martini). Further, Tarsem's Dorothy (played by Adria Arjona) is a young adult nurse, not a child or teen. The show, unfortunately canceled shortly after it was first aired, demonstrates the extent to which Tarsem (who directed all ten episodes and served as executive producer) retained creative control. It echoes the international ethos of *The Fall*, including casting in primary roles Puerto Rican Arjona as Dorothy; Romanian Ana Ularu as (the witch of the) West; Egyptian-German Mido Hamada as Eamonn; English-Jewish-Ugandan Loughran as transgender Tip/Ozma (see Pugh 2008; Jackman 2016; Crawford 2016); and German-Ugandan Florence Kasumba as (the witch of the) East.

Vincent D'Onofrio (who also played the serial killer in *The Cell*) as the sexist and (White-) patriarchal Wizard represents and champions science, while the witches and others of their sisterhood, including Joely Richardson's Glinda/(witch of the) North, take the part of magic. However, as in Tarsem's other fairy-tale works, no simplistic binary of female/magic versus male/science emerges; things are pretty complex. Perhaps this lack of a simplistic dualistic hook of good versus evil, or even of science versus magic, was part of the problem for viewers anticipating them from a Wizard of Oz–themed work. And some of the audience wanted to see closer connections to the familiar Fleming film (see also Newell 2017). Further, the show's negative evaluation of guns and its anti-sexist, anti-patriarchal, anti-war messages would not please a conventional mainstream American audience.

Academic responses to *Emerald City* tend to be more positive than those of other reviewers and audiences. Alison Tedman notes approvingly the lack of "objectification of female characters" (2017), particularly by the use of highly distinctive costuming (another emblem of Tarsem's work). The plot is complex, as in other works intended to reward multiple viewings. Dorothy, a twenty-something nurse, is transported by a tornado from today's Kansas to Oz in a police car with a dog she predictably names Toto, after seeking out her biological mother in a trailer park. She encounters the tribal Munja'kins, rescues the crucified amnesiac scarecrow figure she calls Lucas (played by Oliver Jackson-Cohen), and tricks the witch of the East into killing herself.

While en route to Emerald City, hoping that the Wizard will restore the scarecrow's memory and send Dorothy back to Kansas, she and Lucas gradually learn about the threat of "the Beast Forever," a mysterious destructive force that takes different forms. Since coming to power, the Wizard has outlawed magic because it threatens his dictatorial powers, in return for his promise to use science to protect Emerald City from the Beast Forever. He has, however, sacrificed other locations and realms to save it, such that, for example, many denizens of the Land of Ev drowned in the Wizard's response to the Beast's last attack. And the Wizard blackmails and murders those he suspects of harboring magic, threatening their families' lives and killing them if they fail to choose his side, that of science. The series' concluding episode demonstrates magic's transcendent power, and Dorothy returns to Kansas, but the scarecrow character appears there, indicating that she is needed back in Oz. Despite a petition on change.org, it seems unlikely that there will be a second season to specify what Tarsem intended for the follow-up.

The characters who link back to Kansas—including the Wizard (who, though he has outlawed magic, is not above appropriating it for his own purposes) and Dr. Jane Andrews (played by Gina McKee), who saves Ozma's friend Jack (played by Gerran Howell) by making him a mechanical metal body (including his heart)—mainly use science. However, as with the flying monkeys and Jane's resurrection of Jack, their science is inflected with magic. Those most adept with magic are the female witches. The four witch sisters, despite obvious racialized differences, share a biological mother, and each has sought her own way to cope with the Wizard's patriarchal power, allowing him to direct their use of magic. But the bicultural (born in Oz/raised in Kansas) Dorothy, who proves to be skillful with both magic and science, undermines the simplistic binary. *Emerald City*'s fourth of ten episodes, "Science and Magic," makes the linkage explicit. The relation of Storyrealm and Taleworld does not approach *The Fall*'s complexity, but as in it, a simulacrum of the real present day plays a significant role (see figure 3.6).

That episode offers some plot elements that later prove crucial: Jane's reconstruction of Jack, the Tin Woodsman figure, and his introduction to the multi-masked Langwidere; Dorothy's meeting the child witch Sylvie (played by Rebeka Rea) and her extraordinary powers; the Wizard's choice of new adviser Anna (played by Isabel Lucas); Tip's meeting Glinda and East, representing options, as Tip states, "So you're saying my only choice as a girl is nun or whore?" (respectively); and direct evidence of the Wizard's brutality against those who seek to oppose him. It also includes an exchange confirming magic's centrality to Oz.

> WIZARD: Do you know the difference between science and magic?
> JERMIAH (VILLAGE ALDERMAN, PLAYED BY JOPLIN SIBTAIN):
>   Only that one is a lie.

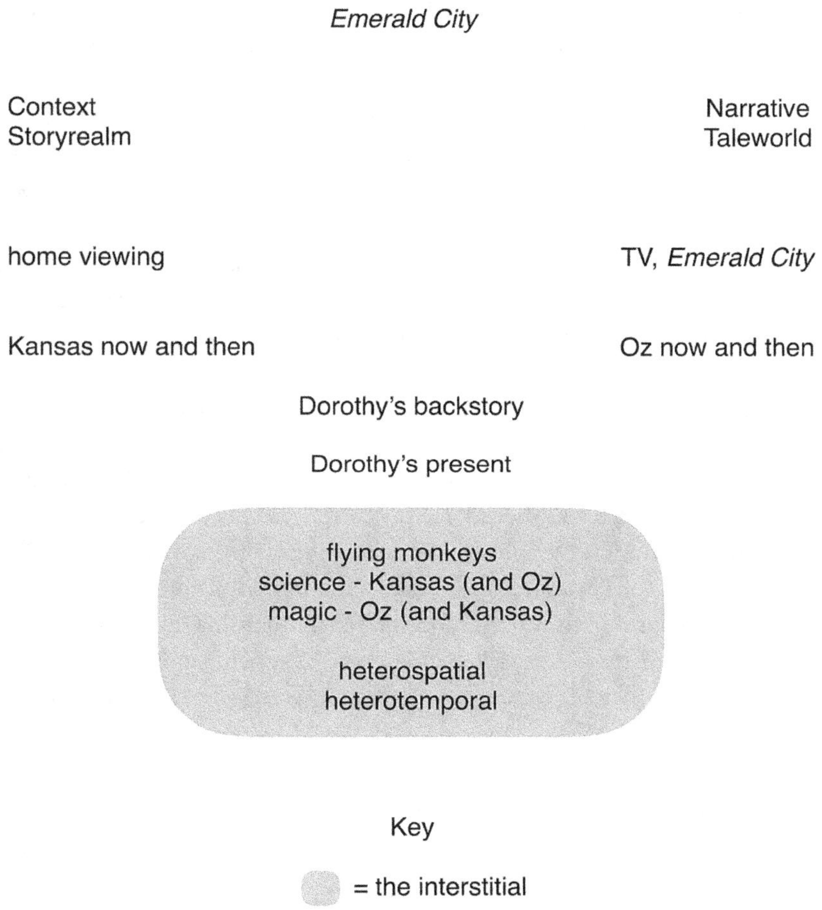

Emerald City

Context Storyrealm	Narrative Taleworld
home viewing	TV, *Emerald City*
Kansas now and then	Oz now and then

Dorothy's backstory

Dorothy's present

> flying monkeys
> science - Kansas (and Oz)
> magic - Oz (and Kansas)
>
> heterospatial
> heterotemporal

Key

⬤ = the interstitial

FIGURE 3.6. Storyrealms and Taleworlds in *Emerald City*.

WIZARD: Ah, which one is that?
JERMIAH: Oz is a land of enchantment. Magic is its heart.

The flying monkeys, machines representing the Wizard's science and mechanics, in part parallel the metaphorical locations of the camera obscura in *The Fall* and the zoetrope in *Mirror Mirror* (see figure 3.7). Like the two mechanical devices, the monkeys are introduced early in the narrative. As some of the arsenal the Wizard uses to spy on magic and the witches, these objects may look a bit like their biological simian relatives, but unlike the hybrid Jack (originally human, and becomes part human, part machine), there's no evidence of any attempt to render them as even partly flesh and blood. They are steampunk science, though the motor for their operation is mysterious. Are they part clockwork? Nuclear? (Part of the Kansas subplot has the Wizard, Jane, and others working in a nuclear power plant.) Battery operated? Or simply magic? Whatever their source, termed "drones," they seem purpose-built for the Wizard.

About a third into episode 1, "The Beast Forever," the first view of a flying monkey shows one airborne over an expanse of water. The creature itself turns the crank that apparently runs the rotor blades beside its body (but it's unclear what powers the monkey itself). The camera circles around behind it, as the monkey drone flies past a stone colossus toward a cathedral-like building. As the camera pulls out from a view behind the apparatus, it shows two of the Wizard's advisers crossing a bridge and entering the Wizard's room, where he plays a keyboard. He says, "Why do I get the feeling, Isabel, when I stop playing you're going to deliver some horrible news?" As the Wizard turns from the keyboard, the viewer has a first look at his face. "Something has happened in the east," Isabel (played by Suan-Li Ong) says. The two advisers cross the room and pick up the drone. They bring it into a room with a large table at which other advisers are at first seated—but they stand when the Wizard enters. "This drone was over the Tribal Free Lands last night. Near the Munja'kin Village," says the other adviser. An extreme close-up shows the monkey face, one eye lit up. It has three lenses that can be rotated

FIGURE 3.7. Monkey drone in *Emerald City*.

into position around it. The light from the eye flashes as the camera moves over the Wizard's face. He watches what it projects. A view from behind shows the hand of one adviser turning a small crank in the side of the monkey's head, as it projects a view of Dorothy's tornado on a screen. "Wait. Slower," says the Wizard. "Closer, closer." The adviser changes to another lens. The projected image, as if from a dirty, optically imperfect lens, reveals the police car in which Dorothy arrived in Oz, falling. The adviser indicates that they have "the first true sign. Now the Beast Forever will rise."

The above-described scene is the first one in the series that does not focus on Dorothy's views and experiences, entering a realm and introducing people she has not yet encountered. It's preceded by an exchange between Dorothy and Munja'kin Ojo, who is the first to talk about the West and North witches and the Wizard. Ojo explains that the Beast Forever "takes many forms"—flood, fire, and "monstrosities that slither and soar"—and that the Wizard used the "Eternal Warriors" (now manifesting as stone giants), who "formed a wall around Emerald City to keep the Beast Forever from flooding our entire world." "Yeah, definitely not Kansas," Dorothy quips.

The flying monkey sequence crucially offers the first view of the Wizard in person and also of his nun-like advisers, costumed in robes with large circular headdresses. It establishes the Wizard's position of power over a multitude of women—he questions, they answer. It demonstrates his use of magic and science in directing the projection of the drone's images, and it also tells the audience that Dorothy's appearance in Oz may portend badly for him. The revelatory scene is immediately followed by the Wizard commanding Eamonn, the head of his (male) human army, to kill or bury whatever has arrived in Oz to ensure that "it doesn't come *back* here" (my emphasis). The Wizard's wording suggests that he suspects who has come (back) and that she threatens his power. It also shows that he's not only a despot, but a ruthless, murderous one. He is in no way the 1939 *Oz* film's well-meaning and benevolent but bumbling ruler.

The applications of the narrative to its contemporary world and its current leaders were noted by at least one reviewer:

> In our real, albeit increasingly nonsensical world, we're witnessing the battle between science and magic play out again, as it has for centuries. Somehow, decades of consistent research from the world's leading experts on topics including climate change, human sexuality, reproductive rights, gender, criminal justice, income disparities and on and on can be legitimately

refuted by people who . . . just don't believe that. . . . Before Enlightenment turned science into a discipline grounded in facts, observation and study, everything could be explained through magic—or religion. But here we are, again. In *Emerald City*, the Wizard is a proponent of science, as long as the science helps him hide his powerlessness, maintain control and furthers his greed and lust. Magic, in Oz, belongs to the people; magic connects them to their culture and their understanding of the world. That's not beneficial for the leader, so it must be suppressed. (Venable 2017)

In the end, journalist Malcolm Venable pulls back from a direct condemnation of (unnamed by him) leaders like US president Donald Trump who resemble Tarsem's Wizard; after all, the piece appeared in the very mainstream *TV Guide*. Venable concludes that "science and faith—not to mention technology and religion, the common folk and the high class—can co-exist peacefully; . . . we need those contrasting forces to push life forward. *No one POV is inherently more 'right' than the other.* That's something we need to hear now more than ever" (2017; my emphasis). It may not be coincidental that this coded commentary (see chapter 1) refers to a conflict on the "right"— Venable could alternatively have used instead, for example, "correct," "factual," or "true." This "everybody's equally right" argument shows a specious relativism; the position of the American extreme Christian right is by no means an accurate representation of the world. But even a coded defense of the left in the context of current mainstream journalism can be alternative (see, e.g., Victor 2017).

Emerald City, like *The Fall* and *Mirror Mirror*, tends to side more with magic than with science; magic can have good purposes, though when co-opted by the Wizard, it is dangerous and destructive. But science on its own seems to have few benign uses. Science, the Enlightenment, and the rational ultimately fail. Not only is it true that "only a witch can kill a witch"—for example, Dorothy tricks East into turning the gun on herself—but the viewer suspects (and turns out to be correct) that witches aren't as easy to simply vanquish as the Wizard thinks. Dorothy's allegiance is clarified in the "Science and Magic" episode. Lucas, the scarecrow, asks her, "Is there magic in your world?"

DOROTHY: Yeah.
LUCAS: Yeah?

DOROTHY: Yeah, but it's different. We have science, and . . . Technology. [She reaches for her cell phone.]
LUCAS: And what's that?
DOROTHY: You'll see. Put this in your ear. Trust me.

After Lucas's initial shock at hearing music from the earphones (Bill Withers's classic 1971 soul number "Ain't No Sunshine"), he guesses, "Science." And Dorothy counters, "Magic." The things Dorothy loves, that are most important to her like great songs, are magical, not scientific. The episode closes, however, with village alderman Jermiah, as the Wizard's guards threaten his daughter and unborn grandchild, renouncing witchcraft and urging the villagers to accept science; the Wizard watching over Anna; and Lucas and Dorothy kissing and then fleeing the Wizard's guards. The resolution of magic and science doesn't come until the tenth and final episode, "No Place Like Home," in which the witches triumph and Ozma is crowned.

Resistant Fairy Tales

What do all these magical and scientific tricks enable or at least make possible in the mind's eye? I argue that they open toward conceptualizing something different—the foundation of any social change. Though not all imagination is subversive or progressive, Tarsem's wild chronotopes and dazzling magic tricks of heterospatial and heterotemporal criticism, deconstruction, and fragmentation invoke multiple viewpoints and what Donna Haraway calls "situated knowledge" and "partial perspective" (1988). It seems difficult to maintain confidence in a position that celebrates multiplicity in the face of politicians best known for cynical falsehoods (Kristof 2017). And rhetorical moves are surely simply wrong when they demonstrate a simplistic cultural relativism and equate White supremacist violence with anti-racist narratives and activism that seek to address, for example, the ongoing marginalization of people of color in North America. Recognizing plural views does not mean presuming they all have equal value.

Thus *The Fall*, *Mirror Mirror*, and *Emerald City* expose how motivations (Roy's, the Queen's, and the Wizard's, respectively) make apparently innocent stories at times toxic and dangerous. Unpacking Roy's narrative flourishes means the audience must enact their own mental heterospatial moves, putting themselves in his and Alexandria's places, to understand not only why they see the world in different ways but also how their experiences have formed diverse ways of seeing. Unlike the Queen in *Mirror Mirror* and the Wizard in *Emerald City*, Roy is not inherently evil. He's (temporarily) a camera obscura, seeing things upside down and backward; circumstances have helped him forget his obligations to treat others humanely.

In *Mirror Mirror*, the Queen's attempts to contain heterotemporality—to be like the zoetrope's rose and renew herself endlessly—avoid the reality that in life, such cycles can't simply be endlessly repeated. Aging and death are inevitable. *Mirror Mirror* does not give the Queen a sympathetic backstory, as does not only *Snow White and the Huntsman* but also *Maleficent* (directed by Robert Stromberg, 2014). There's no evading that, like some politicians, she's simply wrong and evil. Like theirs, her attempts to turn back time have evil consequences. Yet she is defeated by a coalition of the less powerful and ultimately recognized as the tyrant she is.

A similar process manifests in *Emerald City*'s heterospatial and heterotemporal moves and the flying monkeys' conflation of magic and science, as well as their multiple purposes for surveillance, recording, and projection. The Wizard's backstory makes his objection to women's (legitimate) power, in episode 6, "Beautiful Wickedness," even more obviously based in his own megalomania and wish to dominate women, including sexually. His jealousy and manipulation are the reasons why he and Dorothy are in Oz in the first place. As in reality, communities in his fictional realm must act in coalition to defeat him.

Fairy tales like *The Fall*, *Mirror Mirror*, and *Emerald City* present telling instances of fictions offering significant truths and sometimes quite brutal judgments against wrongdoers, whereby they propose something useful—resistances, inspirations—and not only morality narratives and object lessons in the abuses of power. African American feminist Patricia Hill Collins (2002) argues the importance of a free mind, one that can imagine alternatives in advance of manifesting them. The otherworldly realms of fairy tales make them a potential place and time for the play and work of that free mind, and *The Fall*'s, *Mirror Mirror*'s, and *Emerald City*'s fairy tales can literalize a politics of fantasy, what Cristina Bacchilega (2013) calls a "fairy-tale web" of sometimes trenchant subversions and open choices. For those of us who find the world today paralyzingly dystopic, imagining our empowerment—as fairy tales and these films do—can be useful in helping us to enact it.

Where realities and unrealities coexist, sometimes without boundaries, neither ultimately diverts from the other. Bacchilega's call to decommodify magic within the fairy-tale web articulates questions around "the politics of wonder," including querying "what kind of trouble mixing genres makes and for whom" (2013, 28) and "what is the transformative social potential of the varied poetics of wonder that is emerging from different sites in the fairy-tale web?" (29), particularly "in a world that has been characterized as disenchanted" (30). The real world, now more than ever actually experienced by thinking people as a dangerous place wherein despots regularly Trump truth, compassion, and supportive community, may in these films be restrictive and harmful, but their realms of magic offer no anodyne solution. Instead, in *The Fall*, *Mirror Mirror*, and *Emerald City*, communities work together while the apparently weakest find their sources of power to defeat despots. A similar interest in sustaining and encouraging communities manifests in the next chapter, wherein I turn to another kind of interaction between reality and fiction, with intersecting feedback between the thriving actual village of Saint-Élie-de-Caxton and its connections to the magical stories of Fred Pellerin and to two films made from those works.

4

Ça existe vraiment (It really exists)!

Babine, *Ésimésac*, and Ostension at Saint-Élie-de-Caxton

IT'S NOT UNUSUAL FOR EVENTS TO ENGENDER STORIES ABOUT THEM, but sometimes stories—in any medium or form—can also engender events. Folklorists call this mimicry-in-enactment ostension, and it appears most frequently in legend study. Linda Dégh and Andrew Vázsonyi compellingly explore how "not only can facts be turned into narratives but narratives can also be turned into facts" (1983, 12; see also Ellis 1989, 2001). The examples Dégh and Vázsonyi discuss in detail relate to Halloween and extend from adulterating treats for children, to making and wearing costumes, to doing haunted houses, to making and showing films. They trace these events and material culture forms to origins in rumor, memorate (story of personal experience), and legend (story implicating truth, but not always actually believed by all tellers and all audiences). For example, Bill Ellis discusses how murders become imbricated with ideas from legends, so that legends become "paradigms for making the world more horrifying" (1989, 219). But ostension also plays a role in other forms of narrative and media—in this case, fairy tales and films.

At issue here, several processes of ostension operate with respect to two fairy-tale/magical realist[1] films directed by Luc Picard: *Babine* (2008) and *Ésimésac* (2012). Based on narratives by storyteller and writer Fred Pellerin, they are set in his actual birthplace and home, the village of Saint-Élie-de-Caxton, Mauricie, Quebec. Pellerin's own experiences living in Saint-Élie-de-Caxton provide some of the factual basis for his stories, but he also invents magical and wondrous events and characters. Both realistic and imaginary elements ground not only the films but also the presentation within the geographical village of Saint-Élie-de-Caxton of fantasy elements—including *l'arbre à paparmanes*[2] (peppermint tree)[3] and *la traverse de lutins* (elf or gnome crossing),[4] which become tourist visiting sites, along with the graves of the historical figures who inspired characters in the stories/films and the houses or locations where they lived.

Ostension of Pellerin's narratives further enters the lives of Quebecers, even outside Saint-Élie-de-Caxton. For example, my neighbor Annie Bédard's family is from Saint-Prosper, Beauce, in Chaudière-Appalaches region, east of Mauricie. Annie's mother loved Pellerin's stories, and for her wake the florist made a *paparmane* tree. As Annie and her sister Josée discussed in an interview:

> ANNIE: When my mother died—she loved *paparmanes*, and Fred Pellerin's Saint-Élie-de-Caxton is well known for their *paparmane* tree. And when my mother died, Josée decided to ask the florist to create a *paparmane* tree. And then to have a bowl of *paparmanes* that when people would come to give their sympathy, before they would take a *paparmane* and then they would come to give their sympathy. And Josée had written a very nice poem and she made a line with "There's not only in Saint-Élie-de-Caxton that there's

1 I use "magic realist" and "magical realist" interchangeably.
2 *Paparmane* is a Quebec term for peppermint candy; derived from the English "peppermint," it can also be spelled *pepparmane* and *papermanne* ("Paparmane" n.d.). In Pellerin's stories, unlikely objects magically grow into or on trees when left on the ground or buried, including a watch (as in *Babine*) and *paparmanes*.
3 Unless otherwise indicated, translations are mine. Quotations with fewer than ten words in French I leave in the text; for those with ten words or more, I place the original French in an endnote.
4 I use "gnome" because so many of the representations of *lutins* in Saint-Élie-de-Caxton itself would be identified in much of North America as lawn or garden gnomes.

a *paparmane* tree, now there's one in Saint-Prosper" to testify the life of our mother who loved *paparmanes*.

JOSÉE: And when we buried her, because when she died it was in December, we buried her in April, I brought some *paparmanes* and we threw some *paparmanes* in the grave, just to tell her, "Have fun." . . . .

ANNIE: Yeah and it was fun because at the funeral, was this beautiful little tree, like the florist used some cotton balls and in every cotton ball, she put a *paparmane* inside, and it really looked like a *paparmane* tree.

JOSÉE: And people talk a lot about this *paparmane* tree.

ANNIE: And when we were welcoming them to take one, therefore when they were coming to give us their sympathy and shake hands, all of them had the big mouth with a big *paparmane* in their cheek! It was very funny. But at the same time, it was comforting and very touching to see that people were part of it. (Bédard and Bédard 2018)

Here ostension—the creation of a *paparmane* tree, based on Pellerin's stories, in Saint-Élie-de-Caxton—derives a new ostension—the creation of a *paparmane* tree, based on Pellerin's stories and the Saint-Élie-de-Caxton tree, as a participatory element at Mme. Bédard's wake.

This relocation and re-creation confirms the storyteller's own evaluation that "I define myself within Saint-Élie, which is real, which has a distinctive culture and which rings in the universal" (Langevin 2010, 5).[5] As Annie said:

> I grew up with my father telling me stories that were like legends: half fictive, half reality, from the town beside. I was going to bed with those stories. And therefore we have been always interested by storytelling and legend, and Fred Pellerin, I think he revived that in Québec. . . . I think we're touched by those stories, by the memory of our childhood. Because, so, when you're born in a small village, which is our case, every village has their fool, every village has particular characters that you can relate to the stories of Fred Pellerin. They are different, it's different stories, but culturally it's very similar. And I think this way, it's why it's making it

---

5 Je me définis dans Saint-Élie qui est réel, qui a une culture particulière et qui sonne dans l'universel.

universal, about the storytelling and the fact that we all love it. (Bédard and Bédard 2018)

Though his stories invoke the universal, specifics of place are nevertheless central in Pellerin's work, in particular his home village.

Saint-Élie-de-Caxton

The Saint-Élie-de-Caxton tourism website's welcome page notes:

> People from elsewhere and everywhere, we most cordially welcome you to our Saint-Élie-de-Caxton, land of *lutins* and *paparmanes*. In an enchanting setting, you'll be able to meet a population of warm, welcoming and lively people. Take the time to savor our village on foot, by cart or by bicycle. You'll see, Saint-Élie-de-Caxton exists! Really! ("Saint-Élie: Ça existe vraiment!" n.d.)[6]

Saint-Élie-de-Caxton, a parish municipality in the Mauricie region, in the foothills of the Laurentians, was known simply as Saint-Élie before 2005, referencing the name of the first priest to serve the parish, Élie-Sylvestre Sirois-Duplessis (1795–1878; see Thériault 2008, 55), and the Christian prophet Elijah. Caxton was the historic name of the canton (township). Its population now hovers around fifteen hundred, and 95 percent of its people have French as their first language ("Saint-Élie-de-Caxton" 2017; see also Pellerin 2006; Thériault 2008).

The writer's effect on his hometown is frequently noted:

> Pellerin admits that tourism in Saint-Élie-de-Caxton seriously increased since his success and that the village had to organize a guided tour of its handful of streets. Some good people come to attend the Christmas Mass in Saint-Élie, others make a detour to place their order at the now famous potato hut. After hearing Fred boast the wonders of his quiet and zany

---

6   Gens d'ailleurs et de partout, nous vous souhaitons la plus cordiale des bienvenues dans notre Saint-Élie-de-Caxton, pays des lutins et des « paparmanes ». Dans un décor plus qu'enchanteur, vous aurez la chance de côtoyer une population de gens chaleureux, accueillants et pleins d'entrain. Prenez le temps de savourer notre village, à pied, en carriole ou à bicyclette. Vous verrez, Saint-Élie-de-Caxton, ça existe! Vraiment!

life, many plan a return to village life—some even think of emigrating to Saint-Élie! (Gingras 2008, 39)[7]

Annie concurred with these comments:

> Fred Pellerin is definitely an activist, and he's not doing storytelling just because he likes it, but because he wanted to put Saint-Élie-de-Caxton on the map. He wanted to save this village, and to save this village, he said that "I have to be out, I have to talk about it, I have to do something." And his creativity brought the public and they created, as you know, the walk and so many events, but not only that, because he was able to talk about Saint-Élie and staying there. He could have left for Montreal and have another type of career, but no, he still stays in Saint-Élie and he's very proud of it. But his art has also brought a lot of people, new families to Saint-Élie-de-Caxton and they were able to save the school. . . . That, for me, is political. It's the art-in-action, in a way, to save the school and also promoting the arts. (Bédard and Bédard 2018)

A plethora of discourses (re)create Saint-Élie-de-Caxton as a topographical location that instantiates the links between fiction and reality. For example, a reviewer of *Ésimésac* says that in the film "we're in Saint-Élie-de-Caxton not in historical reality" (Protat 2013, 57).[8] And Bertrand Bergeron discusses in detail how Saint-Élie-de-Caxton as a tourist destination mediates experience and imagination, along with his evaluation of Pellerin's place in oral and literary traditions of Quebec. "Saint-Élie-de-Caxton exists in two intimately interpenetrating ways. It reveals geography before accessing the imaginary" (2014, 20).[9]

---

7   Pellerin a avoué que le tourisme à Saint-Élie avait sérieusement augmenté depuis le succès qu'il connaît, et que la ville a dû organiser un tour guidé de la poignée de rues qui la ceinturent. De sympathiques écornifleux viennent assister à la messe de Noël à Saint-Élie, d'autres font un détour pour passer leur commande à la désormais célèbre cabane à patates. Après avoir entendu Fred vanter les merveilles de sa petite vie tranquille et loufoque, plusieurs envisagent un retour à la vie de village—certains songeraient même à émigrer à Saint-Élie!
8   Nous sommes à Saint-Élie-de-Caxton et non dans la réalité historique.
9   Saint-Élie-de-Caxton existe de deux manières intimement interpénétrées. Il relève d'abord de la géographie avant d'accéder à l'imaginaire.

The church, which appears in both films as a studio build and in *Babine*, crucially, on location in the final sequence, as I discuss below, was begun in 1921 after its predecessor burned (as it does in *Babine*) and was dedicated in 1922.[10] Other important sites in the village related to the films are the houses of characters Babine, Toussaint Brodeur, Ésimésac Gélinas, La Stroop (the witch), and Méo Bellemare; the ostension of the gnome crossing and peppermint tree; and the graves of Pellerin's real-life characters. As I discuss in this chapter's conclusion, my June 2018 visit to the village showed me the residents' perhaps surprisingly large degree of participation in the often ostensive creation of a distinct location, including by decorating their houses and properties with *lutins*, *paparmanes*, fleur de lys Quebec flags, and more.

Fred Pellerin

Born in 1976 in Saint-Élie-de-Caxton and a graduate of l'Université du Québec à Trois-Rivières, the musician, singer, storyteller, writer, and scriptwriter Pellerin has been nominated for and won numerous awards. He credits his interest in storytelling to evenings at his parents' home, saying that his taste for telling tales comes from his taste for listening to them and that in the village he listens more than he tells (see also "Biographie" 2016).

> In the sanitized world we're offered, where wonder is extinguished before the great laws of reason, I force myself to reintroduce everyday magic. Storytelling, before being an artistic process, is a personal and community approach. To dream of a village that surrealizes itself, I make frequent gestures seeking to overcome the real. (Pellerin quoted in Gingras 2008, 41)[11]

Pellerin comments that in his artistic process, "I mostly read a lot of novels and spent evenings with the old people of the village, to chat. It's also a form

---

10 On the church's history and construction, see Thériault (2008, 47–49).
11 Dans le monde aseptisé qu'on nous offre, où l'émerveillement s'éteint devant les grandes lois de la raison, je me force à réinjecter du magique aux jours. Le conte, avant d'être une démarche artistique, c'est une démarche personnelle et communautaire. À rêver d'un village qui se surréalise de lui-même, je pose des gestes fréquents à tenter de dépasser le réel.

of cinema" (quoted in Gendron 2009, 16).[12] He sees his work, given its basis in fact, as closer to legend than to folktale and fairy tale (Guindon 2007), an evaluation with which many folklorists would agree.

Pellerin's other movie credits include cowriting the screenplay for *Pieds nus dans l'aube* (Barefoot at Dawn) (2017) with Francis Leclerc, son of the famous singer-songwriter, poet, novelist, playwright, actor, broadcaster, and political activist Félix Leclerc (Roy et al. 2008). The film is based on Félix Leclerc's 1946 autobiographical novel of the same name. Its setting, 1920s La Tuque, Quebec (also in Mauricie, some 150 kilometers north of Saint-Élie-de-Caxton), recalls the pastoral aspects of *Babine* and *Ésimésac* but, designated as "drama" on IMDb, unlike them it remains securely realist. Pellerin also did the voice-overs in both *Babine* and *Ésimésac* and acted in a television movie of his storytelling (which he wrote), a video, and a television series. He has one soundtrack, record albums, and several recorded appearances as himself to his credit.

Pellerin is an important figure in the current revival of oral storytelling in Quebec (see Chrupała and Warmuzińska-Rogóż 2013; Bergeron 2014); one reviewer calls him "*notre barde national*" (our national bard) (Robin 2013, 60). Like so many other Quebec artists and creators, he is socially conscious and politically active. For example, when in 2012 then premier Jean Charest named Pellerin to l'Ordre national du Québec, he declined the honor in solidarity with student protests against Charest's proposal to raise university tuition (see "Fred Pellerin absent." 2012). When Charest's government was defeated, Pellerin accepted the award from successor premier Pauline Marois ("Fred Pellerin reçoit" 2012).

Alex Guindon notes Pellerin's ability to transmute the mundane into the marvelous (2007, 34). Literary scholar Chantale Gingras calls him "*la rock star du conte*" (the rock star of tales),

> a response to the madness of modern times. . . . one can't help but see him as a man who fights against global acceleration, against globalization, against a uniform culture that extends across the planet. Listening to the stories of his hometown, to all these winks about the everyday that he sprinkles with snake oil, we see the ephemeral take a little of the traces of

---

12 J'ai surtout lu bien des romans et passé des veillées avec les vieux du village, à jaser. C'est aussi une forme de cinéma.

time, and we see, again and again, that the universal is best attained in the particular. (Gingras 2008, 39)[13]

Pellerin acknowledges inspiration from filmmaker Tim Burton (quoted in Gendron 2009, 17)—a connection noted by reviewer Helen Faradji, who also links Pellerin with the cinema of Guillermo del Toro (2008). In an article entitled "Réenchanter le monde par le conte" (Re-enchanting the World through Storytelling), calling Pellerin a gifted narrator, Jean-Marc Massie says, "Thanks to the storyteller, we may perhaps hope to reclaim the realm of dreams and thus attempt to put the brakes on the disenchantment of the modern world" (2002, 49).[14] These qualities are shared with Burton, del Toro, and Tarsem (as seen in the previous chapter).

Gingras characterizes Pellerin's style as involving exaggeration, nostalgic philosophy, a touch of simple poetry, an appealing irreverence, charming anachronisms, beautiful old turns of phrase and pronunciation, unexpected metaphors, verbal invention, double meaning, and alteration of well-known expressions (paraphrased, 2008, 40). Such writing, as might be expected, offers great difficulty for translators, which may in part explain why Pellerin's incredible familiarity in French Canada is matched only by his near-unknown status in English Canada. Calling his stories *"trop beaux pour ne pas être vrais"* (too beautiful not to be true) (41), Gingras notes traditional aspects of Pellerin's stories—magic and witchcraft as well as key figures who must succeed at difficult or impossible tasks, "a bit like the many traditional Quebec folktales featuring Ti-Jean" (2008, 40).[15] Pellerin's writing and personality are evident in both *Babine* and *Ésimésac*, but the director and main character actor is also a significant persona in the films.

13   une réponse à la folie des temps modernes. . . . on ne peut s'empêcher de le voir comme un homme qui se bat contre l'accélération globale, contre la mondialisation, contre une culture uniforme qui s'étend à l'échelle de la planète. En prêtant oreille aux histoires de son patelin, à tous ces clins d'oeil du quotidien qu'il saupoudre de poudre de perlimpinpin, on voit l'éphémère prendre un peu les traces du temps, et on constate, encore et toujours, que c'est dans le particulier qu'on atteint le mieux l'universel.
14   Grâce à la parole conteuse, nous pourrons peut-être espérer nous réapproprier le domaine du rêve et ainsi tenter de mettre un frein au désenchantement du monde moderne.
15   un peu à la manière des nombreux contes où figure Ti-Jean, le personnage-phare des contes folkloriques québécois traditionnels

Luc Picard

The actor, director, and screenwriter who directed both films and also played shopkeeper hero Toussaint Brodeur in them, Picard trained at the Conservatoire d'Art Dramatique in Montreal. He has a multitude of acting credits in theater and film and also directed *Les rois mongols* (The Mongol Kings) (2017, released in English as *Cross My Heart*) and *Audition* (2005), which he wrote and in which he also played the main character (see Cailher 2008); he was also one of the nine Quebecois directors (including Micheline Lanctôt, whose work I discuss in chapter 6) represented in the film anthology *9* (2016). His entry in *The Canadian Encyclopedia* notes "his social and political commitment" to left and Quebec sovereignty politics; his role as "spokesperson of the international cooperation organization Development and Peace, of Chic Resto Pop, which provides affordable meals to the less fortunate, and of the Maison des jeunes, which is intended to defend respect for young people and their rights"; as well as his pacifism. Diane Cailher concludes:

> Luc Picard's exceptional artistic talent has won over public opinion and the critics and brought his peers' admiration. His brilliant career has given him the status of a respected star worthy of popular favour and cinema honours. His integrity and courageous political positions have also made him a leading figure with regard to the engagement of artists as responsible citizens. (2008)

Here I would argue that another level of ostension operates. As an actor, Picard brings this personal history, familiar to his Quebec and Canadian francophone audiences, to the work he does, including these two fairy-tale films. His character, Toussaint Brodeur, similarly seeks peace and reconciliation in Saint-Élie-de-Caxton; Toussaint regularly intervenes on behalf of individuals in the interest of fair and reasonable actions, and he also seeks ways to improve the community and to join its members in positive action. As Josée commented: "There is always a Toussaint Brodeur in small communities. People of common sense; people trying to keep equity, not morality in the bad sense. But if you can have a mayor like Toussaint Brodeur, it is a good thing" (Bédard and Bédard 2018).

(How) Are *Babine* and *Ésimésac* Relevant to Fairy Tale?

Babine (IMDb, "adventure, drama, fantasy") and *Ésimésac* (IMDb, "adventure, fantasy, sci-fi") invoke magical realism as well as fairy tales and other forms of folklore and traditional culture.[16] More than thirty years ago, literary theorist Fredric Jameson distinguished magic realism from fantastic literature by noting that "magic realism now comes to be understood as a kind of narrative raw material derived essentially from peasant society, drawing in sophisticated ways on the world of village or even tribal myth" (1986, 302). The films Jameson discusses, like Picard's films of Pellerin's work set in traditional Quebec village society, deal with history and violence, using distinctive, often darkened color palettes.

Alluding to fairy tales—the stories collected as "Arabian Nights" or "1001 Nights"—Wendy B. Faris's "Scheherazade's Children: Magical Realism and Postmodern Fiction," defines her topic in terms of an "irreducible element of magic, something we cannot explain according to the laws of the universe as we know them" (1995, 167); "a strong presence of the phenomenal world" (169); the reader's "unsettling doubts" about "contradictory understandings of events" (171); "closeness or near-merging of two realms" (172), that is, those of the magic and the real; and "question[ing] received ideas about time, space, and identity" (173). Amaryll Chanady seeks to distinguish (literary) magical realism from fairy tales on the basis of her overly constricting views of the latter as "rigid" and "effectively restrict[ing] the imaginary to well-defined models" (1995, 130).

Joel Hancock, in contrast, draws structural links between magical realist author Gabriel García Márquez's novella "The Incredible and Sad Tale of Innocent Eréndira and Her Heartless Grandmother" and some of the more famous tales in the Brothers Grimm's anthology, precisely because he sees in Márquez the Proppian formulae that Chanady argues are absent from magical realism. Hancock argues that Eréndira is a Cinderella-like figure, and he picks motifs from other wonder tales to construct his argument. He sees as fairy-tale-like "the frame of the story; the description and development of

---

16 They are certainly not the only films to connect magic realism and fairy-tale forms; not surprisingly, *Eréndira* (directed by Ruy Guerra, 1983), with the novel and screenplay written by canonical magical realist author Gabriel García Márquez, also links them (see Santos-Phillips 2003).

the characters; the role of ingredients such as cruelty and bloodshed; the mixing of reality and fantasy" (1978, 50).

Similarly, Arnold M. Penuel connects Márquez's short story "El rastro de tu sangre en la nieve" to "Sleeping Beauty" (ATU 410) and other tales, beginning with "the titular image of blood on the snow" (1995, 239) and other motifs Penuel associates with "Snow White" (ATU 709). He suggests, "It should come as no surprise that the master of 'magical realism' should have recourse to fairy tales, in which the supernatural is paramount" (241). Penuel remarks that Márquez's story "diverges from the typical fairy tale in which the hero faces hardships and terror, but in the end overcomes them, symbolically undergoing a process of maturation that enables him (or her) to survive and even thrive in life (live happily ever after)" (1995, 247). As should by now be clear, though, current versions of traditional tales, including those in fairy-tale media, often similarly avoid the predicted happy ending, closings at least temporarily present in both films from Pellerin's stories.

Particularly when discussing written rather than cinematic forms, some theorists distinguish the magical realms of fairy tales, in contrast to the everyday settings of magical realism (see, e.g., Leal 1995; Wilson 1995). However, as this work shows, fairy-tale films and other nonliterary media are frequently set in the quotidian. Claudia Schwabe seeks to sort out the relations between magical and real *worlds* in two fairy-tale television series, *Grimm* and *Once Upon a Time*, both at least partly based in a fictionalized present day. As she points out, it is by no means unusual for media to represent "the real world [as] . . . nuanced with multiple layers of detail and meaning" (2014, 298; see also Lukasiewicz 2010). Vanessa Joosen takes a highly pragmatic approach to the intersections of magical realism and fairy tales:

> Realistic is everything that can be explained by empirical science. In this view, it is perfectly realistic that a servant girl marries a prince, that a mother trades her daughter for a vegetable, or that a poor farmer finds a treasure and buys a castle. Not realistic are animals or objects that communicate in human speech, horses that fly, or fairies that can turn a pumpkin into a coach. (2007, 230)

Joosen advocates understanding "the opposition between magic and realism as a continuum" (230); certainly they appear to act as such in *Babine* and *Ésimésac*. For example, some of the witch figure's powers are simply practical, but others are preternatural. Similarly, the diegetic exercise of planting in *Ésimésac* includes conventional seeds but also *paparmanes*, with an apparently equal expectation that they will grow.

Another reason for considering these films as fairy tale is their popular reputation as such with their audience. Very few Quebec films make their way consistently into English-language venues in other provinces, so several years ago, I inquired of colleagues and students in Quebec in preparation for writing the entry on Canada for *Fairy-Tale Films Beyond Disney: International Perspectives* (Zipes, Greenhill, and Magnus-Johnston 2016). Just about everyone who answered the query concurred that *Babine* and *Ésimésac* were the two most important Quebec fairy-tale films (see Greenhill and Kohm 2016). Others agree, including at times the narratives' creator. Story author and screenplay writer Pellerin invokes fairy-tale wonder and formula in discussing *Babine*: "Initially, the tale is a time out of time. It's 'Once upon a time'. . . . I like to believe in a bubble where everything could exist, where everything could be magic. Because there's a lot of de-magic today; everything is de-magiced, reasoned, calculated" (quoted in Gendron 2009, 16).[17] He also notes that in making *Babine*, "We didn't need to pay attention to anachronisms; . . . we had 'once upon a time'" (19).[18]

Several reviewers similarly highlight the films' interactions between reality, belief, and magic. For example, Zoe Protat's article "Croire à la magie" (Believe in Magic) calls *Ésimésac* "anchored in some truth like magic realism" (2013, 57).[19] And interactions on the film sets and on location, particularly for *Ésimésac*, which was filmed mainly on constructed sets in Saint-Élie-de-Caxton, further complicate the links, as Pellerin describes:

> When I saw Marie-Chantal Perron, who plays Toussaint Brodeur's wife, with Michel Brodeur, Toussaint's son, on his father's tombstone . . . they are there, all three. It can't happen in life, it's difficult to cause, but we went there. Three entities that are not supposed to meet in the course of

---

17 Au départ, le conte, c'est un temps hors temps. C'est « Il était une fois ». . . . J'aime croire en une bulle où tout existerait, où tout serait magique. Parce qu'il y a beaucoup de démagie aujourd'hui; tout est démagié, raisonné, calculé.
18 On n'avait pas besoin de faire attention aux anachronismes; . . . on avait « Il était une fois ».
19 ancré dans une certaine vérité, à l'instar du réalisme magique.

real life: the tombstone of a legend, his son and the woman who plays his wife. (quoted in Gendron 2009, 20)[20]

Filmed in moody, darker-toned colors, Picard's two fairy-tale movies are named for their extraordinary male main characters. They underline the films' loose association with fairy tale but firm basis in traditional culture, manifesting in their concern for what folklorists, avoiding potentially loaded terminology, call "local characters." "Character" may actually be used in English-speaking communities to refer to individuals like "village idiot" Babine or strong man Ésimésac (actual name Onésime-Isaac). Folklorist Diane Tye finds that in Amherst, Nova Scotia, "the term refers to any individual whose dramatic performance . . . is recognized as being in contrast to, or in conflict with, governing social norms," and she notes that most other community members see the character as "non-threatening" and "often humorous" (1989, 182). The apparently intellectually disabled, like Babine, often find the role of local character useful as a way to manage the stigma too often associated with them. The community's evaluation often notes the ways the individual actually manifests greater acuity than others, that they are not stupid (discussed in Tye 1989, esp. 195–96); similarly, some characters in *Babine* note the title character's wisdom. Like many fairy-tale characters, especially those who are boys or men, he's a wise fool.

Though perhaps most often associated in English Canada with the legendary Paul Bunyan, many more strong men characters like Ésimésac—and stories about them—appear in French Canada. In nineteenth-century Quebec, the historical voyageur and logger Joe Montferrand became the subject of both true and apocryphal narratives of his prodigious physical strength (Monteiro 1960a). From the same century, from Trois Rivières, some forty-five kilometers from Saint-Élie-de-Caxton, came Maxime Duhaime; further, "one Giroux . . . took the place of his horse in the shafts of the wagon when his horse was too tired to make the summit of a hill" (Monteiro 1960b, 24). Though Ésimésac was a historical personage (*Ésimésac* DVD Extras), his notoriety appears to be mainly in the region around Saint-Élie-de-Caxton.

---

20 Moi, quand j'ai vu Marie-Chantal Perron, qui joue la femme de Toussaint Brodeur, avec Michel Brodeur, le fils de Toussaint, sur la pierre tombale de son père . . . Ils sont là, tous les trois. Ça ne peut pas se passer dans la vie, c'est difficile à provoquer, mais on est endu là. Trois entités qui ne sont pas supposées se rencontrer dans le cours réel de la vie: la pierre tombale d'une légende, son fils et la femme qui va incarner sa femme.

Local character anecdotes, unlike fairy tales, are not intended to be understood as fictional; their world is recognizably like that of the present day even if they are set in the past; most are thus legends. (However, note the extent to which, throughout this book, media creators set clearly fairy-tale-themed works in quotidian, realistic, present-day settings.) Though *Babine* and *Ésimésac* cannot be securely located as fairy tale alone, neither can many of the works I discuss elsewhere in this book; and these films' associations with that form and with other types of traditional narrative are sufficient to include them here.

Babine (2008)

Babine is based on stories from Pellerin's *Il faut prendre le taureau par les contes! contes de village* (You Must Take the Bull by the Tales! Village Stories) (2003).[21] Babine (played by Vincent-Guillaume Otis), son of local witch La Stroop (played by Isabel Richer), is called "*le fou du village*" (the village idiot) in Saint-Élie-de-Caxton. His mother sends him out into the village one evening to collect icicles with which she plans to weave snow. Coincidentally, while Babine is out, the church catches fire as a result of one of village merchant Toussaint's lightning bug experiments. Babine is first on the scene and raises the alarm. But help comes too late to save *le Vieux Curé*, the old priest, called Father Time in the English subtitles (played by Julien Poulin). The new priest (played by Alexis Martin) inexplicably hates Babine, accusing him of responsibility for the fire, imprisoning him, coercing him into confessing to causing the old priest's death, and sentencing him to hang. Babine's friend Toussaint sabotages the rope, freeing the young man. The priest again accuses and sentences Babine to death, but Toussaint helps him escape.

Babine follows a circus that features a beautiful dark-haired woman and a giant bull. He obtains what he thinks is a lock of the woman's hair and returns home to use his mother's spell book to summon her. But the hair

---

21 The title offers an example of Pellerin's unexpected metaphors, verbal invention, double meaning, and alteration of well-known expressions, as discussed by Gingras (2008). *Prendre le taureau par les cornes*, a traditional expression also known in English, "to take the bull by the horns," requires only two letter changes for *cornes* to become *contes*. The story involves just such decisive action from Babine in a difficult situation. French readers/listeners would also recognize the English homonym tail/tale. The bull who appears in the story is figuratively grasped by both the tail and the tale.

actually belongs to the bull, which arrives instead. It rampages through Saint-Élie-de-Caxton, terrifying the new priest, who flees. As the bull wreaks havoc and partially destroys the church and town, Babine pipes a tune that makes the sun set, and the bull magically leaps into the sun. Babine is again sentenced to die, but Toussaint lets him select the manner, and he chooses to die *"par le temps"* (by time). The closing sequence, discussed in detail below, shot in the actual cemetery by the church in Saint-Élie-de Caxton, moves to the present day, where Babine is being buried just before his 276th birthday. The primary actors from the film (including Otis, thus grieving his own character) as well as Pellerin are mourners, in contemporary clothing.

Seventy-five Saint-Élie-de-Caxton residents were extras, and the film premiered in the church there. Included among those present was an eighty-seven-year-old man who had for twenty years lodged Roger Lafrenière, inspiration for the character of Babine, who died March 13, 2001 (Provencher 2008). After attending a press preview in Saint-Élie-de-Caxton, and under the subhead "Un conte de fées . . . vrai" (A fairy tale . . . true), journalist Frédérique Doyon quotes director Picard saying: "This will be a fairy tale, but it's based on something real."[22] She also quotes Pellerin: "All my stories are approved by the people in the village because they speak about their father or grandfather. It must be done with respect because I live here, and it is my priority to live here, more than to be a storyteller" (2007).[23] And Michel Coulombe notes:

> Although it begins with the classic: "The story that I will tell you . . . ," *Babine* has little to do with the bewitched canoe[24] or other Quebec legends. We discover a pregnant woman who, for years, refuses to give birth,

---

22 Ça va être un conte de fées, mais c'est basé sur quelque chose de vrai.

23 Toutes mes histoires sont approuvées par les gens du village parce que ça parle de leur père ou leur grand-père. Faut que ce soit fait dans le respect parce que j'habite icitte, et c'est ma priorité de vivre icitte, plus que d'être conteur d'histoires.

24 From a French Canadian version of "The Wild Hunt" in which *coureurs de bois* (fur traders) make a deal with the devil so they can go home to visit their sweethearts. If they break interdictions against, for example, blaspheming, hitting a church steeple with their enchanted canoe, and returning after 6:00 a.m., they lose their souls. The group agree not to drink alcohol to ensure compliance. Predictably, the interdictions are violated, but usually the men use a clever ruse to retain their souls. Vincent-Guillaume Otis, who plays the character of Babine, also appears in a 2016 film based on the legend, *Chasse-Galerie: La légende* (directed by Jean-Philippe Duval). Looking much prettier than he

a calendar that reads September 43 and a tree that grows on the place where a watch was buried so that it tick-tocks. Though there's a witch in the village as in tales, the story's magical aspect does not rest on her. *Babine* could be the missing link between tradition and modernity. (2009, 24)[25]

This "missing link" may in part relate to the film's thematic use of time. The heterotemporality here is more extensive even than in Tarsem's films and implicates a variety of modes of real and fantastic time. In *Babine*, the invocations of time include, for example, a tree that grows when Babine buries the old priest's watch, which eventually matures to clock size, as well as the imaginary calendar date of September 43. Play with time takes place most clearly and extensively in *Babine*'s closing sequence.

At first there is no background music. Inside the church, Toussaint stands behind the altar with a gavel, preparing to render judgment on Babine before the congregation. After Babine declares his own death sentence—"*je vais mourir par le temps*" (I'd like to die by time)[26]—a smiling Toussaint pounds his gavel to confirm the self-determined fate; then the camera tracks backward from behind the figure of Babine facing Toussaint at the altar. Though the scene invokes the fictive time of the film's diegetic narrative, the seeming realism of the presentation of the events is in part signaled by the lack of extra-diegetic sound.

As quiet, minor-key piano music with very subtle orchestral accompaniment begins, underlining the fictive movie time, the camera moves back through the partially ruined church, with a broken statue of a female saint, a life-size head of the Madonna, crosses, and other debris strewn along the aisle floor. As the church doors close, Pellerin's voice-over commences,

---

does in *Babine*, Otis plays the lumberwoods boss who tries to steal the main character's fiancée.

25 Bien qu'on y débute par le classique : « L'histoire que j'vas vous conter . . . », Babine n'a que bien peu à voir avec la chasse-galerie ou le répertoire des légendes québécoises. On y découvre une femme enceinte qui, depuis des années, refuse d'accoucher, un calendrier qui indique le 43 septembre et un arbre qui pousse à l'endroit même où l'on a semé une montre de sorte qu'il fait tictac. S'il y a bien une sorcière au village comme dans les contes, l'aspect magique du récit ne repose aucunement sur elle. Babine pourrait être le chaînon manquant entre la tradition et la modernité.

26 Throughout this discussion of the scene, the English translation comes from the subtitles.

another signal of fictive movie time. *"Aujourd'hui, si bien des villages n'ont plus de fou"* (Today, if many villages no longer have idiots), referring to today, the actual here and now, with a dissolve to a close-up of two parked cars, confirming that the scenario itself has changed to the present day, outside the fictive/historical time of the rest of the film, *"il y a surtout bien des fous qui n'ont plus de village"* (many idiots no longer have villages). The latter phrases echo the film's opening sequence assertion that *"à cette époque-là, chaque village avait son fou, puis chaque fou avait son village"* (at the time, every village had an idiot, and every idiot a village). These locutions invoke multiple times: then and now (both understood within the generalized quotidian that is the subject of discussion—village time before and after); then and now (the beginning and the end of the movie); and the fictive magical time of the rest of the film and the apparently real time just introduced.

A close-up begins with a figure seen from the waist down, walking between parked cars, wearing plaid trousers and running shoes. The cars and the clothing signal present-day action, but that their wearer is Pellerin isn't immediately clear. *"Babine a été condamné á mourir par le temps"* (Babin [*sic*—name is given thus in the subtitles] was sentenced to death by time). Happenings return to the narrative time; events described belong to the rest of the film, not the present day. As the orchestra becomes slightly louder, the figure's legs continue along a partly shadowed graveyard path, showing headstones and flowers, *"par le temps qui passe"* (By the passage of time). The walk strongly and correctly suggests a location shot rather than work in a studio (as was the case in the rest of the film), again underlining present-day, now, not the studio/fictive setting. Yet the voice-over content refers to the narrative's fiction—the idea of being sentenced to death by time.

With upward panning, the legs move toward a group of standing people, *"Il a purgé sa peine jusqu'à épuisement"* (He served his full sentence). This idea complexly refers both to the sentencing just witnessed by the audience and to the passage of time between then and the depicted now, an interval not part of the film's actual diegesis. The camera pans further up behind the now fully visible figure as he walks between those standing. *"Quand il est mort, il allait fêter son 276e anniversaire de naissance"* (When he died, he was about to celebrate his 276th birthday). The impossible death at 275 links with the soon-to-be-confirmed location shot in the Saint-Élie-de-Caxton churchyard—and Babine's fictive grave.

Cut to a shot from behind an officiating priest (played by Luc Proulx) standing at a grave with a coffin ready to be lowered, showing the mourners standing in a semicircle facing the grave with the priest at its head. It is now clear that the walking legs belong to Pellerin, the creator of the stories and writer of the screenplay. At first, the abrupt appearance of the actual person of the author, who had no acting role in the film (other than the voice-overs), might suggest to the audience that this is a scene from normal time, a documentary shot. However, with a third priest added to the two in the body of the film, Proulx's presence reminds the viewer of the passage of time within the film (before and after the old priest's death) but also indicates that the current scene, though on location and featuring a nonactor in no other role than as the author Pellerin himself, is fictive, not documentary.

Pellerin has now moved between the two mourners in the center, the actors Otis (Babine) and Picard (Toussaint), both dressed in everyday clothes, at the standing group's center (see figure 4.1). It appears that the cast members are playing themselves. Or are they perhaps playing the roles of playing themselves? Unlike Pellerin, who has hitherto only been present as a voice-over, their embodiments signal that they exist filmicly in the past/magical realm of the film, but also as actual individuals who are actors—a common-sense knowledge not often invoked in fictional films. And yet they are performing a present-day group of mourners for a fictitious character, whose avatar is among their numbers, led by another actor playing a priest. Importantly, many of the mourners in the background are not major players in the film. The viewer may wonder: are they extras or crew? Are they actual residents of Saint-Élie-de-Caxton?

FIGURE 4.1. Mourners at Babine's grave.

The priest speaks: "*Nous retiendrons de Babine de que les rumeurs du village répéteront encore pour les siècles des siècles*" (Babin will be remembered in village gossip repeated forever and ever). The fictitious-time figure being buried also appears in represented present-day village talk. "*Par l'ouïe, avec l'ouïe, et en l'ouïe*" (Through whim, with whim, and in whim). Though *l'ouïe* generally translates to (the sense of) "hearing," the subtitles' English paronym (sound-alike with a different meaning) "whim" (for "him") allows the possibility of the English double entendre that immediately follows. Reverse to the crowd's response: "*. . . à toi, Dieu le Père tout-puissant . . .*" (is unto thee, God the Father Almighty). This is another of Pellerin's wordplays; "*Par l'ouïe, avec l'ouïe, et en l'ouïe*" is a paronym for the Catholic mass's "*Par lui, avec lui, en lui*" (By him, with him, in him), followed by "*A toi, Dieu, le père tout-puissant*" (To you, God the all-powerful father), the words spoken by Babine's mourners. The French words invoke a liturgical time, rendered humorous by the double entendre, and the English a playful replacement of the known object with the quixotic (see Huss 2015).

The music becomes subtly louder, more pensive than sad, a conversation between piano and orchestra, calling on fictive movie time in the midst of a realistic representation on location. Cut to the clock face in the reshaped tree trunk and then a slight pan up to show Babine's gravestone as Pellerin's voice-over resumes, "*Babine entrait dans l'éternité avec une horloge en guise de cercueil. Tous ceux qui l'avait condamné étaient déjà morts depuis longtemps*" (Babin entered eternity with a clock by way of a coffin. All those who had condemned him were long dead), with a cut to Richer (the witch) and Maude Laurendeau, who plays Lurette Riopel, in full face close-up. *Babine*'s fantasy time thus includes the death of the fictitious figures who condemned Babine, in a time not represented in the film's diegesis. Again, arbitrary clock time is partly undermined by the timepiece's location, having itself grown within a tree that also grew. It also recalls Toussaint's wall calendar that shows September 43.

Dissolve to the Lurette Riopel cross grave marker with daisies around it. This view renders Lurette the character, Laurendeau who plays her, and the actual Lurette buried there in the graveyard. The flowers hearken back to the fictional story time, as Lurette constantly picks petals off daisies through the film in a sequence of "he loves me; he loves me not." "*À Saint-Élie-de-Caxton, c'est lui qui avait eu raison*" (In Saint-Élie-de-Caxton, it was he who had been right). *Raison* can also mean "reason"—a double entendre that the fool is the sagacious person; as indicated above, the wise fool is part of local character lore and fairy tale.

"*On venait d'enterrer l'ancien temps, avec le dernier fou de notre village*" (The past had just been buried with our last village idiot). Again the actors' presence on location invokes their characters but also their actual personae. The viewer may wonder if their present-day clothing is their own, chosen by them, or another set of costumes. A series of dissolves between gravestones and actors follow, including Picard partially dissolving to a pan to Toussaint's gravestone, again the triple persona and triple time: fictional Toussaint, actor playing him, Toussaint's grave, dissolving back to Otis close up. It is appropriate that this section closes with the film's two most central characters.

Cut to Pellerin close up and then a view behind his head and shoulders, standing at the foot of the grave looking down upon it. It's clear now that Babine's coffin lid is constructed from the fictional clock tree, with the old priest's watch also visible. The other mourners are gone, and Pellerin turns and strolls out of the shot, with a cut to full view as he walks away from the gravestone toward the church and steeple. His voice-over refers to himself and the present, "*Ce qui reste, par chez nous, c'est des soirs où on se rassemble pour jaser encore*" (Yet, in my village, we still gather some nights to shoot the breeze), as Pellerin walks further out of the shot.

Cut to an extreme close-up of the coffin wood, "*à reconstruire des légendes sur la démesure de notre petit monde*" (rebuilding legends about our outrageous little world), referencing hypothetical future storytellings, panning toward the clock face on the coffin, "*à se répéter qu'il existe une folie*" (reiterating that a certain idiocy) continuing pan toward the grave marker, "*capable de rallonger l'espérance de vie*" (can extend life expectancy). The sequence returns to the fictional/fantasy past and to the magic in the film's story. "*Puis on se force, de notre mieux, pour que les légendes de demain <u>soient encore plus belles à raconter</u>*" (And we do our best to ensure that tomorrow's legends), past the grave marker, with its inscription visible, then behind to a tiny tree with the old priest's watch growing in it, "*que celles d'aujourd'hui*" (<u>are even better</u> than those of today).[27] Again the future links to the story narrated in the film and to arbitrary time as told by the watch/clock. As the piano music rises up the scale and ends, the camera pans in toward the small timepiece, and the sound of a clock ticking manifests. The closing time referent returns

---

27 I have preserved the way the subtitles are rendered. The underlined sections correspond to one another.

to the magical. The orchestra becomes louder and then ends with a loud boom from a drum. Cut to black.

The presence in this scene that most obviously plays with the notions of reality and fiction as well as with different kinds of time is that of actor Otis, who plays Babine. To enumerate, Otis/Babine invokes the actor representing himself and implicating all the roles he has played (and, for subsequent audiences, will later play). But he also signifies a mourner in the scene; the character of Babine elsewhere in the film and in Pellerin's storytelling and writing; the absent presence of the 275-year-old character in the coffin; his name's appearance on the fictitious gravestone; and the actual Roger Lafrenière, buried in the same cemetery with his location also marked by a gravestone. It would be difficult to locate a scene in most other films that successfully manages such complex heterotemporality. Like the convolution of films in general, it includes both magical and realist properties, and sometimes combines them.

I would argue that typecasting is a particular form of ostension, wherein an actor's previous roles make it difficult for them to get later parts playing substantially different characters. Actors justifiably fear typecasting, and in my interview with the Bédard sisters, Josée mentioned that Otis had some difficulty getting roles after *Babine*. IMDb indicates the same. The actor had two features and one television movie between 2005 and 2007, two other features in 2008, and then (barring one short film) a hiatus until 2010 and 2012, when he had television series roles. Since 2016 he has had an ongoing role in the television series *District 31*. In further evidence of ostension in Otis's life, he has been a spokesperson for La société québécoise de la déficience intellectuelle (Quebec Intellectual Disability Society) since 2010 ("Semaine" n.d.).

In addition to other linkages of the real and the fictional, one of Pellerin's signature elements—the magical qualities of *paparmanes*—makes its way into the film: Toussaint licks two and uses them on Babine's underarms, implicitly as a deodorant, before they go out together to give New Year's greetings to the village. But planting (with the expectation of reaping) peppermints is explicitly included in the second film, as is the actual Saint-Élie-de-Caxton.

Ésimésac (2012)

Most magical happenings directly depicted in *Babine* result from an application of spells (in particularly Babine's act of summoning the bull) or are unexplained; we don't know how or why the old priest's watch grew into a clock tree, for example. In *Ésimésac*, in contrast, magical events are the motor for the entire film, beginning with the title character's marvelous birth. Three characters—Ésimésac himself (played by Nicola-Frank Vachon), his sister Marie (played by Sophie Nélisse), and the witch (reprised by Richer)—have magical capabilities and powers. There is much less play with time; as in Tarsem's films, one film implicates time, and in the other, place has a strong presence—in *Ésimésac*, that includes filming on location in Saint-Élie-de-Caxton.

The film's story surrounds Ésimésac Gélinas, whose mother carried him for a preternaturally long time; though only two years old, he looks like a young adult and is magically strong but lacks a shadow. The film's first scene shows Marie's shadow bouncing along a dirt road. Ésimésac is carrying her—but because he has no shadow, only hers is visible. The time period for *Ésimésac* is later than that of *Babine*. (There are a few references to the latter character, but he only appears in photographs.) In the interim, hard times have fallen on Saint-Élie-de-Caxton. The Gélinas family subsists on hot water, stale bread, and salt. Only the blacksmith Riopel (played by Gildor Roy) has money, from making bomb casings. His daughter La belle Lurette (reprised by Laurendeau), called Anna Domini in the English subtitles, with Ésimésac and his sister Marie, rally the village to plant a community vegetable garden.[28] Ésimésac has displaced Riopel as the strongest man in the village, and the latter refuses to support the garden. The two characters play a game of checkers; if Ésimésac wins, Riopel has to make a water tank for the garden. When they shake hands before the match, Riopel lifts Ésimésac off the floor; Ésimésac responds likewise, in a kind of visual representation of a tall tale. But the game leads to a fight between the two players; the audience sees the first evidence of Marie's magic when she halts time to stop the conflict. The game is judged a draw, and without a water tank, the garden withers.

The villagers' attention is diverted when, tired of making bombs, Riopel bargains with a railroad builder (played by Hugo Giroux) to supply cheap

---

28   *Il y a belle lurette* means "long ago." It's an archaic-sounding but apparently actually quite recent expression known in France and across French-speaking Canada. While it would not be used in telling fairy tales (that would be *il était une fois*—"there was once" or "there once was"), its references to time harmonize with both films' concerns.

rails, with the vague promise that his action will bring the railway station and thus much-needed prosperity to Saint-Élie-de-Caxton. Riopel recruits Ésimésac to help with the rail making and delivery; the latter abandons the garden. Comparing himself with Riopel, Ésimésac decides he too wants a shadow, and he gets one from the witch in exchange for an acorn. The shadow is at first acorn sized and shaped. Lurette has been playing "he loves me; he loves me not" with daisy petals, and one falls down the drain. She sees it as a sign that her lover won't return from the war and keeps the village awake weeping. Ésimésac sends his shadow to retrieve the petal. In return for his service making it possible for them to sleep, Ésimésac persuades the villagers to work for the railway without payment until the station comes.

Marie begins to fall ill, sprouting feathers. Ésimésac's shadow looks more like a tree, and he argues with his mother about buying food and medicine on credit. He learns what Riopel has known for some time: the station will go to the village of Charette instead of to Saint-Élie-de-Caxton. In winter, famine becomes desperate; Ésimésac tries to bring a huge rock to stop the train but finds that his shadow has drained his preternatural strength. The village unites at Christmas mass. As the blacksmith Riopel sings "O Holy Night," Marie collapses. Ésimésac takes the apparently dying child to the tracks, and the villagers follow. Marie magically rises out of Ésimésac's arms, and as the train approaches, her angel wings unfurl. Gathered on the tracks, the community collectively halt the train (see figure 4.2). Working cooperatively together with Ésimésac, Riopel, Toussaint, and the barber Bellemare (played by René Richard Cyr) turn the train on its side. It spills a cornucopia of food. As the villagers move toward it, Marie gets the last word, "*La force du nombre, mon frère*" (Strength in numbers, my brother), with a gradual fade to black.

The crucial final scene confirms a moral recurring throughout the film—that to survive and thrive, the community must work together. However, it also underlines that it's not the strongest—Ésimésac and Riopel—who can unite Saint-Élie-de-Caxton. Instead it's the weakest—the young and apparently dying Marie—who succeeds. Fairy tales, like this film, often circle around the weapons of the weak. *Ésimésac* pivots around two young but unusually mature female characters—Lurette and Marie. Both *Ésimésac* and *Babine* have abnormally young or immature males (Babine is intellectually challenged; though Ésimésac appears to be around twenty, he is actually only two). All characters are White-identified Quebecois. Saint-Élie-de-Caxton's isolation and confined space is crucial; even the *possibility* of a railway

FIGURE 4.2. Marie leads the halting of the train.

station brings selfishness and capitalist mentality. The greatest dangers, like the bull and the railroader, come from outside, brought perhaps unwittingly by characters serving their own self-interest. These films offer parables about relationships with greater powers (the English language and the rest of Canada as bull/ies, duplicitous railroaders). Yet the community does not just survive, it flourishes through collective strength and wisdom. Ésimésac needs help from mature men transformed and rescued by a younger woman; in contrast, Babine, who cannot grow up, by implication keeps Saint-Élie-de-Caxton unsullied. Inspired by these works, I decided I wanted to experience the village myself.

Media Tourism in Saint-Élie-de-Caxton

Wednesday, June 13, 2018. I arrived in Ottawa yesterday, and this morning I'm renting a car and driving to Saint-Élie-de-Caxton with my friend Chris Carton, a retired high school teacher living in Ottawa who was a fellow student in the Memorial University of Newfoundland Folklore Department master's program—we've known each other since 1977, forty-one years. Though it's a three-and-a-half-hour drive to Saint-Élie-de-Caxton from Ottawa, compared to one and a half hours from Montreal, I want another experienced fieldworker with me to keep an eye out for things we should be observing and photographing. And I'm not a fan of driving in Ontario and Quebec on the Trans-Canada Highway, having become used to the less congested roads of Manitoba, so company and a driver who's familiar with the area is useful.

I'm a bit apprehensive because the weather forecast says rain; it could really hinder walking around and photographing. Chris and I leave Ottawa around 8:00 a.m. We arrive at the tourist information center just inside the Quebec border around 9:45 a.m. The guide who assists us is clearly surprised and pleased that English speakers ask for material on Saint-Élie-de-Caxton. She's quite familiar with Fred Pellerin but has never herself visited that village. We get maps, instructions, and a tourist book for the Mauricie region. Saint-Élie-de-Caxton is listed as number three on their "Can't-Miss Experiences" following "Lively Urban Life in Trois-Rivières" and "Join the party at the Festival Western de St-Tite." Under the title "Come be amazed in Saint-Élie-de-Caxton," the guidebook says, "One big museum, Saint-Élie-de-Caxton is a magical village that stands out through its originality. A place where **imagination** is at the centre of everything! . . . Visiting Saint-Élie-de-Caxton is like dreaming with your eyes open, with **Fred Pellerin's** tales in the background" (Mauricie 2018–19, 8; boldface in original).

With Chris driving, it's a blessedly uneventful Trans-Canada Highway trip, if not a visually stimulating one. Past Montreal, almost immediately after we turn onto Highway 153, the rolling landscape shows that we're heading for the foothills of the Laurentian mountains. We go through Yamachiche. It has a familiar villagescape: mainly older buildings from the mid-nineteenth century or earlier, cozied up to the road, clearly not accommodating to a widened highway. It makes me happily nostalgic for trips I took as a child with my photographer father around parts of rural Ontario now horribly ruined by urban sprawl, the once rich farmland today covered with industrial buildings and new suburbs. Fred Pellerin's work supports retaining Quebec's heritage landscapes, and I thoroughly approve.

As we go through the village of Saint-Barnabé and turn onto Highway 351 heading for the village of Charette, we pass more lovely countryside. Part of Charette's main road parallels the train tracks; as in *Ésimésac*, the train actually did go there. We reach Saint-Élie-de-Caxton before noon and find *Le bureau d'acceuil touristique*, the tourist information office, easily, in particular because the building has giant posters for both films on its walls. *Babine* has slight pride of place because it's the first one visible when driving in from the highway and main street through town, on the wall with the entrance to the *Centre communautaire*, or community center. The *Ésimésac* poster is on the wall with the entrance to the tourist information office.

Two young women in the office greet Chris and me. I ask if they have the audio guides to the village in English, but no, they're only in French. They assure me we will understand them. I ask if they get many Anglos, and they say no, but they had somebody from the United States, from Oregon, last week. I buy the Saint-Élie-de-Caxton history and photography books, two audio guides, and a bottle of Saint-Élie water. At the front desk they have two bowls of *paparmanes*; I take several to give to my neighbor, Annie Bédard. To the left of the desk, there's a glass case with a doll-like statue of Pellerin, dressed in what appears to be the same red and brown plaid trousers he wears at the end of *Babine*.

As we set out on our walk around the village, I find the descriptive parts of the audio narration easy to follow, but the excerpts from live storytellings by Pellerin are much more difficult for those people, like me, used to listening to a more mainstream French accent. The regional language Pellerin maintains is unfamiliar in the formal circumstances I usually encounter, and his storytelling, as already indicated, is allusive and poetic and the pronunciation very specific: Onésime-Isaac becomes Ésimésac, for example. I'm taking a picture of the Saint-Élie-de-Caxton sign and fountain on the other side of the road from the tourist center. I'm standing too far into the road—Chris alerts me to get out of the way of a driver, and they shout something out the window. Chris tells me they called me "Babine."

I'm multiply grateful that Chris is there, because he's keeping his fieldwork eyes open better than I am and spots a tree with three places where branches were cut away and turned into two eyes and the rest of a face. He also spots a cut-down tree trunk with gnomes, lights, a bird feeder, and tiny maple sap cans as well as a gnome looking out the window of one house, waving. It's getting pretty clear that many, many residents are going along with the theme and putting up their own displays. The Babine house is undecorated, but further along, we see a *traverse de lutin* flag on a porch. The Toussaint Brodeur house is beside a chip wagon, and the Ésimésac house is now the post office; it seems the latter in particular is the location, not the actual building where the Gélinas family lived.

We head toward the *traverse de lutins* and come across a house with giant *paparmanes* on the porch, a wooden horse, and "speak no evil, see no evil, hear no evil" (in that order) gnomes and other figurines. The two women sitting on the porch say it's OK to take a photograph (but I didn't understand the rest of what they said to us) (see figure 4.3). We also come upon a decorated mailbox with a bell, old lantern, gnome, and sign "Le Sonneur"; a

FIGURE 4.3. *Paparmane* house.

property with a for-sale sign that has on one side of the fence an Anne of Green Gables plaque and on the other side a Halloween plaque with a witch, ghost, and jack-o'-lanterns; and another with a two-dimensional Mountie lawn sculpture holding a "Traverse de lutin" (*sic*) sign. By the actual *traverse de lutins* sign, elf footprints cross the road.

Heading back, we come across more gnomes looking out windows; a restaurant and bed and breakfast, Le Lutin Marmiton (with a sign showing the *lutin* carrying a covered platter; *marmiton* means assistant chef); and the church. Behind and to the right of the church is the *paparmane* tree. The graveyard directly behind the church is quite large, with lots of familiar surnames from the movies. We locate the Babine (Roger Lafrenière) gravestone beside a memorial for the village's priests. Standing very near the spot where the Babine burial was represented in the film, I notice how different the back of the church appears; a fence now marking out the parking lot would have prevented Pellerin from walking off-screen as he does at the end of *Babine* (see figure 4.4). We locate the Toussaint and Jeannette Brodeur gravestone. It's a big, black, modern one, unlike the one that appears in the *Babine* closing sequence. On the way back to the car, we see another amazingly

FIGURE 4.4. Church rear view.

decorated house, with a giant fleur-de-lys Quebec flag and hear-, see-, and speak-no-evil gnomes in the window and outside. It takes us over two hours to walk through the village at a leisurely pace, photographing, following the sites on the map, and listening sporadically. When we go back to the tourist information center to return our audio guides, the staff let us know that we just missed meeting Pellerin himself. As we're ready to leave, around 2:45 p.m., it starts raining.

Saint-Élie-de-Caxton has become a tourist site, both formally and informally displaying to insiders and outsiders alike links to magic and to Pellerin's stories and films. This process connects to film and literary tourism, involving visitors to the settings of fictional works or places in the lives of authors/creators. The sources inspiring such tourism are legion (see, e.g., Beeton 2005 on film tourism; Robinson and Andersen 2003 on literary tourism). Undoubtedly the most internationally famous such example in Canada is Cavendish, Prince Edward Island, with all of its connections to Lucy Maud Montgomery's renowned Anne of Green Gables (and other) series (see Gothie 2016). The Cavendish house, now named "Green Gables," has some connection to Montgomery's writing but has been repurposed to become a heritage location in a national park—beside a golf course. The property has been conceived mainly in terms of its representation of Montgomery's literary landscape rather than as a more conventional historic site. Tourism has encouraged the creation of "Anne" connections throughout Cavendish—and, indeed, across Prince Edward Island. Japanese visitors in particular have proved so lucrative that local services have Japanese speakers and much public signage is in Japanese (see Squire 1996). Many residents feel caught between the profits to be made and their perception of the destruction of their local biosphere and culture (discussed in Tye 1994; Cormack and Fawcett 2003; York 2007, esp. 78–95).

As the experience of Cavendish shows, sorting the historical from the literary is by no means an easy process. Similarly, sorting realities from fictions in these kinds of locations becomes even more fraught. As Anne-Li Lindgren, Anna Sparrman, Tobias Samuelsson, and David Cardell (2015) discuss with respect to "Astrid Lindgren's World" in Sweden, fiction is hybrid and interrelated with reality. These researchers cite such linkages as children dressed as characters from Lindgren's novels meeting actors representing those characters and online videos wherein parents name and present their children as if they were Lindgren characters, often enacting scenes from her works. They call this congeries of linkages "assemblages of realunreality" (179) and "materialized fiction" (182)—terms that would also well describe the closing scene of *Babine* described above.

Particularly when contrasted to Cavendish, but even in its own terms, Saint-Élie-de-Caxton seems admirably muted in its calls to literary and filmic connections. Businesses draw on references from Pellerin's work (as described above) but also from fairy tales. One bed and breakfast, for example, uses fairy-tale wordplay, being called "L'Adèle au Bois Dormant"—the proprietor's name, Adèle, constructed into a paronym for *La belle au bois dormant* (Sleeping Beauty). The villagescape isn't obviously commercialized (see figure 4.5). With the exception of the community center and tourist office, there's very little signage at all, and significant locations from Pellerin's stories and movies only have discreet numbers linking to the tourist map. There are no giant intrusive billboards. It impressed me that residents decorated their properties with images of supernatural creatures and *paparmanes*. Of course, their motivations must go far beyond display for tourist visitors, but such participation in the invention of Saint-Élie-de-Caxton as a magical real location suggests they are relatively high on the positive side of George V. Doxey's (1975) Irridex model of host irritation, with a range of

FIGURE 4.5. Streetscape rue Saint-Jean.

reactions from euphoria, to apathy, to annoyance, to antagonism (as noted in Beeton 2005, 122).

With few outside Quebec knowing about Pellerin, Saint-Élie-de-Caxton's clientele is necessarily limited—and, indeed, so is its tourist season. There are Christmas events, but otherwise the tourist office is open only from June to October. Further, a more general terminology of "media tourism," which allows the inclusion of music, television, and other forms that "induce" visits (see Reijnders et al. 2015), seems a better descriptor for this place and its complex relation to Pellerin's work. With its obvious links to an actual place and characters, to legend (see Ellis 1989, 2001), to creative storytelling and writing, and to film, it's most accurate to call Saint-Élie-de-Caxton's form "media tourism."

It might also be seen as one of what Stijn Reijnders calls "places of the imagination," part of a circle of influence where physical places (like Saint-Élie-de-Caxton) inspire artists (like Pellerin) who construct imaginary places (as in the stories and films), which become appropriated by fans, who search for physical references to imaginary places (2011, 17). The tourist materials' affirmation that Saint-Élie-de-Caxton "really exists!" gets confirmation not only in the actual locations where Pellerin's characters lived, and ultimately their gravestones, but also in the official construction of imaginary locations like the gnome crossing and the peppermint tree as well as in the residents' own representation of gnomes, peppermints, and so on, inside and outside their houses. The real-life effect of all of this work has been to support, indeed to grow without simultaneously destroying the ambiance of, the village that also lives in the imagination of Pellerin the storyteller and in the two films made from his narratives.

Not only does his work generally support his own and actor/director Picard's progressive politics, but it also enables the social engagement of actor Otis supporting the causes of folks with intellectual impairments. Pellerin's Saint-Élie-de-Caxton is also about ecology and community. Observers like the Bédards credit Pellerin's work with saving the local school. Apart from increasing the likelihood that young families will come and stay, keeping the village vital, schools serve as a focus for collective action, as well as community centers for all kinds of events. And Pellerin's ecopolitics are evident as well, in the fact that parking in Saint-Élie-de-Caxton by the tourist center has plug-ins for electric vehicles. And so Pellerin's comment as quoted above, that his work is about overcoming the real, finds expression in everyday political effects.

Next, I move into the worlds of particular fairy tales, demonstrating how filmed versions implicate reality and wonder, especially in terms of often resistant and engaged political interventions into serious contemporary matters. In the following chapter, I show how "Hansel and Gretel" not only invokes issues about harms to children, but, particularly in its less realistic modes, bringing magic and science fiction, also addresses possibilities for failure and even apocalypse, implicating the works of significant recent queer theorists.

THEMES AND ISSUES FROM THREE FAIRY TALES

5

"Hansel and Gretel" Films

Queer Death, Queer Failure, Family Horror, and Science Fiction

"HANSEL AND GRETEL" (ATU 327A) CONCERNS CHILDREN WHOSE PARents abandon them in the forest, where they meet a witch whose house at first seems attractive but is, it later becomes obvious, actually a cannibal's evil ploy to attract food. Failure to provide for children due to worldly insufficiency—as Jack Halberstam's "The queer art of failure turns on the impossible, the improbable, the unlikely, and the unremarkable" (2011, 88) and José Esteban Muñoz's "This world is not enough" (2009, 1) might predict—leads to magical encounters. But Jack Zipes calls out the story's "very problematical" handling of hunger, child abandonment, nasty stepmothers, witches, and "the sanctification of paternal rule." He notes that "the readers of [the Grimm brothers'] tales in the nineteenth century and early part of the twentieth century were faced with these problems" (2006, 195).[1] And he continues:

---

1   Zipes also discusses several "alternative Hansels and Gretels" from literature, many of which locate the story in a realistic historical or current location, often as modes for exploring trauma, genocide, abuse, and other difficult topics (2006, 212–21).

> the problems raised by the discourse in this tale have not been resolved in reality: poverty, conflict with stepparents, the trauma of abandonment, child abuse, and male domination.... America is one of the richest countries in the world, and like other rich countries contributes to the impoverishment of children through the social and economic policies of state and federal governments.... "Hansel and Gretel"... became a classic fairy tale in Western culture precisely because it developed a relevant discourse that made a marked impression on listeners, readers, and viewers and caused them to ponder solutions to the dilemma of abused and abandoned children. (220; see also Zipes 2011,193–206)

In fact, "Hansel and Gretel" is frequently cited as an indication that fairy tales deal with actual historical problems. Eugen Weber's article tellingly entitled "Fairies and Hard Facts: The Reality of Folktales" takes a historian's perspective to argue *against* psychological interpretations popular in the 1980s. He gives several examples but begins by suggesting that "Hansel and Gretel," "a story about little children who show quite a lot of initiative in order to cling to a minimum of security or to capture it when lost ... would strike [the historian] as highly realistic and calling for very little interpretation indeed" (1981, 94). Such proposals are best mitigated somewhat; as Maria Tatar suggests: "there is much in every folktale that requires awareness of social realities, just as there is much that defies historical explanation" (1987, 50).

But most of the best-known contours of "Hansel and Gretel" certainly fall within the realm of empirical possibility, to use Vanessa Joosen's (2007) criteria discussed in chapter 4. Starvation, child abandonment, scattering objects to find one's way back, cannibalism, trickery, deceiving someone, and burning a person in an oven are all quite conceivable. And though the foodstuff gingerbread is an unconventional building material, it is a possible though certainly unwise choice. However, the magical assistance of birds, beasts, and/or angels (see Uther 2004, 1:212) can best be explained as supernatural and symbolic (see Tatar 1987, 50–51).

Joosen (2011) suggests that fairy-tale scholarship can influence writers of literature, and it seems plausible to extend her insight to film and television. Given the tale's often-noted links to reality, it is probably not coincidental that "Hansel and Gretel" is the focal fairy tale for episode 11 of season 3 of the television series *Buffy the Vampire Slayer* (directed by James Whitmore Jr., 1999), with its themes of contemporary moral panics and scapegoating. The premise of the episode, called "Gingerbread," is articulated in the following interchange between characters:

> GILES (PLAYED BY ANTHONY STEWART HEAD): There is a fringe theory, held by a few folklorists, that some regional stories have actual, um . . . very literal antecedents.
> BUFFY (PLAYED BY SARAH MICHELLE GELLAR): And in some language that's English?
> OZ (PLAYED BY SETH GREEN): Fairy tales are real?
> BUFFY: Hans and Gre—Hansel and Gretel?
> XANDER (PLAYED BY NICHOLAS BRENDON): Wait, Hansel and Gretel? Breadcrumbs, ovens, gingerbread house?
> GILES: Of course. Well it makes sense now.
> BUFFY: Yeah, it's all falling into place. Of course, that place is nowhere near this place.
> GILES: Some demons thrive by fostering hatred and, uh, persecution amongst the mortal animals. Not by—Not by destroying men, but by watching men destroy each other. They feed us our darkest fear and turn peaceful communities into vigilantes.
> BUFFY: Hansel and Gretel run home to tell everyone about the mean old witch.
> GILES: And then she and probably dozens of others are persecuted by a righteous mob. It's happened all throughout history. It happened in Salem, not surprisingly.
> XANDER: Whoa, whoa, whoa. I'm still spinning on this whole "fairy tales are real" thing.
> OZ: So what do we do?
> XANDER: I don't know about you, but I'm going to go trade my cow for some beans. No one else is seeing the funny here.

In a reversal of conventions—a frequent maneuver in fairy-tale media, especially live action—in "Gingerbread" the Hansel and Gretel characters turn out to be monstrous, not innocent. Benevolent witches Willow (played by Alyson Hannigan) and Amy (played by Elizabeth Anne Allen) along with the slayer hero Buffy—representing the fight against evil—are tied to stakes for burning, escaping only at the last minute. And again, the levels are multiple; the episode, a fictional story, refers to a fairy tale (presumed fictional), which is connected to events with the episode's diegesis (the discovery of the bodies of "Hans" and "Greta" and their gradual demonic overtaking of the town of Sunnydale), but also to actual happenings from history, including the Salem witch trials and persecution in Nazi Germany—examples of "turn[ing] peaceful communities into vigilantes," as quoted above. The episode also refers somewhat obliquely and codedly to moral panics about satanic ritual abuse of children that emerged in the 1980s and 1990s in both the United States and Canada (as discussed, e.g., in Wright 2005). And Xander's (joking) reference to trading a cow for beans refers to the idea of ostension, the live enactment of ideas and images from stories, as discussed extensively in chapter 4.

Like another exception to the feature-film Disneyfication of fairy tales, "Little Red Riding Hood" (ATU 333; see, e.g., Kohm and Greenhill 2014), "Hansel and Gretel" has been the subject of many filmic versions. The story has been adapted for theatrical, television, and video/DVD release, including American, Australian, British, Canadian, Czech, Dutch, French, German, Israeli, Japanese, Polish, South Korean, Soviet, Spanish, and Turkish productions. Zipes's *The Enchanted Screen* (2011, 413) lists forty-one "Hansel and Gretel" films produced between 1909 and 2007 but overlooks *The Night of the Hunter* (directed by Charles Laughton, 1955) and *Poslední motýl* (The Last Butterfly, directed by Karel Kachyna, 1991). And many more have appeared since, a significant number in the horror genre, but also, in realist mode, works as divergent as *H & G* (directed by Danishka Esterhazy, 2013) and *Koca Dünya* (Big Big World, directed by Reha Erdem, 2016).

Across cinematic genres—drama, science fiction, noir, horror, slasher, thriller, comedy, and adventure—recurring themes and ideas in live-action "Hansel and Gretel" films involve including lost or abandoned primary characters; portraying the Hansels and Gretels as teenagers or (young) adults, not small children; rendering them vengeful/misbehaving rather than innocent; dealing directly with child abuse and violence, sometimes as motivating adult behavior; using the name Grimm (grim); creating an identity/homology between stepmother and witch; and/or playing with the stepmother/witch characters' gender. In this chapter I explore live-action (not animated, because of its conventional associations with escapist family entertainment)[2] cinema; with a present-day or near-future setting; aimed primarily at adult audiences (not child and/or family fare, therefore not

---

2   For a discussion of one fairy-tale exception referencing "Little Red Riding Hood" (ATU 333), *Jin-Rô* (Jin-Roh: The Wolf Brigade, directed by Hiroyuki Okiura, 1999), see

censoring or mitigating harm); not based on the late nineteenth-century Humperdinck opera (generically distinct); feature length (rather than shorter works, which do not always allow more extended exposition of issues); and not originally made-for-television serials (which often necessarily lose direct focus upon fairy-tale themes).[3] Of course, the foregoing characterizes tendencies, not hard-and-fast empirical rules. Nevertheless, these characteristics help winnow the otherwise completely daunting number of ATU 327A films—which as of March 2019 totals eighty in the International Fairy-Tale Filmography (IFTF).

Because they seem to offer slightly less obvious references to reality—though, as I will argue, they nevertheless implicate many of its aspects—I work here with "Hansel and Gretel" movies that invoke the supernatural and/or science fiction. In the films I consider, the setting is apparently current or future times implicating the real and/or the now, but they include magical elements and/or not yet possible technology. These works, like many others using the same tale type, explore family relationships—sibling to sibling and parent to child (including adoptive)—as well as broader issues, comprising—as in the previous chapter—dealing with community or lack of community. To a large extent, the films' stories implicate major failures of their human characters to fully overcome their supernatural or mechanical adversaries or interlocutors, even to the extent of an actual or potential apocalyptic failure and the end of *Homo sapiens* itself.

In particular, they offer telling opportunities to explore how the central ideas expressed in Lee Edelman's *No Future: Queer Theory and the Death Drive* (2004) and Jack (Judith) Halberstam's *The Queer Art of Failure* (2011) manifest cinematically beyond the examples given in those works. These theorists work with the rhetorics of success associated with heterosexuality and heteronormative thinking and of failure as queer. As Halberstam puts it, "the negative thinker can use the experience of failure to confront the gross inequalities of everyday life in the United States" (2011, 4)—and, I would add, elsewhere.

Greenhill and Kohm 2013. And as discussed in chapter 2, animation can also be associated with serious, non-escapist, dramatic films.
3   Media scholars enjoin recognition of the vast differences between feature film and television production (see, e.g., Bignell 2013). For a discussion of American and British television episodes based on or referencing "Hansel and Gretel," many of which implicate the horror genre, see Tresca (2014).

I discuss concepts of queer in greater detail in chapter 7, but my usage in this chapter refers to all forms of sexualities and sexual expression outside heteronorms; in effect, it may include anything from nonreproductive heterosex to forms considered much more problematic. As in Gayle Rubin's (1984) exposition, I avoid moral judgment of that system. Conventionally, differences in sexuality are coded in terms of the presence or absence, aligned respectively with heterosexuality and homosexuality, of reproductivity and of success and failure at perpetuating the species and the social order. Thus heterosexuality becomes emblematic of life and success, and homosexuality and the queer of death and failure. I do not, of course, argue that queer folks cannot reproduce—they have the same capabilities for conception and nurturance as other members of *Homo sapiens*. Nor do I associate them with the apocalypse—straight people need no help in ushering in all kinds of toxic results in human-engineered disasters from climate change to nuclear war. However, as these "Hansel and Gretel" films explore, queer folks—indeed anybody whose sexuality is outside the most conventional and heteronormative—are too often suspected of seeking the end of the human race (discussed extensively in Edelman 2004, 111–54; see also Bernini 2017).

But Edelman's and Halberstam's analytical perspectives haven't been uncontroversial, even within queer theory and queer communities. For example, José Esteban Muñoz criticizes Edelman's and others' "anti-relational" theory as being based on "a single trope of distance" and "romances of the negative, wishful thinking, and investments in deferring various dreams of difference" (2009, 11; see also Johnson 2015). Both Edelman and Halberstam critically embrace the tropes of death and failure, but they also refuse their binary limits—as, perhaps surprisingly, do these "Hansel and Gretel" films. As I'll show for the films I discuss, their calls to reality, despite simultaneous calls to supernatural and/or futuristic elements, may offer conservative viewpoints, warning of a queer menace (and thus invoking the perspectives on which Edelman and Halberstam, as well as other theorists and activists, riff). Or they may implicitly and/or explicitly call for a halt to heteronormativity, conventional nuclear families, and indeed the exploitative capitalist dominance of *Homo sapiens(?) TrumpAmericansis* even at the expense of the end of humanity.

But I also draw on Muñoz's utopian vision of queer as "not yet here" (2009, 1), a futurity "always on the horizon" (110), and Halberstam's call that "rather than resisting endings and limits, let us instead revel in and cleave to all of our own inevitable fantastic failures" (2011, 187). These films' explorations sometimes seem a direct instantiation of Muñoz's political arguments, that "the present . . . is impoverished and toxic for queers and other people who do not feel the privilege of majoritarian belonging, normative tastes, and 'rational' explanations" (2009, 27). The films' magic and future settings both imagine alternatives.[4] Similarly, Zipes (1983) seeks and invokes fairy tales' liberatory potential, and Kay Turner (2012, 2015) conjures up their lesbian and queer possibilities. She notes that "if fairy tales seem to hurtle headlong toward normative reunion, marriage, and social stability, often the route navigates topsy-turvy spaces filled with marvels, magic, and weird meet-ups" (2015, 46).

I have eliminated a few movies, exclusively for purposes of this chapter's length and focus, but my perspective applies equally well to them. Specifically, while Walter Rankin identifies *What Lies Beneath* (directed by Robert Zemeckis, 2000) as "Hansel and Gretel," some of his connections are somewhat tenuous (as discussed, e.g., in de Vos 2009). I also decline to explore in detail films that have audience score ratings below 25 percent on Rotten Tomatoes, an arbitrary number that nevertheless evokes a failure to engage successfully with viewers. Wikipedia (correctly I think) asserts that two were "sparked" by *Hansel & Gretel: Witch Hunters* (directed by Tommy Wirkola, 2013): *Hansel & Gretel* (directed by Anthony C. Ferrante, 2013), a "mockbuster" ("Hansel & Gretel: Witch Hunters" n.d.) that went directly to DVD[5] (Rotten Tomatoes audience score of 16 percent on May 18, 2018); and *Hansel & Gretel: Warriors of Witchcraft* (directed by David DeCoteau, 2013), which also riffs on the Harry Potter franchise's concept of a high school for witches (Rotten Tomatoes audience score of 18 percent on May 18, 2018).[6] *Hansel Vs. Gretel* (directed by Ben Demaree, 2015, Rotten Tomatoes audience score of 10 percent on June 5, 2018) also recalls Wirkola's film. Otherwise, I have not cherry-picked; I discuss every example that fits my criteria above, available to me in English.

---

4   See also Tison Pugh's (2008) analysis of L. Frank Baum's Oz as queer utopia.
5   Note that the choice in *Hansel & Gretel: Warriors of Witchcraft* to give the young adult siblings Hansel and Gretel the surname Grimm recalls other films based on the same tale that also draw links to the collectors, notably *Grimm* (directed by Alex van Warmerdam, 2003).
6   I defer to later work more examination of queer Canadian-American dual-citizen director DeCoteau's campy fairy-tale films, which also include *Snow White: A Deadly Summer* (2012).

"Hansel and Gretel"—Cannibals and Other Horrors

The best-known traditional versions of "Hansel and Gretel" concern a father persuaded by his wife, the children's stepmother, to abandon his daughter and son in the woods. Twice the kids find their way home, but eventually they become lost and encounter a gingerbread house, wherein a cannibal witch lives. She confines Hansel to a cage and forces Gretel to do housework. The boy deceives the witch by proffering a stick or bone instead of his finger when she wants to test whether he is sufficiently fattened up for cooking. When she decides to cook him anyway, Gretel tricks the witch and pushes her into the oven. The children take the witch's treasure and, sometimes with supernatural help, bring it home to their now (again) widowed father. The tale can incorporate striking images evoking appropriate and inappropriate food, many of which have become cultural clichés, like the trail of breadcrumbs, the gingerbread house, the imprisoned Hansel's bony "finger," and the witch shoved into the oven. Many films for adults use these images—sometimes *only* these images.

Yet even within Europe, traditional versions of ATU 327A vary extensively. Zipes comments that in the manuscript on which the Grimms based their story:

> the children are not given lovely names; their mother is their biological mother; the children do not need the help of God to save themselves; they automatically return home with money that will guarantee a warm welcome. Indeed, the Grimms . . . demonized a stepmother, transformed the children into two pious innocents with cute names who trust in God, and added a silly duck that helps them across a pond to sooth[e] a sobbing father, who does not show any grief about his dead wife, nor does he apologize for abandoning them. (2011, 194)

The cannibalistic figures include not only witches but "ogres, giants, . . . demons, and magicians" (Zipes 2013, 121). There may be one child protagonist, or three, male and/or female, who may simply be lost, not abandoned. The house in the woods may have quite conventional construction materials. In an Italian version, the boy Peppe drinks from a magical brook that turns him into a sheep and his sister Maria "more beautiful than the sun" (136). Maria grows up and marries a king. Her stepmother, jealous that Maria's success has exceeded her own daughter's, plots against the young queen.

Both stepmother and stepsister are explicitly evil and receive gruesome punishments in the end, but their powers are not supernatural, and they are not cannibals. The stepmother (not a supernatural creature in the woods) as evil cannibal is also found in a Romanian version, in which (like the Italian story) the boy transforms, this time into a cuckoo (121–53).

These extreme variations in tradition are not unlike those in the films, which can stray far from the familiar Grimm version. Indeed, filmmakers sometimes produce readings that are (ironically) closer to tradition than they may suspect. However, most animated and live-action films for children closely follow Grimm, though many North American productions mitigate or code its horror. In the *Faerie Tale Theatre* version (*Hansel and Gretel*, directed by James Frawley, 1983), Gretel's witch murder resuscitates the children's predecessors, who have been turned into a gingerbread fence. Rather than dying in the oven, the witch turns to gingerbread. *Hansel & Gretel* (directed by Gary J. Tunnicliffe, 2002) includes lengthy interludes when the children meet the Sandman, played by comedian Howie Mandel in a multicolored coat and rabbit slippers, as well as a comic bogeyman, a flatulent troll, and a helpful blond wood faerie.

Marking an identification between the (step)parent and the evil witch the children encounter, the same actor can take both roles. The latter combining takes place also in "Hansel and Gretel" shorts and family films, as in Joan Collins's stepmother/witch in the *Faerie Tale Theatre* movie and Delta Burke's stepmother occupying the witch's house at the close of the Tunnicliffe work. In Tom Davenport's *Hansel & Gretel: An Appalachian Version* (1975), female actor Marlene Elbin plays both, but the witch is voiced by male actor Julian Yochum. A transgender (step)mother/witch played by (Michael Yama) also appears in director Tim Burton's (1983) Disney television version.

Avoiding psychological explanations, Zipes sees the story as dealing with "abandonment and the search for home" (2011, 200) and links "Hansel and Gretel" with "Tom Thumb" (ATU 700), "The Pied Piper" legend, "Donkey Skin" (ATU 510B), and "The Juniper Tree" (ATU 720; see, e.g., Greenhill and Brydon 2010; Greenhill 2014; chapter 6, this volume). He says that cinematic adaptations of these works "comment metaphorically on modern attitudes toward the maltreatment of children, the causes of physical abuse and violence suffered by young people, and the trauma of incest" (Zipes 2011, 193). Child disappearance, especially as motivated by stranger-danger/pedophilia fears, is remarkably absent from these films, despite being a common trope in crime films since the 1980s (see, e.g., Kohm and Greenhill 2011). Child sexual abuse can appear as an explanation for ambivalent or evil Hansel and Gretel characters' actions, as it does in movies based on the theme of "Little Red Riding Hood" (see Kohm and Greenhill 2014). Live-action films often exploit their medium to enact and highlight the abuse theme, also present in some traditional versions. Zipes argues that most such works

> tell the story of child abuse and abandonment from an adult perspective that diminishes or excuses the consequences of adult actions harmful to children. Even if the tale may point to the parents as culpable, there is a certain amount of rationalization of guilt and responsibility that shapes the telling of the tale. (2011, 195)

The mitigation of parental guilt seems less prevalent in the supernatural and science fiction versions of "Hansel and Gretel." If anything, most clearly amplify culpability through horror, which, as already indicated, many ATU 327A films invoke. Brigid Cherry's work includes the observation that for women "habitual viewers" of the genre, "the taste for horror often began well before adolescence—several reported that their first experience of horror involved being enjoyably frightened by Disney-animated films and other dark children's films based on fairy tales—and has persisted long after" (2002, 173). She notes horror's complex relation to genre, as a constantly shifting discourse of "aesthetics, affects and audiences" (2009, 3). She details some of the contents of its subgenres, such as supernatural, occult, and ghost films, psychological horror, and monster movies, well represented in works derived from "Hansel and Gretel." She also explores audience reaction, that "any film that shocked, scared, frightened, terrified, sickened, or disgusted, or which made the viewer shiver, get the goosebumps, shudder, tremble, jump, gasp or scream in fear could be classified as horror" (2009, 16). Who that audience might be is always in question—sometimes film studies theorists rely on their own perspective and those of other writers in the form of reviews, professional and otherwise. Film studies using ethnographic methodology are relatively rare.

Cherry's example of cannibal horror films (one possible subtype for "Hansel and Gretel"), *Cannibal Holocaust* (directed by Ruggero Deodato, 1980), is a mockumentary (fictional, usually humorous, but offered as if it were a documentary), and she argues that such movies "are evidence of the strong social taboos set up to maintain the clean and proper body" (2009, 118). Cherry's analysis links to compelling arguments by Barbara Creed

(1993), using the work of Julia Kristeva on literary horror (1982). Both look at the (gendered) role of abjection—the corpse, the crossing of bodily borders, and "the construction of the maternal figure as abject" (Creed 1993, 11). The maternal abject involves the child (of any gender) seeking to free themself from the mother's power, absent fathers, and blood, including the "gaping wound," symbolic not only of the castration of the male but also the fear of women's sexual physiology and menstruation. These processes tend to be visually represented in "Hansel and Gretel" horror films, where their Freudian implications sometimes seem overdetermined, as in most versions of the tale: fear of the (step)mother/witch; Hansel's bony finger as phallic; and the implicit linkage of starvation with the mother's abjection, including her production or withholding of sustenance and the suggestion that her wish (when in the witch's form) is to completely consume the child, in the literal form of cannibalism.

As John Rieder details, many theorists strictly divide science fiction as a genre from fairy tale, but internationally, recent films link them (2018). In defining science fiction, Adam Roberts (2006) attends to three theorists. Darko Suvin considers forms with "the presence and interaction of estrangement and cognition, and whose main device is an imaginative framework alternative to the author's empirical environment" (1988, 37); Robert Scholes attends to work that has a radical discontinuity with the world "we know, yet returns to confront that known world in some cognitive way" (1975, 2); and Damien Broderick invokes (among other issues) "metaphoric strategies and metonymic tactics" (1995, 155). All the qualities those three theorists use to define science fiction could equally describe fairy tales and fairy-tale cinema. Roberts ultimately lists a series of topics "liable to be thought of as science fiction: spaceships, interplanetary or interstellar travel; aliens and the encounter with aliens; mechanical robots, genetic engineering, biological robots; computers, advanced technology, virtual reality; time travel; alternative history; futuristic utopias and dystopias" (2006, 12). These matters are not commonly associated with fairy tales—but the alien and computer link supports my contention that *The Cabin in the Woods* (directed by Drew Goddard, 2012) is science fiction as well as "comedy, horror," as it's designated on IMDb. And on several counts above, *I, Robot* (directed by Alex Proyas, 2004) is science fiction, though called "action, adventure, crime" on IMDb.

Vivian Sobchack argues that (North American) "horror film, family melodrama, and science fiction film" alike express fears of American bourgeois patriarchy, "terrorized by its own past, not able to imagine and image its own presence in the future . . . trapped by its desire to escape the present" (1987, 191). Thomas Doherty (2015) similarly links these issues. (The single non–North American example I discuss here, from South Korea, also addresses family horror.) Rieder notes that "genres themselves, within the mass cultural milieu, attain a certain quasi-archetypal quality, so that 'romance' or 'the fairy tale' or 'science fiction' come to operate as signifiers not so much of a category of fiction as of an imaginary realm, a domain of possibilities, a collective fantasy" (2017, 56). Seeing links between fairy tale, science fiction, and horror in these films, I discuss them in the order of their release.

The Guardian (directed by William Friedkin, 1990)

William Friedkin directed two iconic 1970s films, the action, crime, drama *The French Connection* (1971) and the horror *The Exorcist* (1973). Though Friedkin's later work never quite reached the status of those two, he had considerable success as a director. *The Guardian* (drama, horror, mystery) was initially panned, including by Roger Ebert (1990), but it has more recently gained a following and cult status. Originally intended as a "deliberately arch, body-count rich, blackly comic horror film" to be directed by Sam Raimi, it moved with Friedkin to become a "human drama," evidence of "a flesh and blood auteur reaching through the slick veneer of a studio-produced entertainment and making a beautiful mess of things" (Alexander 2015). In the DVD commentary to *The Guardian*, Friedkin indicates that he does not see his film as horror, because "it was based on an actual case." His remark is a telling example of the confusion of fiction with unreality that remains a concern throughout this book. Yet Friedkin also indicates that his personal interest in the narrative came from his own experience of "the nanny from hell"—again, fiction and reality combine (2011).

"What I set out to do with *The Guardian* was to make a contemporary— to that time—Grimm fairy tale. The Grimm fairy tales are very disturbing. They're very frightening, they are not the Disney version that most people are familiar with. They are, let's face it, horror stories" (Friedkin 2011). After opening type that explains that this is a film about Druids, who are sometimes evil, the narrative begins with a young boy reading "Hansel and Gretel" to a baby, as their parents prepare for a weekend trip. Because the woman forgets her glasses, the couple turn back and discover the nanny and baby gone. The baby's face appears in a tree, to which the audience understands the nanny has given it as a sacrifice. The main action concerns Kate (played by Carey Lowell) and Phil (played by Dwier Brown), who move from Chicago to Los Angeles for his job. When Kate gives birth to Jake, she continues working as a decorator because she is "having such a good time" and does not "want to miss out on anything"—by implication, there is no financial requirement for her to earn a wage. They interview nannies, and after their first choice has a serious bike accident, they settle on Camilla (played by Jenny Seagrove).

Three would-be rapists who encounter Camilla with baby Jake in the woods are promptly skewered and burned by the Druidic tree. The couple's friend Ned (played by Brad Hall) pursues her, seeking a date. He follows and observes her naked at the foot of the tree. Coyotes chase Ned back to his home, where he calls for help and then leaves a phone message warning the couple against Camilla. The coyotes smash into Ned's place and rip him apart, but his body and blood magically disappear. The mother from the opening sequence also warns Phil against the nanny. He fires Camilla.

Jake gets sick but recovers, and Camilla tries to steal him from the hospital. Kate and Phil flee with the baby to their house. When coyotes surround Jake, Phil takes him to the woods. Kate in the couple's Jeep and Camilla flying through the air follow. At the Druid baby tree, Kate hits Camilla with the vehicle; she appears dead. The police investigate, but they see the babies as merely carvings; Camilla's body has disappeared. Phil takes a chainsaw into the woods. Camilla appears in the house. When Phil cuts the tree, blood spurts from it—and in the house, Camilla also bleeds and loses limbs, eventually falling through a window. The couple and baby are reunited.

This film recapitulates 1980s conservative backlash against feminism, as outlined in Susan Faludi's bestseller (1991). The implicit blame for the happily married heterosexuals' problems lies with Kate's selfish (in the film's terms) wish to return to work, compounded by the fact that she relinquishes the baby to a nanny so (too!) quickly after the birth. Kate's difficulties with breastfeeding simultaneously punish her for abandoning Jake to Camilla and lead to the nanny's ability to bond readily with the baby. The (feminist backlash) implication is that biomothers *must* stay home and *never* think of their own needs and wishes, subordinating them unquestioningly to what is simply presumed—a priori, without proof—to be the best interests of the child, as I discuss in chapter 6. Further, the nanny is not only a danger to the child but also a danger to the marriage. A husband's eye will ever wander to a younger version, and women are implicitly always replaceable and interchangeable as wives, although never ever as mothers! In the conclusion, the biomother's attempt on her rival's life is only a stopgap; success requires the phallic father's phallic chainsaw on the nanny/stepmother/witch/abject/phallic mother's tree to overcome her.

In terms of "Hansel and Gretel," Camilla is the familiar simultaneous stepmother and witch. In both roles, she's bent on destroying baby Jake—consuming him in her avatar tree. In many versions of ATU 327A, the biomother abandons her kids by dying, thus implicitly as much, if not more, to blame as the father for all that happens in the story. A symbolic homology between parental decease and parental neglect makes it so. In *The Guardian*, Kate plays the biomother's role as the one who abandons, but in this version she also plays a part (if an ultimately relatively unimportant one) in rescuing her child. The woods are dangerous because the witch's tree is there, but home is also perilous. The supernatural aspect increases and overdetermines the stepmother/witch's threat, but the plot of the psychonanny does not require it, as evidenced, for example, in the contemporary *The Hand That Rocks the Cradle* (directed by Curtis Hanson, 1992; see Hubner 2018, 179).

The film's and the director's perspectives are more conservative than some other "Hansel and Gretel" films. They clearly present stepmother/nanny/witch Camilla in terms of the monstrous feminine, particularly via uncontained flows of blood from inappropriate places, including the phallic tree. The heterosexual biofamily, in its most conventional expression, becomes an explicit ideal. The threat of sex outside marriage not only is linked with rape but, even when implicitly consensual, is punished with death but also literal disappearance. Nevertheless, resistant viewers might see Camilla's attractive anti-heteronormative perspective—her interloping presence in the conventional nuclear family—and her instrumental use of babies for her own purposes as foreshadowing Edelman (2004). Indeed, in part, *The Guardian* offers one example of Edelman's concept that a current politics makes self-evident the idea of reproductive futurism—the idea of perpetually desiring and enacting improvements *for* children (2–3). Camilla, of course, is fighting for the child—but in her own interests, implicitly contrasted with Kate and Phil's uncontested presumed interest only in Jake's own welfare.

Camilla offers one answer to Edelman's question, "What . . . would it signify *not* to be 'fighting for the children'?" (3)—that is, to be fighting for one's own survival instead. His response, "that *queerness* names the side of those 'not fighting for the children'" (3), invokes Camilla as a perverse figure, in terms also envisioned by Halberstam (2011), discussed below. The film's view of the family is difficult to read as anything but anti-feminist and conservative; threats to the nuclear family must be excised at all costs. If firing the female threat doesn't work, kill her. If killing doesn't work, destroy her symbolic power. The queer Camilla fails rather spectacularly with Jake, but there's no guarantee she won't magically resurface as she has before. (I imagine a sequel, so familiar in horror franchises, *The Guardian 2: Camilla Returns*.) But for a manifestly counterculture Hansel and Gretel, the next film may be exemplary.

Freeway 2: Confessions of a Trickbaby (directed by Matthew Bright, 1999)

Director Bright followed his successful *Freeway* (1996), updating "Little Red Riding Hood," with an even edgier take on "Hansel and Gretel." Though this film is *not* identified as horror on IMDb, it clearly references the genre, combining an evil transforming witch figure with psychological explorations of serial killing (see Cherry 2009, 5). It is mainly realist, but the witch's transformation at the end as well as some of her powers are preternatural. Its teen primary protagonists are involved in extensive criminal behavior—and much queer negativity/failure. "White Girl" (played by Natasha Lyonne), sent to a prison hospital for bulimia treatment before serving her twenty-five-year sentence, escapes with her cellmate, killer "Cyclona" (played by Maria Celedonio). They head for Tijuana and Sister Gomez (played by Vincent Gallo), who, Cyclona says, can cure White Girl's eating disorder. Their journey includes drinking, drug taking, and robbery by both young women and several murders by Cyclona. White Girl's sleazy lawyer/pimp Mr. Butz (played by David Alan Grier) gets her sentence overturned on a technicality, and goes in search of her.

The escapees locate Sister Gomez, a composite witch/stepmother, who feasts White Girl but requires that she continue robbing johns. White Girl finds Cyclona seminude in a bondage swing in a basement filled with children. Cyclona explains that she was forced to watch while Sister Gomez filmed children being raped, killed, and eaten. White Girl frees the captives, and she and Cyclona discover Sister Gomez, revealed as biomale, performing a ritual surrounded by people in bondage gear. White Girl shoots them and wounds Sister Gomez, whom the young women stuff into the oven to burn alive—where she transforms into a conventional hook-nosed witch figure

FIGURE 5.1. Trans witch transforms.

(see figure 5.1). The *Federales* and Butz catch up with them and surround Sister Gomez's bordello. White Girl kills Cyclona at her behest (she cannot face more prison), brokers a deal with the *Federales*, and leaves with Butz, declaring, "I'm not hungry any more."

In *Freeway 2*, young people's evil comes from adults' abuse and exploitation. White Girl and Cyclona manifest behaviors contrary to middle-class morality, but the former retains a clear, explicit moral code that abhors drug selling to children, child abuse, and murder. She even leaves a trail of rocks of crack cocaine, despite their street value, so that she and Cyclona can find their way back to the train on which they travel to Mexico, but the rocks are gathered by birdlike human characters. White Girl tries unsuccessfully to get Cyclona to take the medications that dampen her homicidal tendencies and tolerates Cyclona's murders because White Girl recognizes them as a symptom of Cyclona's insanity—but beats her severely after one killing spree. White Girl verifies to Cyclona that Sister Gomez caused her mental illness and that her incestuous family compounded the damage. In Old Testament, eye-for-an-eye style, White Girl affirms that Cyclona was right to kill her family. Vengeance may be her right as a victim, but Cyclona cannot survive it.

The film offers no details about White Girl's family, though she is probably the title's trick baby. There is genuine affection between her and Butz; if not family per se, he offers her support against the system. Their closing reunion is no unequivocal happy ending, but since White Girl proclaims herself no longer bulimic, it seems unlikely that Butz is the source of the angst that made her obsessively binge and purge. She seems to revel in the (vengeful) work he presumably taught her, robbing and beating White men who seek sex with a teenager. The audience may join her satisfaction in this vocation, as in the rightful murders of Cyclona's evil family and the evil Sister Gomez. The film implicitly celebrates Butz's and White Girl's unconventional family relationship, unassociated with reproduction, as Halberstam and Edelman might predict.

The gender bending and play with sexuality in *Freeway* 2 begins with the two main characters who become lovers. Though while they are on the run White Girl occupationally dresses in a feminine style and Cyclona's (frankly quite unconvincing) initial disguise is as a boy, director Bright (personal communication, 2012) identified the former as the Hansel figure. White Girl is physically and psychologically stronger than Cyclona, and she is the prime mover in the Gretel-like immolation of Sister Gomez. Yet the children's gender differentiation in the Grimm version is, as indicated above, not the sole tradition.

Evil, arguably transgender characters abound in films—from *Psycho*'s (directed by Alfred Hitchcock, 1960) Norman Bates to *The Silence of the Lambs*'s (directed by Jonathan Demme, 1991) Jame Gumb and beyond (see, e.g., Halberstam 1991). The male-to-female Sister Gomez complexly signifies both stepmother and witch. When her face appears in the oven window, the actor's makeup closely resembles the hyper-pointed nose and chin of the Wicked Witch in *The Wizard of Oz* (directed by Victor Fleming, 1939). Making Sister Gomez a literal fairy-tale witch does not excuse the othering ploy involved. Further, Gallo's performance implies that Sister Gomez, like Cyclona, is insane. If White Girl, representing the film's ethos, forgives Cyclona's murders because her mental state obviates her responsibility, why must Sister Gomez meet such a grisly fate? Is it because her victims, unlike Cyclona's, are children (so she instantiates the associations between queer and death) or because, in the end, the Grimm story's image of the slaughtered witch forced Bright's hand?

Making Sister Gomez (as stepmother/witch) transgender fits with cultural stereotypes that say that no (normal?) mother hurts her children—a presumption I explore in chapter 6. White Girl's and Cyclona's biomothers are absent (dead? in jail? voluntarily abandoning?); they're not part of the equation. Making Sister Gomez supernatural, and the food she gives White Girl implicitly enchanted, so that it never satisfies, and only feeds the young woman's appetite, both overdetermines the threat and increases the viewer's recognition of why that danger was so difficult to overcome. No evil act in the film is ultimately the Hansel and Gretel characters' fault. Again, the adults in their lives are responsible, the heterosexual nuclear family more the problem than the solution, and the two children must save themselves—and each other—whatever safety might actually mean. The underlying problem, of child exploitation, remains. As Edelman might predict, queer links to death and failure, and the heterosexually inflected—if not precisely heteronormative—relation between White Girl and Butz fosters survival.

A.I. Artificial Intelligence (directed by Steven Spielberg, 2001)

Critical reception of this film, begun by Stanley Kubrick and completed by Spielberg after Kubrick's death, was mixed. Many reviewers compare the work with what they imagine Kubrick would have done with it (Gordon 2008, 229–30). Along with several other scholars, Naarah Sawers discusses this film as a version of "Pinocchio"—a story it frequently references—making the argument that *A.I.* explores modes of contemporary capitalism, warning that "modern consumer society has . . . set its sights on human bodies" (2010, 57). But this adventure, drama, sci-fi film also explores the consequences of child abandonment, disparages the nuclear family, and ultimately dispenses with human life from the earth. It has strong ATU 327A aspects as well as some horror, particularly associated with the Flesh Fair.

In the future, humans are allowed only one biochild. David (played by Haley Joel Osment), a mechanical child "Mecha" acquired by Monica (played by Frances O'Connor) and Henry (played by Sam Robards), substitutes for their son, Martin (played by Jake Thomas), who has been placed in suspended animation awaiting a cure for his disease. Though initially ambivalent, Monica imprints David so he will irreversibly love her forever. Monica gives David Martin's robot "supertoy" teddy bear. When a cured Martin returns, jealous of David, he manipulates the Mecha so that his parents fear for the family's safety. Henry wants Monica to return David to the factory to be destroyed; child Martin and by implication father Henry get the blame for the abandonment, but (step)mother Monica is its instrument. She leaves David and Teddy in the forest rather than sending him to immediate death (see figure 5.2). When he realizes what's happening, David cries, "Mommy, if

FIGURE 5.2. Monica abandons David in the woods.

Pinocchio became a real boy and I become a real boy, can I come home?" Monica replies, "That's just a story," and David counters, "But a story tells what happens." Monica says, "Stories are not real! You're not real!" David's last words to Monica are, "I'm sorry I'm not real. If you let me, I'll be so real for you."

Captured for a Flesh Fair that destroys outmoded Mecha for the entertainment of its human audience, David escapes with Mecha prostitute Gigolo Joe (played by Jude Law), who has been framed for murder. The two seek the Blue Fairy to transform David as she did Pinocchio. Mechanical oracle Dr. Know tells David to find Allen Hobby (played by William Hurt) at the end of the world (Manhattan, now inundated). There David encounters other Mecha exactly like him, which Hobby has built as a replica of his dead son. But Hobby asserts David's distinctiveness: "You are a real boy. At least as real as I've ever made one, which by all reasonable accounts would make me your Blue Fairy," Hobby tells a skeptical David. But the Mecha child, despondent, leaps into the water.

He is rescued by Gigolo Joe, who is immediately captured. David and Teddy are submerged and find the Blue Fairy statue in a (now underwater) Coney Island Pinocchio-themed area. A Ferris wheel traps them, and David repeatedly begs the Blue Fairy, "Please make me real." After two thousand years, the ocean has frozen, and no humans remain. Evolved Mechas rescue

David; they access the boy's memories to reconstruct his home. They provide a Blue Fairy, who says, "I cannot make you a real boy" but affirms that he is "unique in all the world." The Mechas create a Monica clone from DNA in a lock of her hair that Teddy kept, but she can live only for one day. Monica tells David, "I have always loved you," and with Teddy the two fall asleep.

With gender reversal from most "Hansel and Gretel" narratives—in *A.I.* the father persuades the (step)mother to abandon the child, not vice versa—this film nevertheless arguably compounds maternal responsibility for David's abandonment in the woods. Its futuristic world recalls 1950s wealthy White American suburban social arrangements; only father Henry works outside the home, and mother Monica apparently has no connection with paid employment. Similarly, there's no option for the Mecha to imprint on more than one family member, so in the film's ethos of course it must be the mother who does the deed. Henry is distant, even epiphenomenal to the family; he brings David to Monica but makes no connection to him. Indeed, Henry affirms of David that "He's a toy." Monica can't bring herself to have David destroyed, but she also fails to fight for him as a family member with a right to stay with them; even she believes that he is "not real."

Concerns around David's realness and the Mecha child's desire to become "a real boy" go beyond the issue of transformation in the Pinocchio story. David recognizes that for him to become real is within *Monica*'s—not his own—capability; "If you let me, I'll be so real for you," he says. But the fulfillment of his wish at the film's closing doesn't actually involve any change in him; instead, it gives him exclusive—if only daylong—access to Monica. The Mecha child blames himself for his mother's failings, but he is in no way responsible for them. Being human and being real aren't the same thing; David's nonhuman loyalty to all his friends, not just his "imprinted" love for Monica, marks him as superior. Similarly, the care and compassion that the other Mechas show David demonstrate by implication that they are better, indeed much more humane, than the humans in the film—from David's nuclear family members who each betray him in their own way, to the husband who murders his wife and frames Gigolo Joe, to those who run the Flesh Fairs and the audience who attend.

The film displays problems of human exceptionalism—the belief that species *Homo sapiens* is fundamentally unique and different from all other beings—at its worst, while clearly criticizing it and the heteronormative family who cruelly abandon David because he's not "real." As Marina Fedosik's consideration of the film as an adoption narrative demonstrates, it offers an extensive reflection on "the difficulty in drawing a distinction between the real and the artificial" (2018, 183). She argues that in the film "David is not recognized for what he really is—neither a human child nor a non-human object . . . whose origin in the sociotechnical is both a reflection and a harbinger of possible human ontologies" (185). He is, nevertheless, "what women and slaves used to be and children still are . . . aspiring to and experiencing the human condition with no access to full human rights" (194). As indicated above, David asks to be "real," not "human" or "orga[nic]"; he links his realness to his uniqueness, and though discovering many others who look like him initially shocks him, the conclusion points to his relationship with Monica, and his survival into the literally posthuman future, as unique. And yet, like Hansel and Gretel's lack of connection to their stepmother, his relationship with Monica is ultimately painfully abusive because of the woman's inability to connect with David as her "real" child.

The nuclear heterofamily fails both literally and figuratively; the relationship of an adult male Mecha Gigolo Joe to child male Mecha David offers nurturance (parental, both conventionally motherly in the form of non-self-regarding care and conventionally fatherly in the form of direction and advice); and ultimately the human race destroys itself to be replaced by kinder, gentler beings in the form of advanced Mechas. The death drive of *Homo sapiens* and its failure are reversed in *A.I.* Hansel's (David's) mechanical witches. Both Gigolo Joe and the advanced Mechas, far from consuming David (which is what his nuclear family does), encourage his growth and aspirations. But the failure to continue the human race is by implication straight, not queer. It appears that in part because of the limitation of reproduction (represented in the film as implicitly heterosexual) to a single child, humans are eventually replaced by Mechas—which, given the failures of the humans, is perhaps not such a bad thing.

I, Robot (directed by Alex Proyas, 2004)

Men are called fathers when they create specifically designated "unique" robots in both *A.I.* and *I, Robot,* and the result is, or could be, the end of humans. Male parturition occurs not only in myth but also implicitly in the traditional tale "The Juniper Tree" (Warner 1998; see chapter 6). Another apparent literal impossibility (now rendered a reality by transmen), the pregnant man finds expression in fairy tales and fairy-tale media. The exceptional robot in *I, Robot,* not coincidentally called Sonny (played by Alan

FIGURE 5.3. Hansel & Gretel book.

Tudyk), refers to his maker, Alfred Lanning (played by James Cromwell), as his father. Perhaps because its science fiction credentials are so obvious, the film is described as "action, adventure, crime" on IMDb. The links with "Hansel and Gretel" appear in different locations, including placement of a book (see figure 5.3) of the tale in Lanning's lab leading to the hero's understanding that he must follow a "trail of bread crumbs." Of course, the irony in that fairy-tale metaphor is that breadcrumbs are the least successful trail markers Hansel uses, since they are eaten by birds so that the kids can't find their way home.

Wisecracking police detective Del Spooner (played by Will Smith) hates and distrusts robots because one saved him from an accident, leaving a young girl to drown—in Edelman's terms, the robot failed to presume child futurity as the sole and transcending desideratum. The robot instead followed the three laws of robotics: first, a robot cannot injure or allow harm to a human; second, a robot must obey orders from humans except when they would conflict with the first; and finally, a robot must protect its own existence except if it would conflict with the first or second law. The robot elected to save Spooner because statistically he was more likely than the girl to survive. Spooner receives cybernetic replacements for his injuries from Lanning, who later appears (inexplicably) to have committed suicide. The detective's mistrust of robots leads him to instead suspect Sonny, personally built by Lanning with programming that allows him to ignore the three laws, of killing his creator.

With the help of Susan Calvin (played by Bridget Moynahan), Spooner seeks to learn what happened, certain that "Lanning was locked down so tight he couldn't get out a message. All he could do was leave me clues. A trail of bread crumbs like 'Hansel and Gretel.'" Spooner and Calvin discover Sonny's recurring dream of a robot savior. When Calvin is about to destroy Sonny's brain because a robot that is not absolutely bound by the three laws would shake public confidence, he makes an observation that David in *A.I.* also realized. Seeing a series of robots around him, he says, "They look like me, but none of them are me," and Calvin confirms, "You are unique."

Upon arriving at the location depicted in Sonny's dream, Spooner discovers a group of the newest model NS-5 robots, soon to be launched to replace all previous models, dismantling older robots. The NS-5 robots begin taking over, killing humans who refuse to accept them. Spooner realizes the robots are being controlled by computer VIKI. Guided by the three laws, but "evolved," VIKI recognizes that humans' self-destructive behavior threatens their survival and so reprograms herself to save humanity from itself. Lanning arranged his own death as a way to stop VIKI. Spooner and Calvin destroy VIKI, and the NS-5 robots are deactivated and sent to storage. Sonny returns to the storage location, where the robots turn expectantly toward him.

Sonny's uniqueness prevents Calvin from destroying him. In turn, Sonny declines to kill humans to save them, affirming that he sees the logic of VIKI's plan but won't go along with it because "it just seems too . . . heartless." Spooner's prejudice against robots makes him ideal in Lanning's plan; it's the police detective's human flaws that make him useful in decoding what has happened. However, a robot (Sonny) needs to save humans from other robots (VIKI and her avatars), and in the film's conclusion, Sonny stands before the other robots as *their* leader and savior also. The film implicitly raises the question that Sonny may again have to choose between saving humans and saving robots—and his next decision may not be the same. If VIKI was correct about humans' ultimate rage for self-destruction—and crucially no one in the film argues that she is wrong—the future may vindicate her.

But mere survival, without what makes *Homo sapiens* human (which does, perhaps contradictorily, appear to be their death drive), proves unpalatable for most of the protagonists—that's why they object to VIKI's plan. From the robot who saved Spooner rather than a child to VIKI, who seeks to kill humans to save them from themselves, a queer futurity reigns in *I, Robot*. The queer family of Sonny with his father, Lanning, stepparents Calvin and

Spooner, and a multitude of robot siblings proves durable. While VIKI might be the witch character, by implication so is her mechanical relative Sonny. To echo Glinda's memorable query, is he a good witch or a bad witch? Or to restate, will he allow the human death drive to prevail to its ultimate inevitable conclusion—in Edelman's terms, "no future" for *Homo sapiens*? The film's ending leaves that question open.

Henjel gwa Geuretel (Hansel & Gretel) (directed by Pil-sung Yim, 2007)

IMDb calls this *Hansel & Gretel* "drama, fantasy, horror," but Zipes sees this work as "not a horror film" but "more surreal meditation about what we do to children when we bring them into a vicious world and when home can be a savage place" (2011, 206). In an again familiar reversal, the witch characters are male, but the (somewhat mitigated) savior is male also. The children do not ultimately get what they want, as they do in most traditional versions of ATU 327A; the three abused kids in Yim's version want loving, willing parents, but they end up without them. The future may seem promising for the hero and his girlfriend (now wife) and child, but the film never lets us know whether the three children will continue to search for parents (albeit perhaps in a more favorable urban location) or if they remain as wandering spirits. A notebook depicts them as happy together, but that doesn't preclude a continuing search.

As Björn Sundmark puts it, "the new equilibrium—the child régime—is dangerous. . . . [The] film dwells on the precariousness of the situation" because the children need "an endless supply of adults" (2017, 102). Within the film, representations of the "Hansel and Gretel" book and the children's notebook indicate that behind what seems to be taking place—that a family takes in lost travelers—is the reality that the kids are serially killing and replacing heterosexual couples who wander into their realm but are found inadequate as parents. Again the live-action diegetic reality is initially deceptive and the viewer doesn't realize what is actually happening, just as hero protagonist Eun-soo (played by Jeong-myeong Cheon) at first is unaware. The apparent fictions within the diegesis indicate greater truths.

Eun-soo crashes his car while arguing on the phone with his girlfriend, Hae-young (played by Eun-joo Kim), about terminating her pregnancy. Eun-soo recovers consciousness in a forest, and Young-hee (played by Eun-kyung Shim) leads him to the "House of Happy Children," where her parents, older

FIGURE 5.4. The house in the woods.

brother Man-bok (played by Eun Won-jae), and younger sister Jung-soon (played by Ji-hee Jin) welcome him (see figure 5.4). After a strange breakfast of pastel-colored cakes, Eun-soo (whom the children call "Uncle") tries to leave but cannot—all paths lead back to the house. When he returns, the parents are gone. On Eun-soo's third day, he meets Man-bok on the path, bringing the Deacon (played by Hee-soon Park) and his wife (played by Lydia Park). Eun-soo finds the wife stealing but also comes across a "Hansel and Gretel" book.[7]

On the final day, the two girls beg for a story, and Eun-soo, beginning "Once upon a time," narrates about his relationship with his dying mother and girlfriend and about wanting to leave because if he doesn't the "baby could die" and he wouldn't see his mother. Eun-soo follows Man-bok into the woods, where the boy enters a blue door. Eun-soo finds inside a notebook that reveals the parents' arrival and deaths, as well as documents indicating that the children are adult aged and were residents in the "House of Happy Children" orphanage. The Deacon, having found expensive jewelry, threatens the children, trying to get the deed to the house to turn it into his church. He reveals that he murdered his own father, and the children defend themselves supernaturally. Eun-soo warns the children not to kill the Deacon,

7 See Bacchilega (2013, 101–7) on the significance of books in the film.

saying, "You'll be like him if you do this!" but Man-bok counters that "Bad grown-ups must be punished" and shows him the "Hansel and Gretel" book, saying "The bad witch got punished." Eun-soo replies, "That's a fairy tale." "No," says a crying Jung-soon. "This book granted all our wishes."

A flashback reveals that they and other children were horribly abused—beaten, starved, raped, and murdered—in the orphanage by "Father" (played by the actor who plays the Deacon). But a visiting Santa gives them candy and the "Hansel and Gretel" book, telling them, "From now on just imagine whatever you want, and your wish will be granted. You can get everything you need this way." The kids reenact the witch burning in "Hansel and Gretel" and kill "Father." In the present, the children ask Eun-soo to stay, but he urges them to end the curse, leave the house, and grow up with his help. They refuse. Young-hee shows him the children's notebook called "Being Happy Forever with Uncle." She instructs him to burn it to escape; he does so and awakes in the woods near his wrecked car.

Later, at Christmas, Eun-soo, home with his wife and baby, finds the children's notebook, all pages blank except for the final one with a drawing of the three, smiling. He weeps. Outside in the snow, the three children, now in the city, turn and walk away from the camera. As Cristina Bacchilega puts it, Eun-soo "confronts his childhood trauma of abandonment, and emerges transformed into a responsible and loving family man" (2013, 99). The children are ambivalent figures, punishing evil people but also those who are not apparently guilty of anything except trying to escape them—or, alternatively, failing to reproduce the unquestioned primacy of all children. The kids are "not to be held responsible for compulsively repeating the cycle of violence they seek to leave behind. Neither are they simply to be indulged in their wish for an impossibly endless and happy childhood" (104). Crucially, the children discover that though "Uncle" Eun-soo wants to leave and the Deacon wants to stay—saying, "I'll protect you forever. Forever. I'll stay by your side"—their expectations can change. What they think they want—above and before all else, only "parents" who will stay—is not in fact what they need (or truly want). If the parents who decide to remain don't love the kids, they potentially reproduce the conditions that brought them to the "House of Happy Children," underlined by the Deacon and Father being played by the same actor.

Like its North American counterparts, Yim's film literally doubles the roles of the most obviously evil stepfather, the Deacon, and the evil orphanage "Father" witch, played by the same actor. It also reverses their expected sex/gender. The children's final confrontations with the Deacon and witch are presented together, further cementing their links, with quick cuts between the two contexts, sometimes overlapping their content. The Deacon holding a knife to Eun-soo's throat as he sings a hymn juxtaposes with flashbacks of "Father" raping Man-bok in front of Young-hee and Jung-soon, then smoking a pipe, then threatening the children, saying, "If you didn't exist, those sweets would be for me," and approaching Man-bok with a hot poker. Young-hee in the present tells Man-bok, "Eun-soo's right. This man is like the Father at the orphanage." Voiced parts of the confrontation with the Deacon juxtapose with visuals of the orphanage, concluding with "Father" burned in the oven and the Deacon stabbed to death. But the children also have supernatural witchlike characters, and they are denizens of the gingerbread house with the quite un-witchlike initial Father and Mother. Are the latter, along with the Deacon and his wife, and Eun-soo himself, the Hansels and Gretels, with witch children preventing their departure? Other than the evil stepfather/witches, "Father" and the Deacon, mapping roles from ATU 327A on this film's characters is by no means straightforward.

While it's not explicitly apocalyptic, the film's representation of (queer) failure makes it impossible for children, so horribly abused, to recover. No family within the diegesis is without significant problems. Throughout most of the film, Eun-soo wants to escape parenthood with his girlfriend and being Uncle to the three children; with the exception of Eun-soo and his girlfriend/wife, heterosexual couples are ambivalent to explicitly malevolent. Presumably staying children forever, Man-bok, Young-hee, and Jung-soon won't be part of a reproductive continuation of humans;[8] given the damage they have endured, that result is one to be wished for.

Hansel & Gretel Get Baked (directed by Duane Journey, 2013)

As in *Freeway 2*, the Hansel and Gretel characters in the "comedy, horror" film *Hansel & Gretel Get Baked*, with numerous arch fairy-tale references, are adolescents—not-quite-adults yet with adult roles and responsibilities and minimal support from parents or parental figures. However, the films' contexts could hardly be more different. In contrast to their underclass counterparts in *Freeway 2*, the *Baked* main protagonists live in obvious

---

8   They certainly invoke Kathryn Bond Stockton's (2009) idea of queer children; they definitely do not grow up, but instead arguably grow sideways.

privilege. Suburban siblings Hansel (played by Michael Welch) and Gretel (played by Molly Quinn), left alone while their parents visit the Stiltskins, encounter an intense new marijuana strain, "Black Forest High." When Gretel's stoner boyfriend Ashton (played by Andrew James Allen) goes to buy more weed while she makes gingerbread cookies, he encounters witch Agnes (played by Lara Flynn Boyle) with a gingerbread house in her living room. "Don't touch my gingerbread house," she says, but Ashton has the munchies and eats some. He passes out; when he awakes the witch is preparing him for cooking. He mistakes her interest as sexual, but she dismembers and eats him. The next morning Gretel and Hansel go to the witch's house looking for Ashton and then to the police, who are unhelpful. Local gangster Carlos (played by Reynaldo Gallegos) finds out the witch is selling weed on his turf. Ashton's dealer, Manny (played by Eddy Martin), warns the witch but she slits his throat. Carlos takes two thugs to Agnes's house; she and the zombified Manny kill two and cage a third.

Gretel works with Manny's girlfriend, Bianca (played by Bianca Saad), to investigate Agnes and her house. Bianca diverts Agnes, and Gretel sneaks into the basement and locates the Black Forest High crop, caged henchman Octavio (played by Celestino Cornielle), and the remains of people Agnes has killed. Gretel leaves a trail of Skittles to help her find her way back, but Bianca eats them. Hansel comes to the witch's door. Zombie Carlos tries to kill him but is killed in turn. Agnes knocks Hansel out. As the witch prepares to cook Hansel, she discovers he's a virgin and requires extra preparation. As Gretel and Bianca try to rescue Hansel, Agnes kills Bianca, but Gretel pushes the witch into the furnace and locks the door. As the oven explodes and the house burns down, the siblings escape. A police officer finds a cat and takes it to his van; after a commotion therein, Agnes reaches out and adjusts the rearview mirror and then drives away.

Agnes connects in multiple ways with those who arrive at her door; she may simply sell them Black Forest High weed; she may drug, eat, and/or kill them; she may steal their youth; she may have sexual encounters with them; she may imprison them; she may zombify them. It would be difficult to argue that she is not a queer character. Viewers discover at the end that this resilient, omnisexual witch not only shape-shifts between older and younger versions of herself but can also become an animal. With so many forces to invoke, she may in fact be indestructible. Again, the witch or magical figure lives on. Humans are in danger from her; not even explosion and fire can destroy her. No limits to her power emerge in the narrative.

A familiar trope of horror films, the unkillable monster, the omnisexual Agnes clearly retains her own queer futurity—perhaps more like Muñoz's always-on-the horizon form (2009, 11) than like Edelman's. Hansel and Gretel may return to their parents, but they bring no bounty from the witch's house. Her artful queer failure, in Halberstam's terms, only presages her return. Their friends gone, Hansel and Gretel are fortunate to escape with their lives. They clearly represent normative heterosexuality, in contrast to so many other characters who die, like Bianca, who makes out with Agnes, and Gretel's boyfriend, Ashton, who is willing to have sex with a much older woman. And yet Agnes, the most polymorphously perverse of all, not only lives but also by implication goes on to more of the same—no death for her. That she uses capitalism—selling Black Forest High not for monetary gain but instead to get access to young people whose essence she employs to stay youthful—makes her further something of an anti-capitalist hero. *Baked*'s Hansel and Gretel may be radically transformed by their tussle with a queer supernatural adversary; others don't survive that experience.

The Cabin in the Woods (directed by Drew Goddard, 2012)

Like *Baked*, the meta-horror reflection *Cabin* is classed on IMDb as "comedy, horror." But as might be expected given its association with auteur Joss Whedon and his troupe of actors and crew, it offers the viewer a cerebral (yet extremely entertaining) experience, in the form of "a pointed critique of neoliberalism" (Blouin 2015, 83). The dystopian premise of a group of technical bureaucrats focused on efficiency instead of on the human implications of their actions is all too real, from historical examples like Nazi Germany to the current US presidential dictatorship.[9]

Technicians Sitterson (played by Richard Jenkins) and Hadley (played by Bradley Whitford) learn that a ritual in Stockholm has failed, and only Japan and America are left. Meanwhile, American college students Dana (played by Kristen Connolly), Holden (played by Jesse Williams), Marty (played by Fran Kranz), Jules (played by Anna Hutchinson), and Curt (played by Chris Hemsworth) leave in an RV for a weekend at Curt's cousin's off-the-grid

---

9 Director Goddard's second film, *Bad Times at the El Royale* (2018, mystery, thriller), with links to historical reality (incorporating events and film from the 1950s, 1960s, and 1970s), is even more explicit in its political message about government corruption, the evils of religion, and ubiquitous surveillance.

cabin. Sitterson and Hadley manipulate the students with mind-altering drugs to hinder rational thinking and increase libido. Exploring the cabin cellar, the students find various objects, including the diary of Patience Buckner (played by Jodelle Ferland), abused by her sadistic family. Despite stoner Marty's warnings, Dana recites Latin inscriptions from the journal, which summons the zombified Buckner family. Curt and Jules have sex and then the Buckners decapitate her; Curt escapes to alert the group. Marty discovers concealed surveillance equipment, but the Buckners drag him away. Sitterson and Hadley learn that the ritual in Japan has also failed; the American cabin ritual is humanity's last hope.

Curt, Holden, and Dana attempt to escape in their RV, but Sitterson triggers a tunnel collapse to block them. Curt jumps a ravine on his motorcycle seeking to get away and alert the authorities but is killed when he crashes into a force field. Holden and Dana retreat to the RV, but one of the Buckners fatally stabs Holden. The RV crashes and sinks into a lake. Dana escapes and swims ashore—she seems to be the "final girl," as described by Carol Clover (1992). As the Buckners attack her, Sitterson, Hadley, and the rest of the institutional staff celebrate the successful ritual but are interrupted by a phone call. Marty has survived because his heavy marijuana use made him immune to the technicians' drugs. He rescues Dana. In a hidden elevator they descend into the underground facility, where a menagerie of monsters correlate with the objects in the cabin's cellar. The items each group chooses make them the associated monsters' victims—the unwitting agents of their own ritual deaths. Cornered by security forces, Dana and Marty release the monsters, which wreak havoc and slaughter the staff. Dana and Marty flee, and Dana accidentally mortally wounds Sitterson, who begs her to kill Marty so she can be the final girl and complete the ritual.

The two students discover an ancient temple. The facility's leader, the Director (played by Sigourney Weaver), explains that they are participating in an annual ritual sacrifice of the young to appease the Ancient Ones, gods who once ruled the earth. Each facility's ritual follows rules from its culture; in America, sacrifices conform to horror archetypes: the whore (Jules), the athlete (Curt), the scholar (Holden), the fool (Marty), and the virgin (Dana). To complete the ritual, the virgin must survive or die last. If all facilities fail, the penalty is the human race's extermination. The Director tries to kill Marty, but zombie Patience Buckner appears and kills her instead. Deciding that humanity is not worth saving, Dana and Marty share a joint. The temple floor collapses, and a giant hand emerges, destroying the facility and by implication the world.

Here again scholarship influences the fictional narrative; Japanese and American horror film archetypes offer sources for their specific rituals. Youth may succeed in playing the game (thus failing the human race by not completing their ritual) through love and affirmation as the Japanese girls do; or they may refuse to sacrifice themselves or each other for similar reasons as Dana and Marty do (see Mayo 2014). Like in *A.I.*, at the close of *Cabin* humanity is destroyed. Another apocalyptic "Hansel and Gretel" ends with a family playing a role in that result. It's not coincidental that the sadomasochistic zombie—but apparently heterosexual—Buckners cannot win against Marty's Hansel and Dana's Gretel. The latter two explicitly don't enact a heterosexual relationship within the diegesis (despite references to a brief freshman dalliance). Refusing the heterosexual, replacing it with the heterosocial, by implication places Marty and Dana in the realm of nonreproductive relationship, imputed as queer in American popular culture, as Edelman outlines. The (temporarily!) surviving two save one another, and they vanquish not only the Buckner family but also the witch/Director. But their success is also queer failure; by Dana choosing not to kill Marty, and by Marty choosing not to commit suicide, this Hansel and Gretel bring the Ancient Ones forth, and the result is the end of the world (see figure 5.5).

The "neopostmodern" (Och 2015) narrative plays humorously and ironically with ideas of science linked to fictions using stereotypes. For example,

FIGURE 5.5. Hansel (Marty) and Gretel (Dana).

"HANSEL AND GRETEL" FILMS * 157

the ritual directors biochemically manipulate the students—including via blond hair dye to make Jules less intelligent and more sexual. But the narrative also indicates that the five protagonists are actually aware that their behavior in the cabin is not what they expect of themselves and each other. Though all but Marty are affected by the drugs they are given, they do not lose themselves entirely. Their awareness and their discussion of each other's behavior, however, is all that we know of the characters' usual identities. The film lacks a requirement for extensive characterization because the protagonists have literally become archetypes (see Och 2015, 206). The ritual fails, its directors fail, and the world ends. And as might be expected, the queer (heterosocial, not heterosexual; nonreproductive) relationship between Marty and Dana leads to the world's termination—no future, in Edelman's terms, or "the association of failure with nonconformity, anticapitalist practices, nonreproductive lifestyles, negativity, and critique" (Halberstam 2011, 89). Remarkably, given its denouement, it appears that the film's creators do not rule out the possibility of a sequel (see, e.g., O'Connell 2015), a fitting link to Halberstam's and Muñoz's concepts!

Mama (directed by Andy Muschietti, 2013)

The family is again deconstructed in the "horror, thriller" film *Mama*, which opens with letters being spelling out in a childish-looking print, "once upon a time . . ." During a devastating financial collapse, Jeffrey Desange (played by Nicolaj Coster-Waldau) shoots people at his workplace, kills his wife, and takes his children, three-year-old Victoria and one-year-old Lilly, to an abandoned cabin. Jeffrey holds a gun to Victoria's head, but a mysterious figure kills him. Five years later, Jeffrey's artist identical twin brother Lucas's private investigator, Burnsie (played by David Fox), finds Victoria (played by Megan Charpentier) and Lilly (played by Isabelle Nélisse) deep in the woods in a feral state. Psychiatrist Dr. Gerald Dreyfuss (played by Daniel Kash) seeks to find out how they survived, and the girls refer to "Mama" (played by Javier Botet). Dreyfuss supports Lucas's custody claim over that of the children's aunt, Jean (played by Jane Moffat), in exchange for a furnished house and permission to monitor their progress. Lucas's punk rock musician girlfriend, Annabel (played by Jessica Chastain), reluctantly agrees to the plan. Dreyfuss hypnotizes Victoria and asks her to tell him her story.

VICTORIA: It was a long time ago. A lady ran away from a hospital for sad people. She took her baby. They jumped into the water.
DREYFUSS: How could you know that story, Victoria? Did Mama tell you that story?
VICTORIA: She showed me.
DREYFUSS: How?
VICTORIA: In a dream.

Victoria thrives with Annabel and Lucas, but Lilly retains feral qualities.

Mama attacks Lucas, putting him in a coma and leaving Annabel to care for the girls alone. Annabel's nightmare reveals Mama's past. She is the ghost of the institutionalized Edith Brennan, who jumped from a cliff to prevent her baby being taken from her; Edith drowns but the child's body catches on a branch. Victoria grows close to Annabel and fearful of Mama. Dreyfuss visits the cabin; Mama kills him. Initially screaming at Annabel's touch, Lilly eventually accepts her hold. Annabel hears the rest of Dreyfuss's interview with Victoria.

VICTORIA: She fell into the water but the baby didn't.
DREYFUSS: Why?
VICTORIA: I don't know.
DREYFUSS: What could have happened to the baby, Victoria?
VICTORIA: I don't know.
DREYFUSS: Mama didn't show you?
VICTORIA: She doesn't know what happened to her baby. She went walking in the woods, looking for it. She searched for a very long time.
DREYFUSS: And then?
VICTORIA: (crying) Then she found us.
DREYFUSS: Why are you crying, Victoria?
VICTORIA: 'Cause she's sad.
DREYFUSS: Is she sad, or are you sad, Victoria? Where is Mama? Is she here, with us? Can you show me Mama?
VICTORIA: She won't come here.
DREYFUSS: Why not?
VICTORIA: Because she knows you're watching.

Aunt Jean enters the house, seeking evidence for her custody case. Mama inhabits her body. Annabel awakes to find the children gone. She takes the baby remains that Dreyfuss had found and speeds away in her van, finding Lucas on the road. They see Mama and the two girls on the same cliff from which Edith leapt. Annabel offers Mama her child's remains, but when Lilly calls for her, she nearly kills Annabel and Lucas. Victoria asks to stay with Annabel. Mama lets her go but takes Lilly. Annabel begs her to bring Lilly back, but Mama and Lilly fall, becoming happy spirits, embracing and smiling, and then turning into a shower of moths. Annabel holds a weeping Victoria. A bright blue moth lands on Victoria's hand. "Lilly?" she asks. Lucas crawls over, and the film concludes with the three embracing on the cliff as the moth flies into the camera.

Given the extensive use of psychological analysis in horror film theory, especially the idea that monstrous figures are the projection of realistic fears and other feelings, *Mama* tellingly links the ghost to reality—she's not Victoria's projection, but actually exists. Psychiatrist Dreyfuss's death perhaps results from his need to find empirical verification of the supernatural figure's existence. Mama kills him only when he visits the cabin, though she manifests elsewhere, including in Dreyfuss's office; he becomes a threat to her projects of getting Victoria and Lilly back, and finding her lost baby, when he appears in the location where Edith suffered at the hands of other authority figures.

Played by a male actor representing a female character, mother/stepmother/witch/ghost/Edith/Mama offers an ambivalent figure. Unlike most ATU 327A stepmothers, Mama seeks to protect not only her biological baby but also her stepdaughters, Victoria and Lilly, from those who seek to take them away from her, ostensibly for their own good. But she conflicts with another stepmother, Annabel, whose presence overdetermines Edith/Mama's association as simply witch (as does her transgender cinematic representation). Edith's fight with the nuns and priests who run the institution where she is incarcerated ends with failure for all—Edith dies and loses her child, but the religious authorities also fail, being unable to apprehend the woman or save her baby. And yet the heterosexual family also (partially) fails; heterosexual couple Lucas and Annabel get Victoria, but single ghost mother Edith/Mama gets Lilly. As in Yim's *Hansel & Gretel*, apparently implausible stories initially taken as fiction—or in Victoria's case, psychological projection—turn out to be literally true. And queer failure succeeds while heteronormativity fails, at least in part.

Queer Endings and Beginnings

As is often the case with horror films, long prone to sequels, the endings of these films may also be beginnings: Camilla might return; White Girl's life continues; Mechas shape the future; Sonny and the other robots may become dominant; Man-bok, Young-hee, and Jung-soon keep searching; Hansel, Gretel, and Agnes all live on; the Ancient Ones return; two unconventional families—Lucas, Annabel, and Victoria but also Edith and Lilly—persist. Two futures are explicitly human free—in *A.I.* and *Cabin*; one is quite possibly human free—in *I, Robot*; and *Baked* offers an unpromising potential result if followed to its logical conclusion since Agnes seems unkillable. Hansel/Gretel child figures may remain at least somewhat lost or abandoned, especially White Girl; David; and the three in Yim's *Hansel & Gretel*. Witch Agnes survives, as do stepmother/witch Edith and Lilly literally in spirit.

In most realist present live-action "Hansel and Gretel" films, families are both a sanctuary and a problem (see Greenhill and Kohm forthcoming)—which certainly reflects most human experiences. Nuclear families offer few solutions in these science fiction and supernatural films—as is also the case for familiar versions of the fairy tale. When children—Hansels and Gretels—are wronged in the films I discuss in this chapter, the result is more ambivalent than in the more realist films. The sole example in which the nuclear biofamily survives, and the threat to it apparently does not, is *The Guardian*. Perhaps the director's wishful thinking and explicit link to his own experience overdetermine his presentation of the conclusion. Baby Jake may be safe, but the tree indicates that the baby body count is enormous. The film clearly represents a prevalent point of view about the need for the nuclear family and the threat of queer intrusions into it and of powerful women who can't be controlled by men.

However, the conventional nuclear family gets a pretty thorough (and often quite realistic) trouncing in the other films. In *Freeway 2*, the family and religion cause White Girl and Cyclona's problems, and the pimp is the hero. The cruelty of the nuclear family against figures who intrude into it (contra *The Guardian*, it's the family, not the intrusion, that is the problem) literally causes the end of the world in *A.I.* There is no conventional nuclear family in *I, Robot*, and humans are simply self-destructive, whereas robots at least try to protect them, if somewhat misguidedly at times. The character who refuses to kill people because it's "too heartless" is the nonbiological

Son(ny). And though there's a happy nuclear biofamily in Yim's *Hansel & Gretel*, the parentless magical children are still out there, apparently indestructible. Who knows what they might do? The same can be said of Agnes in *Baked*. Brother and sister Hansel and Gretel have survived, but so has their nemesis. *Cabin* joins *A.I.* in rendering administrative systems responsible for human destruction. Specifically, not only do those who run the rituals simply acquiesce to the threat they're dealing with, but they do so with satisfaction and relish. And in *Mama* it's the system (economic collapse) that is the apparent motor, but the nuclear family is the object and the father the instrument of harm.

Even when the human world is not wiped out entirely, threats remain: Baby Jake seems safe, but other children may be in peril; and people are certainly in danger from Agnes. Not only queer death and failure but also straight death and failure prevail. The reality to which these films refer is perhaps apocalyptic—that the future cannot be guaranteed if humans continue on their current route. Expecting deus ex machina solutions proves unreasonable, and if the individual and collective messages in these films seem confused, so does the reality to which they refer. In present-day America, caging children is policy (see "Separation" 2018). Perhaps as *A.I.* and *Cabin* suggest, such a society does not deserve survival.

In the next chapter, children and their biological mothers and stepmothers encounter witches and witchcraft, again in the context of horror, but this time as approached by women feminist directors exploring family dynamics expressed using the fairy tale "The Juniper Tree," and the ideas of witnessing, disclosure, etiology, and coping. The reality represented in these films is maternal—indeed, more broadly, parental—ambivalence, and society and institutions won't help. Individual women must find their personal resources (as they do in *The Babadook* and *The Moth Diaries*); if they don't, watch out (as in *The Juniper Tree* and *Le piège d'Issoudun*).

6

Witches, Mothers, a Vampire, and a Babadook

Women Coping with Crimes and Harms in "The Juniper Tree" Films

"WITCH STORIES ARE NOT PRETTY THINGS. . . . THEY ARE CHRONICLES of hard looks, hard words, hard luck. They *are* dramatic, however. . . . [They] arise from situations in the everyday world and feature real enough protagonists" (Rieti 2009, xiii). Folklorist Barbara Rieti's *Making Witches: Newfoundland Traditions of Spells and Counterspells* talks about witchcraft in twentieth- and twenty-first-century Newfoundland as a "casual mix of ordinary and extraordinary affairs" (2009, xvii). She notes that "Witchcraft is all about power, imagined and real" (3). Her descriptions also aptly fit the intersections of the natural (probably real) and preternatural (perhaps unreal) represented in the four films I discuss in this chapter as witch stories. These otherwise very different movies—*The Babadook*, by Australian director Jennifer Kent (2014), *The Moth Diaries*, by Canadian director Mary Harron (2011), *Le piège d'Issoudun* (The Issoudun Exit/Trap; Juniper Tree) by Quebec director Micheline Lanctôt (2003), and *The Juniper Tree* by the late American director Nietzchka Keene (1990)—use or include feminist considerations of the traditional wonder tale type ATU 720, "The Juniper Tree."

Having access to unexpected, unconventional power means that witch characters in these films (as in Newfoundland, described by Rieti) have a particular capability of preternatural *vision*—that is, they *see* manifestations and actions that others within the film's diegesis do not. I use "preternatural" when I draw attention to appearances and activities as extraordinary, unusual, and unexpected, outside or beside the natural and usual, without judging the specific contours of their diegetic reality. That is, preternatural avoids deciding whether or not the film seeks the audience's acceptance that something impossible, beyond normal experience, actually takes place; questions whether it does so only within the mind of one character (or, in *The Babadook*, two characters); or leaves that conclusion ambiguous.

That women filmmakers should be so interested in reproducing and reflecting on a story based on or implicating a fairy tale about perhaps the most abject, monstrous woman in conventional mainstream society—the murderous mother—offers issues for feminist analysis.[1] That they do so in the context of vision in particular offers issues for feminist film analysis that, at least since Laura Mulvey's (1975) work, has been concerned with the gaze—who looks at whom and to what effects. Usefully summarized by Gray Cavender and Nancy Jurik (2007), Mulvey examines who conventionally looks (the camera; male characters within the diegesis; and male spectators as presumed audience) and who is conventionally looked at (women and in particular their bodies). Despite film theorists' (including her own) extensive criticism and nuancing of Mulvey's initial statement (see, e.g., Kaplan 2000; Chaudhuri 2006; Van den Oever and Human 2015), many conventional mainstream films continue to reproduce this "taken-for-granted" pattern (Cavender and Jurik 2007, 280). Unquestionably, the greater participation of women filmmakers, especially when they work outside the Hollywood machine (as is the case for those I discuss in this chapter; see also Greenhill 2014), has amended the processes of looking and seeing. In particular, these changes include the camera taking the role of representing women's perspective (Ramanathan 2006); the presumptive audience being women and not men and not necessarily heterosexual or heteronormative (see Thornham 1999); and the nuancing of the concept of the look when, as in these four films, women protagonists are also the diegetic lookers and seers (see also Hollinger 2012).

---

1 For a discussion of motherhood in films, see Fisher (1996).

These ATU 720 films deal with various crimes and harms, from maternal filicide to suicide to arson. As Cavender and Jurik point out, "traditionally, in the crime genre, women rarely see; instead they are seen, either as femme[s] fatales or victims. For this reason, the crime genre has long been characterized as misogynistic" (2007, 281). Cavender and Jurik seek alternatives in what they call "progressive moral fiction . . . works that"

1. draw in insights from the experiences of those who are socially marginalized and oppressed,
2. locate the experiences within their larger social context,
3. reveal fissures in the predominant ruling apparatus, and
4. offer *vision* or hope for collective empowerment and challenges to unjust social arrangements and organizations. (283; my emphasis)

These perspectives can be discerned in the films I discuss. With these theorists, I note that while filmmaker intention is a valuable addition to the repertoire of knowledge, films themselves "take on a reality of their own, a reality that is ever emergent and changing with subsequent viewings over time" (Cavender and Jurik 2007, 285).

Babadook, *Issoudun*, and *Juniper* feature murderous mothers who are seeing witches or witchlike figures (though the two most capable seeing witches in *Juniper* are not themselves murderous; indeed, one is a murder victim). *Moth* has a somewhat distant mother and a young woman identified as a vampire, but the primary character is witchlike in her capability of vision. All the films have dead, missing, or absent all-consuming fathers and offer preternatural, uncanny, extraordinary moments seen by primary characters and the film audience, but not by others within the diegesis—flashes that appear to "contradict[] the laws of nature as experience has taught us to define them" (Todorov 1970, 27)—within otherwise realist, live-action representations.[2]

All the films leave open the question of whether or not the preternatural happenings result from the disturbed psychological states of the witch

---

2 The International Fairy Tale Filmography (iftf.uwinnipeg.ca) lists additional ATU 720 films with male directors. For further analysis of *Juniper* and *Issoudun*, see Greenhill and Brydon (2010); Zipes (2011, 221–23); Greenhill (2014, 2017a); and Greenhill and Kohm (2016).

characters who see and experience them.³ That is, these works imply parallel possible explanations for preternatural events. They are either the characters' delusions or supernatural happenings actually taking place as the film audience sees them; either they are explainable in conventional realistic terms or they are fantastical. Arguably, the respective genres of realist drama and horror might suggest that (realist) *Issoudun* and *Juniper* offer the psychological explanation and that (horror) *Moth* and *Babadook* provide the supernatural. However, all the films ultimately avoid absolutely confirming or denying either, and the situation is much more complex.

In *Juniper* and *Issoudun*, seeing the dead comes in the form of apparitions, experienced by the witch seers but (again) *not* by others within the films' diegesis. In *Moth* and *Babadook*, the focal scenes show impossible happenings, again seen only by the primary protagonists. The film audience, vouchsafed a glimpse of what the witch/seer sees, recognizes denotations of crimes and harms affecting both the witch/seers and those they see: a murdered woman, murdered children, a vampire suicide, and an angry bogeyman figure. As elsewhere, feminist fairy-tale filmmakers' concerns (see Greenhill 2016) make central not only women's looking but significantly their seeing, rendering that seeing as a special and particular knowledge.

Thus, despite their manifest differences, these four movies have in common diegetic moments when the audience sees the witch characters' preternatural visions. The audience's power, like that of the filmic witches, resides in their ability to see what others within the diegesis cannot. "Seeing" is also significant for Newfoundland witches, though it is mainly about prediction. In contrast, more than foretelling the future—though the film visions may suggest ominous expectations of (more) death and harm—*seeing* in these movies directly references actual sight. In *Juniper*, a daughter sees her murdered mother; in *Issoudun*, a mother sees her murdered children; in *Moth*, a young woman sees her vampire schoolmate slit her own wrists in a deluge of blood; in *Babadook*, a mother and son see the monstrous eponymous creature (who sometimes appears as her dead husband). Visions in these films implicate those dead by violence (including at their own hand), and all the primary characters mourn a nuclear family member—mother, father, or husband.

---

3   Nicole Rafter and Michelle Brown explore cinematic representations of psychological theories of crime (2011, 47–66).

I focus on four striking visual filmic moments, which represent the supernatural/magical in the context of the real/natural. These offer flashes of the uncanny, "an experience of disorientation, where the world in which we live suddenly seems strange, alienating or threatening . . . which permit[s] ostensibly rational people to encounter . . . unnerving feelings" (Collins and Jervis 2008, 1).[4] The sequences express anger (externalized reaction to death) and despair (internalized reaction to death), via literally gloomy and actually weeping or bleeding landscapes and locations.

Who looks but also who sees are obviously crucial issues in film and film viewing. Scenes in which the main characters' looking gives primary focus, then, offer vital information. Filmmakers resist the idea that a single scene may be taken as more fundamental than any other. And yet while one might seek a wholistic view of movies, in which each segment, shot, or image is equally significant, filmmakers also design pivotal, critical shots, scenes, and "aha moments"—key, revelatory scenes specifically calculated to be memorable. Decisive scenes in these four "Juniper Tree" films combine a visual focus with an openness to interpretation. Their diegetic viewers clearly understand them as indicating something true and authentic, if not in the realm of normal reality. Notably, the films engage concerns of trauma not only as tragedy but also as fantasy, explored in other fairy-tale movies like Terry Gilliam's Alice in Wonderland–themed *Tideland* (2005; see Kérchy 2016, 75–94) but also in Tarsem's works discussed in chapter 3 and the "Hansel and Gretel" films in chapter 5.

Engaging with crime and harms linked with looking and seeing, these are critical crime films, as defined by Nicole Rafter and Michelle Brown: "In contrast to conventional narratives characterized by easy resolutions, critical films are dominated by open endings and characters who are neither good nor bad but inscrutable. In these contexts, the world, the self, and truth are volatile, unpredictable, and never fully knowable" (2011, 6–7). Specifically, these films' uses of seeing the preternatural[5] explore issues around *witnessing* (not only literal visual but also in the sense of acknowledging harms and crimes);[6] *disclosure* (letting the seer and audience know—or confirming their suspicion—that a crime has been committed or a harm has taken place);

---

4 See also the discussion of uncanny in chapters 1 and 2.
5 I have found little work that considers uses of the preternatural in crime films. Exceptions include Linnemann (2015).
6 Thanks to Steven Kohm for suggesting this increasingly significant aspect.

and *etiology* (in the interplay between psychological and supernatural, which parallels internal and external sources for criminality and harms). Another possibility, *revenge* (retribution for protagonists' or others' actions), commonly seen in supernatural crime/harm films, is tellingly absent from these works. The films are *postmodern* in the sense that "viewers are . . . left . . . with no clear way of making sense of the criminal; such films challenge the very idea of criminological explanation" (Rafter and Brown 2011, 6). With respect to both psychological and supernatural explanations, these films have little truck with diagnosis and cure (and thus with specific psychological theories), but a great deal with *coping*. Such work is significant because with critical crime films, as Rafter and Brown, argue:

> one cannot really pull apart image and meaning. We are not claiming merely that movies create cultural focal points and reproduce the emotional textures of crime in ways that formal criminology cannot. Rather, we are claiming that images organize our worlds and that representations are central to our lives. Representations shape how we think about crime. (2011, 5)[7]

"The Juniper Tree" Tale and Films: Seeing the Dead and Creating Audience Witches

Maria Tatar calls "The Juniper Tree" "probably the most shocking of all fairy tales" (2004, 209), singling it out despite her inventory of the Grimm tales' "murder, mutilation, cannibalism, infanticide, and incest" (1987, 3). Hans-Jörg Uther (2004, 1:389) summarizes the traditional narrative:

> A boy is born but his mother dies. The little boy is slain by his cruel stepmother who closes the lid of an apple chest on him. . . . She cooks him and serves him to his father who eats him unwittingly. . . . The boy's stepsister gathers up his bones and puts them under a juniper tree. . . . A bird comes forth and sings about what happened. It brings presents to the

---

7   Direct effects of media are controversial. Notwithstanding occasional acts of ostension, as discussed in chapter 4, the direct relationship between audiences relating to a character (Till et al. 2013) and their actually acting out the fictional behavior they see is questionable.

father and the sister and drops a millstone on the stepmother, killing her. . . . The boy is resuscitated.

Theorists as well as filmmakers have addressed this tale. Tatar notes the story's conclusion in which "the motherless household becomes the happy household" (1992, 224). Perhaps not surprising, given the feminist predilections of their directors, these films do not end thus. Marina Warner's discussion focuses on the father's cannibalism (1998, 62–66), an aspect of the tale that is not superficially part of every film but that illuminates some underlying themes, especially in *Moth*. As indicated in chapter 5, Jack Zipes includes it in his group of cinematic tales about "child abuse and abandonment" (2011, 221–23). However, this group of films tells a variety of different stories.

Keene's *Juniper*, with its explicit title reference and re-vision[8] and realist aesthetic, is transcultural[9] and transnational, the product of an American writer, director, editor, and producer who filmed a German version of this international tale in Iceland with Icelandic actors speaking English. It explores fraught family relations in a premodern Icelandic setting, incorporating elements of local traditional magic and invoking issues of heterosexual and sibling love and jealousy within what would now be called a blended family. The film presents its preternatural events quite matter-of-factly, though clarifying that only one character sees them.

Lanctôt's *Issoudun* (the English title is *Juniper Tree*, an explicit reference) addresses the inchoate desperation of an early twenty-first-century privileged woman. Metafictionally, it juxtaposes the incorporation of a stylized theatrical performance directly based on a Brothers Grimm version of "The Juniper Tree" with a social realist/neorealist[10] evocation and re-vision of the same narrative set in suburban Quebec, Canada. *Issoudun* directly addresses the complexities of the culturally tabooed subject of child murder by

---

8 Using Kevin Paul Smith's schema for understanding how fairy tales work in literary adaptation (2007, 10), discussed in chapter 1.
9 As discussed in chapter 3.
10 Neorealism, best known as associated with Italian cinema, is "a particular sort of narrative realism based upon the construction of an internally coherent and plausible fictional world . . . that aspires to be taken as essentially consistent with our social world because actions are linked together temporally and causally, a fictional world in which characters act for the same sorts of reason that cause us to act in the social world" (Knight 1992, 126–27). Canadian film neorealism is sometimes termed social realism (see, e.g., Giovacchini and Sklar 2012).

mothers—maternal filicide—without offering pat psychological or sociological explanations.[11] Within the context of the realist representation, it presents a single preternatural event without comment or question.

Harron's *Moth*, closely based upon the book by Rachel Klein (2002), focuses on interactions in a girls' boarding school, in which one young woman, whose father committed suicide, concludes that another student, whose father's death was also a suicide, is a vampire. Though *Moth* offers various references to fairy tales, the primary link to "The Juniper Tree" happens with explicit incorporation, when the preternatural suspect sings a version of the bird's song that formerly gave the tale type its name, "My Mother Slew Me, My Father Ate Me." Again, only one character sees the uncanny events; others explain them away in realist mode as dreams or tricks of light.

Kent's *Babadook* links to ATU 720 in re-vision mainly through its widowed mother who is at her wit's end dealing with her difficult young son. However, it also creates new tales, not only the film's overall narrative but a story within it, the book *Mister Babadook*, which appears and narrates of a monster who inhabits the mother and makes her kill her dog, her son, and herself. Though, unlike in ATU 720, *Babadook*'s mother never reaches the point of actually murdering her son, their conflictual relationship, and the film's focus on it, recalls the traditional tale type. Both mother and son experience preternatural events, but others do not.[12]

Moth and *Babadook* both include scenes showing one character having preternatural experiences, the evidence of which subsequently disappears. Nevertheless, both films suspend judgment about their witch characters, never, on the one hand, simply dismissing them as delusional or, on the other hand, confirming the external reality of what they see. *Issoudun* and *Juniper* offer visions that clearly externalize their witch characters' emotions; to a great extent the apparitions' empirical reality or lack thereof is epiphenomenal. What is most important is that they offer their witch

---

11 In particular, Lanctôt avoids creating the scary career woman stereotype too often seen in American television and film (see Seidel 2013, esp. 85–89). She also avoids creating the monstrous mother so familiar in the horror genre (see Creed 1993, 16–32).

12 A thematically similar film, *Lights Out* (directed by David F. Sandberg, 2016), is unequivocal about the reality of the ghost-monster and her supernatural connection to the psychologically damaged mother. It includes a stepsister who seeks to save her stepbrother. Unlike the films by women, though, it focuses much less on the mother than on the stepsister, who becomes the primary female character.

characters (and, as always, the seeing film audience) insights into what is happening to them.

The Juniper Tree (directed by Nietzchka Keene, 1990)

In Keene's film, sisters Katla (played by Bryndis Petra Bragadóttir) and Margit (played by Björk) flee the region where their mother has been burned for witchcraft. The elder, Katla, finds a widower, Jóhann (played by Valdimar Örn Flygenring), to take care of them, seeking to magically bind him with spells. His son, Jónas (played by Geirlaug Sunna Þormar), is immediately suspicious, but young Margit, supported by her visions of her dead mother (played by Gudrún Gísladóttir), bonds with him over their shared grief at the loss of their mothers. Jónas resists all his stepmother's attempts to gain power in her relationships with him and his father. Eventually a pregnant Katla taunts Jónas, and he falls from a cliff and dies. Katla sews one of Jónas's fingers into his mouth and puts another into a stew for the family. Margit finds it. When a raven appears on a tree that grows from Jónas's mother's grave, where Margit buried his finger, she tells Jóhann that Katla killed his son. Katla flees, and Jóhann leaves in search of her. Margit's concluding voice-over tells a haunting tale of two children whose mother was a bird and whose human father fails to recognize them when they return from the land of the birds.

Though it is mainly Katla who practices magic, Margit periodically uses incantations and spells and has inherited her mother's gift of sight and is thus herself a witch. In the focal sequence, an indoor shot cuts to Margit sitting alone, off-center and screen right, in a rugged landscape. Birds sing. Margit's mother walks into the frame and kneels before her daughter, the background landscape mimicking the slight upward direction of her shoulders. The sun shines on her face, and the treed landscape and sky share the frame, creating a feeling of openness. She smiles gently. Margit is closed in by the dense rocky hills behind her, the lines of which dip inward toward her head. Margit breathes deeply twice and smiles. The mother gazes at her daughter and then looks down and begins parting the front of her dress.

In reaction, Margit's eyes look down apprehensively. A close-up from Margit's point of view reveals a black void between her mother's breasts, framed by her parted clothing. Margit's face registers fear and apprehension before her gaze raises to her mother's face. Her mother smiles and nods as if

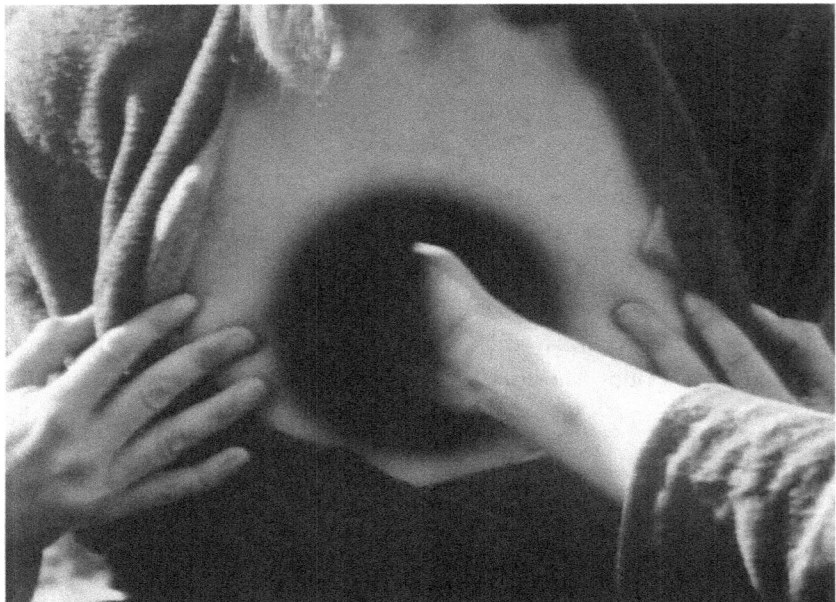

FIGURE 6.1. The black hole.

to encourage Margit. Margit looks down and begins to reach her right hand toward her mother. Another shot of the mother gently smiling. A brief shot of Margit's trepidation as she reaches further before another quick cut to the void in her mother's chest from Margit's point of view. Composer Larry Lipkis's choral "vision music" begins suddenly as Margit's fingers reach into the dark hole from the bottom right (see figure 6.1). A quick dissolve shows a flock of birds soaring and wheeling in the sky, singing more loudly as the vision music crescendos.

This sequence, about three-quarters of the way through the film, is followed immediately by one escalating the conflict between Jónas, Katla, and Jóhann, and then by the scene in which Jónas strides through long grass, slashing it with a stick, as he repeats his mantra, "She's a witch, she's a witch, she's a witch, she's a witch." Ironically, of course, the witch with the greatest power is not Katla, whom Jónas hates and to whom he refers in this scene, but his beloved friend Margit. Jónas knows that Margit sees. It's a source of some conflict between the children, but since Margit's power does not seem to threaten his, the knowledge does not destroy their friendship; indeed, at various points Margit tries to share her visions with Jónas, and he is puzzled and uncomprehending but not resistant.

This scene primarily *witnesses*. It draws attention not only to the crime against Margit's mother (her murder) but also to its effects on Margit. Keene's choice to decline to explicitly confirm or deny Margit's visions, and to present them matter-of-factly, suggests that the director intended the audience to see the sequence as an exploration of the affective relationship between Margit and her mother but also its links to landscape. First, it offers the overall impression of the relationship between Margit and her mother as loving. Of the two, arguably Margit is the one with a hole in her heart, and her intention to enter her mother's void by inserting her hand projects her profound sense of loss upon her mother's image/ghost. The two are inseparable—not even death can part them—but also parallel each other, both seers.

Second, following the landscape background gives a visual metaphor; the mother is beyond the world, and her literal movement out of the picture is symbolized by the hills behind her, which direct up, toward the heavens. In contrast, Margit's background points inward toward her, focusing the audience's gaze toward her centered image. Her ultimate betrayal of her sister—telling Jóhann that Katla killed Jónas—demonstrates that Margit is indeed emotionally and even socially closer to the dead (Jónas and her mother) than to the living. In this brutal landscape and story, Margit (the seer) and Jóhann (who is remarkably unperceptive) are the survivors; Jónas, who doesn't cease mourning his mother and for whom a stepmother makes the loss more acute, and Katla, who yearns for Jóhann's love but apparently never gets it, don't remain part of the diegetic scene.

The black hole scene's *witnessing* underscores the depth of Margit's loss; her mother has become a void into which she apparently wishes to venture. Her travels around the bleak landscape only remind the audience that Margit can never return to her original home and that her wish to return to her mother is equally impossible, not only because her mother is dead but also because she represents the witchcraft and visions that Margit herself may need to repudiate in order to survive. Margit's visions don't help her, and they certainly don't help Jónas. It's not clear whether he falls to his death from the cliff because he stumbles or is caught by the wind or he actually leaps because he truly believes his biomother can supernaturally save him. Either way, he is literally swallowed by the landscape, as Margit's hand is swallowed by the black hole in her mother's body.

The realist, quasi-documentary-style filming presentation suggests that the audience should take what is happening at face value. The film presents the visions both from the camera's (as at the beginning of the sequence) and, specifically, from Margit's point of view (in the black hole scene). Thus, the visions' *etiology* appears to be both within her (thus psychological) and external to her (supernatural). The visions underline Margit's continuing connection with her mother and simultaneously enforce the audience's connection to both. As seeing witches, the audience can question what the mother and her apparitions do for Margit. They underline her role as a witch seer—and thus that her life may be endangered; she could meet her mother's fate. Yet Jónas's witch accusation is against Katla, not Margit. Though the film visually suggests the audience should accept that the mother actually appears to Margit—that she is not delusional—the supernatural offers a way for Margit to *cope* with her mother's death. Thus, the etiology of the visions is doubled. Through her supernatural visions of her mother's continuing presence, Margit's psychological state as well as her grief, anger, and despair at her mother's murder are mitigated through her ongoing spectral existence.

Le piège d'Issoudun (directed by Micheline Lanctôt, 2003)

Lanctôt's film begins before dawn on a wintry day, when Esther (played by Sylvie Drapeau) jumps fully clothed into her backyard pool with her two children. The kids drown, but when Esther's suicide fails, she speeds along a highway, weeping and distraught, trying again to kill herself. Police officer Laurier (played by Frédérick De Grandpré) stops her at the exit to Issoudun, a Québec suburb, and eventually agrees to drive her home. Their intense interactions en route, during which Esther repeatedly taunts Laurier, reveal some of her personal background but little about her motivation for the murders beyond her extreme fears. She says, "As soon as I started having children, I stopped living. I started to be afraid that something would happen to them. Understand? Afraid, terribly afraid, afraid every single minute, afraid for the rest of my life!" The divorced Laurier is forthcoming about his life; he has not seen his three boys for five months but plans to meet them to explain why his marriage ended. His love for children, and his horror when he discovers the deaths, leads to the film's conclusion. In realist scenes, Esther has only one scene of preternatural vision, but it, along with her haunted and desperate appearance and state, makes her witchlike. Like Katla, and to an extent Margit, she seeks to manipulate the living, while also being haunted by the dead.

The sequence on which I focus continues a long handheld shot. The ambulance that Laurier has called for Esther is delayed, so the cop decides to let her go. The lighting is flat. Colors are muted. Even Esther's red sweater looks dull. The trees are barren of leaves, and the ground is the sage/brown of a transitional season, autumn or early spring. The only ambient sound is cars passing on the highway. Laurier snatches Esther's coat from the hood of the police car and opens the back door. He motions with his head for Esther to get out of the back seat. He helps her with her coat and guides her around to the front of the car.

> LAURIER: I can't wait for the ambulance to get here. Go back home, lady, and try to drive carefully.
> ESTHER: Thank you.
> LAURIER: When you get the ticket, you won't thank me. You're lucky. Normally, I should confiscate your car.
> ESTHER: Normally. Is it the only word you know?

Laurier hands Esther the ticket. She smiles sardonically. Laurier raises his finger to point Esther to her car. The gesture bisects Esther's head. As she turns, her left hand moves to her mouth. Her wedding ring is visible. Ominous background music—piano chords and a brief single note on the cello—commences. The camera follows Esther as she walks to the left of the frame and stops by her car.

Esther faces away from the camera toward the highway beside her car. Her hand moves to the top of her head, perhaps pulling her hair slightly. She puts her hand down, turns toward the car, and opens the door. Cut to a fixed camera shot through the driver's side front windshield of Esther's car. In the reflections on the windshield, two figures are visible: the dead children's floating bodies (see figure 6.2). Esther enters the frame from the right, in a close-up, as she gets into the car. Except for Esther's face, everything is in shades of blue. The two figures are transposed on Esther's face. Her eyes are closed. As she opens them, a stream of water flows down the windshield, and she looks up in horror toward the apparitions, which partly frame her head as more copious torrents run down. The music stops with the cut back to Laurier starting his car and the sound of brakes squealing. To the noise of more brakes and car horns, Laurier leaps from the police vehicle, swearing,

FIGURE 6.2. Esther's vision of her dead children.

and takes Esther's place in the driver's seat of her car. "I'm afraid of killing somebody," she says tearfully.

Significantly, cementing the audience's witch power, they see the vision of Esther's children on the car window before she does. Yet she may know it's there, because she palpably hesitates before opening her eyes. The apparition's (supernatural) reality, then, is established so that the audience does not question what Esther sees, magical and uncanny[13] though it obviously is. Esther's vision is the sole nonrealistic event in *Issoudun* outside the fairy-tale play. Though observation is slightly obscured by the windshield and by the water flowing down it, focus attends to Esther's haunted look of horror. She is the author of the event that leads to the apparition and arguably also of the image; it is clear she can escape neither the event itself nor its consequences. The vision simultaneously *witnesses* the deaths of her children and *discloses* her responsibility for it. The process of rendering meaning is complex and

---

13 Todorov distinguishes the uncanny, in which "the laws of reality remain intact and permit an explanation of the phenomena described," in contrast with the marvelous, wherein "new laws of nature must be entertained to account for the phenomena" (1970, 41). Nicolas Royle talks about "a feeling of something not simply weird or mysterious but, more specifically as something strangely familiar" (2003, vii). The concept is discussed in chapter 1.

postmodern. The context of this vision is, not surprisingly, a surfeit of water, though to this point the muted, overcast skies give no hint of the torrential rain that would result in the amount of water that flows down Esther's windshield. Perhaps she has brought that on, along with the vision. The connection to the flowing of copious, uncontrollable tears is obvious. The scene offers a visual literalization of the extensive references to weeping and water in the Grimm version of "The Juniper Tree."

The weepers in the Grimm story are the biological mother, the husband/father, and the stepsister, Marlene. Specifically, in her eighth month of pregnancy, "in tears," the biomother says to her husband, "If I die, bury me under the juniper tree." After she dies "of joy" on seeing her child, the husband "wept day after day" and then "still cried from time to time," and when he stops, he remarries (Tatar 2004, 211). But the most incidents of weeping, and the greatest overabundance of tears, come from Marlene. When in a tragicomic scene, she knocks her brother's head off, "she began to howl and weep." When her mother cooks a stew of the brother, the stepsister "wept so hard that the stew didn't need any salt because of her tears," and when her mother brings in the stew, Marlene "was weeping so hard that she couldn't stop" (213). She "began weeping bitter tears while she was putting the bones down in the green grass under the juniper tree" (214). When the magical birdbrother appears, "Marlene just sat there weeping," and indeed, "She held her apron up to her eyes and cried so hard that it was completely soaked with tears" (219). With the bird's singing she "put her head in her lap and just kept crying and crying" (220). Like the inexplicable water flowing down Esther's windshield, Marlene's tears are not only abject but also excessive—sufficient to flavor a stew or soak an apron.

In *Issoudun*, the physical setting literally mirrors Esther's feelings, rainwater as tears, while the windshield plainly reflects her vision of her children's floating dead bodies. In the Grimm story, the stepmother never cries; and indeed, like her, Esther seems more panicked by her actions than in mourning. The film's flowing water, then, particularly in its overabundance, presents the absent Marlene character's tears. They suggest that perhaps, just as Laurier is stepson as well as father from the Grimm version, Esther may be Marlene as well as mother. The landscape weeps for the children on her behalf.

Again, when the film ensures that the audience sees the apparitions *before* Esther does, it suggests that these visions are diegetically present and are thus supernatural. It would have been equally possible to show them only from

Esther's point of view, for example, or to make the audience's and Esther's views simultaneous, not sequential. What director Lanctôt has said about the difficulties of mothering (see Greenhill 2014), and her move to implicate the audience as co-seers of the supernatural, suggests that they, as members of a society and culture that fails to support mothers, share guilt. Though Esther actually killed the children, others (including society/culture/audience) are partly responsible. The isolation and loneliness of Esther's position is underlined by her sole (within the diegesis) and lonely vision of her dead children. They are inescapable, and as a result, like so many actual maternal filicides, Esther will seek her own death as a *coping* response (see Greenhill and Kohm 2016, 250–56). In a film that offers few explanations, the vision is thus implicitly *etiological*. When it externalizes the result, it may also externalize the cause; that is, if Esther's act can be literally seen as outside her volition and normality, arguably so may its reasons be understood thus.

The Moth Diaries (directed by Mary Harron, 2011)

Suicide explored as a solution to a woman's problems is also part of Harron's *The Moth Diaries*. Sixteen-year-old Rebecca (played by Sarah Bolger) returns to her boarding school two years after her poet father has committed suicide. She particularly looks forward to seeing her best friend, Lucy (played by Sarah Gadon), but a mysterious new student, Ernessa Bloch (played by Lily Cole), Jewish like Rebecca, whose father also committed suicide, supplants Rebecca in Lucy's affections. Rebecca attributes various deaths and other events to Ernessa, who she thinks is a vampire. When several members of the community leave or die, and Lucy, who is Ernessa's lover, becomes ill and dies, Rebecca blames Ernessa. Rebecca finds in the school basement an old trunk on which Ernessa's name is engraved and documents suggesting that Ernessa killed herself many years ago. Rebecca returns to pour kerosene on the trunk, with Ernessa in it, and to set it afire, which also burns the school. As Rebecca is driven to the police station, she drops out the car window a razor blade apparently given to her by Ernessa in the sequence described below.

The connection of the focal sequence's incorporation/quotation of the traditional tale type occurs in the two fathers' metaphorical cannibalization of their daughters wherein their suicides become excessively salient in the young women's lives. Ernessa's vampire obsession with death supports Rebecca's hitherto repressed fixation by separating her from the friendship group that maintained her through her first year of mourning. As Avril Horner and Sue Zlosnik note, the vampire often appears "as an object of desire or a fascinating icon of transgression" (2014, 67). Indeed, Ernessa exemplifies female vampires as Gina Wisker describes them: "Disruptive and troublesome, female vampires are an embodied oxymoron, a thrilling contradiction, fundamentally problematising received notion of women's passivity, nurturing and social conformity. Female vampires destabilise such comfortable, culturally inflected investments and complacencies and reveal them as aspects of constructed gender identity resulting from social and cultural hierarchies" (2016, 150).

A staple of horror films, the lesbian vampire is too often othered, especially in films by men, to (re)establish heterosexuality in "the hegemonic notion of 'woman'" (Case 1991, 9). However, in this film, when women—both the director and the characters in the diegesis—look at the vampire, as Linda Williams's work indicates, they are "en-tranced" themselves (1984); there is a "shared identification between monster and woman . . . a special empathy" (Case 1991, 10). Sue-Ellen Case argues that viewing the lesbian vampire as monster prescribes her from a heteronormative perspective (see also Kosonen 2015). *Moth* avoids normalizing heterosexuality, especially given the homosocial setting of the girls' boarding school, where the male teacher is not only the exception but, in his sexual interest in Rebecca, part of the problem. Rebecca has no heterosexual rescue.

The sequence I explore below overdetermines the relationship between Ernessa and Rebecca in terms of suicidality and blood, while directly quoting "The Juniper Tree." In the previous scene, Rebecca recalls walking into her home bathroom and discovering her father's dead body—he has slit his wrists. She leans against a doorframe and cries as she remembers. Cut to the windows near the ceiling of a circular, ornate room. The camera tilts down slowly to reveal the book-lined walls of the school library. Rebecca sits at a desk, center frame. She looks up. Ernessa's voice says: "Books won't save you." From Rebecca's perspective, hands folded in front of her, Ernessa moves toward Rebecca's table. "Your writing won't save you." Cut to Rebecca, her hands on an open book, another open book beside her, and other books screen left on the table. "The past won't save you." She continues to move toward Rebecca's table. "Mr. Davies won't save you. Daddy can't save you."

"My father wanted to save me," Rebecca replies. She smiles slightly, "He loved me. I know he did." In a low-angle shot, Ernessa says: "He's the one who caused you all this trouble in the first place." Cut to Rebecca, the camera pushing closer in: "You're wrong." She pauses, "The good things I remember about my father, [she smiles slightly] the walks we took, the fairy tales he read to me, they all really happened." Reverse to Ernessa, "He read you other fairy tales that you forgot." She leans in and sings, "My mother, she butchered me / My father, he ate me / My sister, little Anne-Marie / She gathered up the bones of me / And tied them in a silken cloth / To lay under the juniper." Ernessa, center frame, raises her arms and slowly flaps them, birdlike: "Tweet, tweet / What a pretty bird am I." A slight sound of rushing air begins and then crescendos. Still flapping her hands, Ernessa moves them in toward her body. A medium shot of Rebecca shows Ernessa's hands and forearm in the foreground. Then comes an extreme close-up from Rebecca's point of view of Ernessa's hands as Ernessa raises her left sleeve to show cuts on her wrist and says, "It's time to free yourself." A quick close-up of Ernessa's face, looking down as in a Madonna painting, then of her hands, as she makes an additional slice with a razor. The air sound becomes significantly louder.

On Ernessa's wrist, the blood begins to spurt from the slice she has made. The noise becomes a roar as blood sprays into Rebecca's face. She screams. Cut to Ernessa's arm, covered in blood, and then to gobs of blood splattering on an open book. Ominous music begins, as the roaring sound continues. A downward-tilting shot of the windows, as blood rains, shows Ernessa looking slightly up, her arms extended on either side. Rebecca screams and looks up at the blood raining down. Cut again to Ernessa, raising her arms further with her eyes closed. Rebecca, as her screams continue, tries to cover her head with her hands, leaning forward (see figure 6.3). The blood splashes on the books on the table. Ernessa's face looks ecstatic, eyes slightly closed, mouth open, head tilted back (see figure 6.4), again in Madonna pose. She tilts her head down and opens her eyes. As the screams and rain of blood cease and she lowers her arms, there is a fade toward, but not to, black.

Cut to Rebecca, centered in the lower half of the frame, in a pristine library; she breathes in and moves slightly forward, touches and rubs her arm and then looks at her hand, which has no blood on it. She looks up. Reverse shot from Rebecca's point of view to where Ernessa was standing— she is gone. The camera moves up toward the windows. Rebecca looks down onto the library table and reaches for a razor now lying in front of her open book. She takes it, turns it over in her hands, and closes her hands around it.

The film declines to dismiss Rebecca's perspective on the preternatural happenings as the result of "borderline personality disorder complicated by

FIGURE 6.3. Rebecca in rain of blood.

FIGURE 6.4. Ernessa in rain of blood.

depression and psychosis" (Klein 2002, 2), as in the book.[14] The suspension of a possible decision on Rebecca's visions as real or not real renders the relationship between witch/seer Rebecca and vampire Ernessa much more complex. Again, this sequence's reference to fathers confirms Rebecca's and

14 Klein's book (2002) refers frequently to fairy tales in addition to "The Juniper Tree," including "Rumpelstiltskin" (ATU 500); "The Old Woman in the Forest" (ATU 442); and Lewis Carroll's "Alice in Wonderland."

Ernessa's shared experience of being consumed by them. The structure mainly uses medium or close-up shots of Ernessa. It lacks the obvious two shots in *Juniper* or the clear audience disclosure in *Issoudun* that help to confirm the supernatural in those films. With a single, quick shot in the entire sequence wherein the audience sees anything of Ernessa that does not come from Rebecca's perspective—a view of Ernessa's hands and arm in the foreground with Rebecca in the background—the film downplays a supernatural explanation. Indeed, multiple reverse shots suggest Ernessa being seen explicitly from Rebecca's point of view, thus favoring an explanation that Ernessa as vampire/supernatural exists in and for Rebecca's mind—which does not make her any less real.

However, since Rebecca in this scene primarily *witnesses* as the scene *discloses* Ernessa's suicide, and the film elsewhere establishes Rebecca as credible, the single shot is sufficient to confirm that the audience should see what is happening as being real for anyone/everyone. Though usually Ernessa's supernatural shenanigans seem to be viewed only by Rebecca, one other key scene involves another diegetic seer, but student Dora (played by Melissa Farman) dismisses what she sees as a trick of light and falls/jumps to her death from a window that same night. The question, then, is whether the audience as witches are themselves credible witnesses of what is going on, and there is nothing to suggest they are not.[15] Opening the question of *etiology* helps to justify Rebecca's subsequent act of arson. Since Ernessa truly is a vampire murdering her classmates, as Rebecca suspects, the sequence described clearly shows her extensive powers, and justifies Rebecca's work to get rid of her to prevent further damage.

The sequence also *discloses* Rebecca's own struggles with the harm of suicide. As she *witnesses* Ernessa's reenactment of her suicidality, the scene externalizes Rebecca's intentions. It also contributes to Rebecca's *coping* not only by expressing her hitherto unspoken wish for her own death but also by giving her the resolve to deal with Ernessa. One could read Ernessa as encouraging Rebecca to commit suicide, with her words taking away hope of rescue. Alternatively, especially since "the vampire, most particularly the boundary-breaking lesbian vampire, is liberated, refusing the constraints of gender, time, space and conventional power relationships" (Wisker 2016, 158), Ernessa may instead offer Rebecca choices. She proffers the result—the

---

15 Think, in contrast, of the films of M. Night Shyamalan, which seek to trick the audience into drawing false conclusions.

surfeit of blood—and then withdraws it, providing Rebecca with what she apparently thinks she wants. In *coping* with her difficult situation, Rebecca clearly decides after the above sequence that she needs to get rid of what is holding her back, as Harron confirmed in an interview (2017). That Ernessa is the victim of that decision seems less brutal since the film suggests the audience should believe that she's a long-dead vampire, and indeed she reappears in ghostly form after her coffin's burning, advising that she is not so easy to simply destroy.

As in *Issoudun* and the following film, *The Babadook,* even if the apparitions are real and Ernessa is truly a vampire, psychological benefit ensues from Rebecca's externalizing the causes of her anger and despair in Ernessa as significant parts of *coping*. Rebecca can divest of her suicidal aspect by getting rid of Ernessa, who all too clearly instantiates and abjectly but extravagantly expresses it. The etiology again becomes less important than how the preternatural works for the primary women characters, the protagonists of these tales.

The Babadook (directed by Jennifer Kent, 2014)

Though *The Babadook* is the most recent of the four, this female gothic film has already received much academic attention (e.g., Balanzategui 2017; Howell 2018). Director Kent sees its combination of reality and fantasy:

> It is a film that could be played out without that monster; without that energy. But for me it is integral; I couldn't have made one without the other. I couldn't have made a straight creature feature and I couldn't have made a straight drama. This story demanded to be told in this form. . . . If it was just a straight kitchen drama, it could have been melodramatic, and it would have been a shame. (quoted in Risker 2017, 15)

Kent sees horror film as a positive influence on individuals, similarly to claims made in psychological analyses of fairy tales:

> I think all of us have a need to face our fears, and maybe horror films and scary books and stories . . . kind of illuminate this idea that the world isn't perfect; that it is not a happy ever after and that it is important to face the dark side. . . . These stories . . . can give us courage and help us to face our fears. . . . I think it was a psychologist who said: "People who like horror

films are usually quite well balanced." [Laughs.] . . . I like to think that it is true. (quoted in Risker 2017, 17)

Sound design, not only visuals, was crucial for the director, as it often is for horror films with their semantics of music and noise. Yet Kent sought to use sound in a more nuanced way:

> I am particularly obsessed with sound, and so we ran way over schedule on sound. But for me it is as important as vision. . . . I think a lot of modern horror films tend to just think a loud sound is an assault, and that's a way to scare people. . . . I feel it is a bit of a cheap shot. So we worked very hard with the *Babadook* soundtrack to make something that was truly unsettling, and . . . you don't have to use loud sounds to do that. Sometimes it is about being quieter, and sometimes it is about taking sound out altogether. . . . We had a brilliant sound designer: Frank Lipson who we worked very closely with to arrive at that. . . . It was for us when it could no longer be sound that it turned into music. I wanted that to be a very blurred line and so there is not much music there, but when it is there it is pretty strong. (quoted in Risker 2017, 17)

Though none note its use of "The Juniper Tree" tale, most scholars use the film to address the difficulties of motherhood (e.g., Briefel 2017; Buerger 2017; Quigley 2016)—surely a central idea in the traditional narrative. In Kent's riff on the horror genre, Amelia (played by Essie Davis) is raising her troubled six-year-old son Sam (played by Noah Wiseman) after her husband's death in a car accident as he drove her to the hospital to give birth. Amelia clearly resents Sam for his involvement in her husband's death. These feelings manifest in her ambivalent, alternately loving then cold and harsh, behavior toward the child. Sam's preoccupation with monsters leads him to increasingly violent actions. Amelia blames strange and dangerous events on Sam; he blames them on the malevolent Babadook. As his *Mister Babadook* book with its threatening and (as in *Issoudun* and *Moth*) suicidal expressions continues to reappear, Amelia rips it up and throws it away. When the reassembled *Mister Babadook* reappears, with new words and pictures that directly involve her, Amelia becomes more and more disturbed. A confrontation between Amelia, Sam, and the Babadook results in her directly challenging the monster and then relegating it to the basement of her house, where she can control it.

The book first appears when Amelia lets Sam pick his bedtime storybook and he chooses *Mister Babadook*, which she clearly does not recognize. It's a black-and-white pop-up book, and she reads the text (as rendered in the book, supplemented as necessary from subtitles):

> If it's in a word, or it's in a look, / you can't get rid of the Babadook. / . . . A rumbling sound then 3 sharp knocks / ba BA-ba DOOK! DOOK! DOOK! / That's when you'll know that he's around / . . . . See him in your room at night / And you won't sleep a wink. / [Amelia stops reading aloud to the child at this point.] I'll soon take off my funny disguise / (take heed of what you've read . . .) / And once you see what's underneath . . . / YOU'RE GOING TO WISH YOU WERE DEAD.

The focal sequence is prefaced with a scene in which Amelia gives Sam a sleeping drug. She awakens to check on the child. Seeing him sleeping, she moves out of frame as non-diegetic music fades. She walks down the stairs, looking relaxed but somewhat stoned, smiling. There are three firm but conventional knocks on the door. Amelia turns, closing her sweater over her nightgown. Hard cut to her opening the door. A brief handheld point-of-view shot of the front yard shows no one. Amelia turns and slams the door. The camera follows behind as she walks back toward the stairs and kitchen. There is a sound of three loud, pounding, ominous, reverberating knocks; Amelia turns apprehensively. She again opens the door; she walks out and looks from side to side. Cut to a handheld shot from her perspective; again no one. Wind chimes sound as Amelia looks down. Her point of view, as sudden ominous music booms, shows the *Babadook* book outside on the doormat. Jump-cut to a close-up of the book. Reverse to Amelia's close-up, as she shrinks out of frame to pick the book up. The menacing music continues. Amelia walks through her living room quickly, breathing hard. The camera follows as she sits down.

The book, reassembled, shows the rips quite clearly. Cut to close-ups of the pages as Amelia turns them, looking horrified and frightened. New pages manifest in a series of rushed camera pans over the words: "I'll WAGER with YOU, / I'LL MAKE you a BET. / ThE MORE you DENY, the STRONGER I GET." As she turns the pages, a scary Babadook face pops out with a word balloon saying "LET ME IN." An extreme close-up shows the threatening face, with eyes empty circles, mouth open, teeth showing. Cut to a close-up of the Amelia figure, mouth also open in terror, then to "LET ME IN!" and then to Amelia herself, terrified. The book's pop-up Amelia mirrors the pose of the Babadook looming behind her as a black shadow.

"You start to CHANGE when I get in." Back to a close-up of the Amelia drawing, "the BABADOOK growing right UNDER YOUR SKIN." Close-up on Amelia's terrified face. "Oh COME! Come SEE see what's UNDERNEATH!" As the page turns, a headless Babadook pops up, followed by an Amelia pop-up holding the family dog by its neck. The Amelia pop-up shakes the dog until its head drops sideways with a slight snap, the X on its eyes demonstrating that it is dead. Amelia gasps in horror. Cut to the Amelia pop-up, now holding Sam by the neck, an X over his eye also. The camera tracks up to the Babadook drawing behind and then back to the Amelia figure shaking Sam from side to side as slight sounds indicate his neck snapping too. In close-up, the shape of the Amelia figure's eyes and mouth mimics the Babadook's previous close-up. Another close-up shows her hands around the boy's neck, shaking him (see figure 6.5). With a sudden sound of metal scraping, another Amelia figure pops up holding a knife, her face still mimicking the Babadook, with its shadow behind her. The Amelia figure slashes its own throat. Realistic-looking bright red blood immediately flows from its neck.

Cut to an exterior shot. Amelia douses the book with fuel on her barbecue and sets it alight. The music stops as centered Amelia looks up, nearly directly into the camera; cut to Sam, screen right, who looks at her sadly.

Amelia is the sole seer of this sequence. Rather than watching harm or crime, the scene *witnesses* the mother's increasingly disturbed state and gives

FIGURE 6.5. The murderous mother.

warning; it *discloses* the crimes and harms that are the possible ramifications of her continuing on the path she has apparently started. The entire sequence offers all the supernatural material from Amelia's perspective. Though there are objective shots of Amelia with the book, the sequence never confirms from the camera's view that the content she sees is actually there.

Throughout the film, only Amelia and Sam ever see the Babadook. In scenes when the child observes it, the audience does not see the bogeyman figure, only Sam's terrified reactions. Friendly, helpful neighbor Mrs. Roach (played by Barbara West), whom the film presents as sensitive, knowledgeable about Amelia and Sam, and trustworthy, affirms that "He sees things as they are." Though her specific reference in the latter comment is to the boy's frankness about her Parkinson's disease, the audience understands the extension to Sam's general perceptiveness and truth telling. When in the dramatic scenes of confrontation with his mother he says, "I know you don't love me. The Babadook won't let you," the monster allows Sam to externalize and thus cope with his mother's rejection and anger.

In contrast, the film *discloses*, and the audience shares, Amelia's initial skepticism but increasing abilities to perceive the Babadook, not only its sounds but also its manifestations: as glass shards in soup, clothing at the police station, cockroaches, a face in the car's rearview mirror, a figure in films by Georges Méliès that she watches on television, another she sees through her window inside the neighbor's house, and a black shadow and eventual physical manifestations inside her and Sam's house. The film presents most of the evidence explicitly or implicitly from Amelia's point of view, though a few camera's eye views confirm some of the more dramatic manifestations, such as when Sam is whisked up the stairs by an invisible force. The perspective does not undermine her reliability as a witness but instead underlines the extent to which the film approaches her empathically and sympathetically, even when she does terrible things like threatening Sam with a knife.

In a non-supernatural reading, Sam introduces the Babadook and the monsters idea to Amelia, which triggers her own anxieties, anger, and despair over her husband's death, soon exacerbated by lack of sleep. Her actions then feed his quite understandable issues about fear of death, in particular, of losing another parent, which he's dealing with by externalizing into monsters in general and the Babadook in particular. As with Rebecca in *Moth*, the solution presented in *Babadook* is that women must save themselves—but here, also their children. Amelia *could* become *Issoudun*'s Esther, but she does not.

A supernatural reading might begin with the idea of possessed children—which is what Sam initially appears to be (as in *The Exorcist*, Creed's type case [1993, 31–42]). However, Amelia soon gets implicated. Initially, her views of the Babadook are obscured and limited, seen through a sheet she pulls over her head or in the darkness of the corner of a room. One of his few clear, extended manifestations is as the dead husband/father, as well as when Amelia herself becomes possessed. The film's solution to the Babadook problem focuses on Amelia's (and by implication Sam's) *coping*. As with death and other harms, facing fears leads to the potential of controlling them, and that is precisely what Amelia ends up doing. *Coping* comes when she confines the actual Babadook to the basement, visiting him daily to acknowledge and feed him so he ceases tormenting her and Sam. In effect, she externalizes her psychological problems but relegates them to the metaphorical basement, where she can regulate and thus deal with them.

Retroactively, then, though the Babadook is frightening—as are the feelings of despair and anger he instantiates—like many others he also serves as a supernatural helper. The book scene forces Amelia to confront the direction her actions are taking, as the bloody library scene does for Rebecca in *Moth*, and while the Babadook appears to threaten her, he also protects her in part from herself by *disclosing* her problems. Perhaps his looming presence keeps her safe, as his eventual confinement in the basement makes possible the rapprochement between Amelia and Sam. The book's initial manifestation underlines the importance of seeing and the contingent significance of accepting the Babadook so that he can be "A friend of you and me." The new book pages in the focal scene may seem threatening, but they are also truthful; as long as Amelia denies her anger and despair, they only get stronger. She needs to find a way of dealing with them, or dire consequences will follow, including the likelihood of turning her into a suicidal maternal filicide like Esther in *Issoudun*.

Magic and Reality: Power, Imagined and Real, Making Audience Witches

What does all this have to do with reality? As director Lanctôt's own *Le mythe de la bonne mère* (The Myth of the Good Mother, 2006) and countless academic works clearly demonstrate, maternal anguish is all too common, even pervasive (discussed in Greenhill 2017a). And as Rafter and Brown (2011) comment, crime films like these have significant implications for the real world. But these are also filmic reflections on how the commonplace becomes extraordinary. "The world has to be fundamentally *ordinary* before being invested with an uncanny aura; or the uncanny works *through* the ordinariness of the world, even produced *by* it, as though a de-sacralised, disenchanted world becomes uncanny in its very essence" (Jervis 2008, 28). All four films discussed in this chapter deal with a presumption that the world is ordinary, before rendering it anything but. As witch stories chronicling "hard looks, hard words, hard luck" (Rieti 2009, xiii)—particularly hard *looks*—these films render trauma in the context of the fantastical, the magical, but also the psychological. Offering alternatives to a "hegemonic version of the maternal that offers only compliance or abjection" (Carpenter 2016, 46), the films underline that, even for the most privileged, mothering is difficult (*Issoudun* and *Moth*); that dealing with a parent's death (especially by murder or suicide) has consequences for children in their relationships and in their parenting (*Juniper* and *Moth*); and that handling a difficult child makes mothering hazardous for both parties (*Juniper* and *Babadook*).

Power, both imagined and real, thematically echoes in both films. The women's magical seeing powers mitigate somewhat their abjected social positions: Margit's as pubescent, homeless, and subject not only to her older sister but also to her brother-in-law; Esther's as a victim of patriarchy, despite her privilege; Rebecca as othered in her Jewishness at a Christian school but also as a young woman subject to decisions by her elders, including a sexual predator male teacher; and Amelia's as a single mother. In all the films, male hegemony derives in part simply from gender; women's power is personal and individual. The control of seeing as a particular kind of knowing sets the four protagonist witch women apart—and joins them with the films' audiences. The men in their lives know only what is most obvious and manifest; the women's ability to see beyond the present and the quotidian demonstrates how much more knowing they are.

Magical, preternatural scenes are not generally associated with realist/ neorealist/social realist films like *Juniper* and *Issoudun*. If something impossible happens in such movies, it may represent a dream or a drug-induced hallucination, for example. But even that is rare. The bizarre nature of Esther's vision, in particular, is juxtaposed with her profession as an engineer—avatar of a most practical, empirical science. Katla's approach to the magic she performs is also empiricist and practical; she seeks to use it to manipulate the world—in particular, to bind Jóhann to her and obtain his love. Yet both Esther's and Margit's visions are beyond their control; they can't conjure them, even if they wanted to. They take place in an everyday world, and yet they point to horrific events.

Horror films commonly incorporate events that go beyond the normal and natural. Indeed, they often present such happenings as simply supernatural rather than offering them as problematized, as they are in *Moth* and *Babadook*. In particular, all four films' realism incorporates and queries—both directly and indirectly—ideas about magic. Justice links with the supernatural: in the island cultural setting of Iceland in *Juniper*, where vision and seeing connect with the in/ability to control the human world; in the rational, scientific suburban Quebec world of *Issoudun*, in which unseen forces compel human actions; at *Moth*'s elite girls' school, where outsiders enact their power through natural and supernatural forces; and in *Babadook*'s domestic nightmare, where the mother may be the monster or the savior. Crucially, when the audience sees what Margit, Esther, Rebecca, and Amelia see, they participate in the women's perspectives and in their culpability. That the audience and these women see and others don't doesn't mean that what happens is all in their heads. The capability of seeing is not equally distributed in the Newfoundland communities Rieti describes or in these films.

Here, magic operates as an inchoate background. Believing in magic and fairy tales, as these films show, does not mean being deluded. Fairy-tale truth about family relations in particular explores the (realistic) emotional positions of anger and despair associated with those relations—found also, too often, in actual experience. The supernatural and magic can offer solutions to ameliorate—or, in contrast, exacerbate—problems of dealing with emotion and/or imagined alternatives. Crime and harm create trauma, and with the power of vision, fantasy offers viable solutions for coping with problems. Not all films can offer progressive moral perspectives, give realistic (if not per se realist) views of oppression, critique relations of ruling, or offer empowerment and alternatives. However, these films do so, in the context of cinematic artistry and entertainment alike. Similarly, the next chapter's renderings of "Cinderella" outside White heteronormative colonial presumptions offer political critiques of culture and society.

7

Transforming Cinderellas and Cinderfellas

Intersectional Perspectives

ACROSS NATIONS, CULTURES, AND LINGUISTIC GROUPS, FAIRY TALES in all their media-crossing adapted forms address sex, gender, sexuality, race, ethnicity, and more. Yet their heteronormative reputation presumes that oral, literary, and other mediated fairy tales deal exclusively with cisgender[1] women and men, in conventional heterosexual relationships. But like other versions of these stories, fairy-tale films—sometimes with subtlety, sometimes quite explicitly—can undermine or even revolutionize concepts of identities and relationships. This chapter shows that though most American (US)[2] fairy-tale films, especially mainstream studio productions, remain

---

1   Cisgender folks' gender identity matches their conventional gender assignment; the term contrasts with transgender, in which folks' gender identity does not match their gender assignment (see Aultman 2014). The older, medical/psychological "transsexual" (now usually understood as derogatory) should be replaced with transgender or trans (see also "Glossary of Terms: Transgender, Transsexual, Trans" n.d.).
2   By "American," I mean the United States specifically. I identify the sources of films made in locations other than the United States.

unrelentingly White in their characterization and perspective, some sterling exceptions merit attention, and alternatives also manifest from elsewhere. Applying queer/transgender, critical race, and intersectional theory assists my exploration of "Cinderella" (ATU 510A) films. These nonmainstream movies invoke reality by associating that fairy tale with credibly diverse characters, locations, and manifestations—some magical, some not.

Queer theory deconstructs presumptions of normal and deviant sexualities—both understood as social constructions, not neutral descriptions—and their manifestations in practices and texts (e.g., Jagose 1996; Sullivan 2003), including folktales and fairy tales. Transgender theory, similarly antiessentialist (understanding sex as well as gender as culturally constructed, not biologically determined), deals with sex/gender variance, the production of sex/gender norms, and the embodiment of sex/gender in humans and discourse (e.g., Stryker and Whittle 2006; Stryker and Aizura 2013), including folktales and fairy tales. Fairy-tale films can be queer in multiple senses: in the nineteenth- and twentieth-century usages to mean odd, strange making, eccentric, different, yet attractive; in implicating lives and theories relating to sexes and sexualities beyond the mainstream and deviating from the norm; but also in the verb sense of spoiling or ruining.

Anyone giving public talks about fairy tales and fairy-tale films as queer texts often finds herself defending the very idea of sullying these allegedly innocent stories by suggesting they might not be always exclusively and resolutely heterosexual. The experience recalls film scholar Alexander Doty's work interpreting beloved films as queer and the enthusiastic resistance he encountered: "Rarely do such battles produce more rancor than when you are trying to convince people, queer and straight, that a 'popular,' 'mass,' 'mainstream,' 'classic' text might be understood queerly" (2000, 4). Yet normative heterosexuality and cisgender are not the only possibilities these narratives work with. In addition to their overt queerness, many fairy tales' deep structure, represented by the realm of magic, is antimoralistic; agency oriented; and gender, sexuality, and species anti-normative (see Greenhill 2018b; Greenhill and Turner 2016; Turner and Greenhill 2012; Seifert 2015a, 2015b)—as are many films based on or using ideas from fairy tales (see, e.g., Duggan 2013; Greenhill 2015).

Intersectional and critical race theories focus on inequalities and subordination but also seek remedies for those marginalized and othered in mainstream theories and practices. Critical race theory eschews color blindness, acknowledging how White supremacy and racial othering infiltrate all aspects of existence (see Delgado and Stefancic 2001; Bakan and Dua 2014). For example, as Sara Hines (2010) argues, the illustrations for Andrew Lang's *Yellow Fairy Book*, rather than offering disinterested interpretations, encode racialization in rendering the beautification of the "black" main character in "The Glass Axe" (ATU 480) as a transformation to being White, though nothing in the fairy tale's text suggests racial alteration. For feminist theory in particular, the work of African American scholar Patricia Hill Collins (2002) is crucial. She employs the concept of standpoint, crucially suggesting that an individual's social but also their political identity—their perspective—strongly influences how they see, and theorize about, their world.

The concept of intersectionality, coined by African American scholar Kimberlé Williams Crenshaw (1991), shared Collins's insight that being a woman and being Black cannot be considered separately, that the mutual interactions of oppression are complex rather than a simple sum of gender plus race. Crenshaw's ideas have since been applied, particularly by feminist scholars, to deal with the multifarious connections between not only race and sex/gender but also class, sexuality, ability, ethnicity, relation to colonialism, and much more. These concepts are evident in the collection edited by Vivian Yenika-Agbaw, Ruth McKoy Lowery, and Laretta Henderson, *Fairy Tales with a Black Consciousness: Essays on Adaptations of Familiar Stories* (2013). Its "multicultural" perspective is "grounded in Critical Race Theory" (Yenika-Agbaw 2013, 8) and comes primarily from the contributor educators' view of fairy tales as children's literature. For example, Deborah L. Thompson talks about a plethora of literary Cinderellas who "counter the pervasiveness of the blond, blue-eyed Cinderella" (2013, 80). Yet the applications of critical race and intersectionality theory to fairy-tale films have been rare, beyond critiques of the persistent Whiteness of Disney princesses. An exception is Cristina Bacchilega's intersectional examination of cinema and television (2013).

So, inspired by Venezuelan-born filmmaker Fina Torres's undeservedly obscure *Mécaniques célestes* (Celestial Clockwork, 1995), I look at films using and/or associated with "Cinderella." I look chiefly at late twentieth-century and millennial live-action, current-setting films beyond the usual (Disney/mainstream US) suspects to show how character and story, as well as audiovisual elements, further subtle alternative intersectional agendas. But first, some background.

Cinderella as Heterosexual, White Subject: Mainstream Romantic Comedies

As Lewis C. Seifert notes, fairy tales are "overwhelmingly perceived as heterosexual" (2015a, 16). The traditional tale of "Cinderella" is often cited by those who wish to argue that fairy tales are hopelessly, irredeemably heterosexist, gender-normative, heteronormative, and White identified.[3] The story of a young woman, persecuted by female (step)relatives, seeking to attend a ball and ultimately to marry a prince, has been cross-culturally and intermedially interpreted mainly in heterosexual terms. The recent *Cinderella across Cultures: New Directions and Interdisciplinary Perspectives* (Dutheil de la Rochère, Lathey, and Woźniak 2016) includes three queer readings in eighteen chapters—none referring to films. Yet as Jack Zipes argues, Cinderella "has assumed various guises from persecuted stepdaughter to feisty orphan and underdog" (2011, 172). Many twentieth-century American films

> discard fathers who enable their second wives to maltreat a stepdaughter . . . omit the fact that Cinderella was born into a well-to-do family . . . dispense with religious connotations. They patch up the narrative in response to the changing role of women, but they still insist that Cinderella use her talents and beauty in a public spectacle so that she can impress a young man and wed him. (172–73)

The visuality of the focus of "Cinderella" on physical transformation, the befores and afters of a young woman maneuvering between roles as drudge and princess, seems ripe for filmic treatment. Many "Cinderella" movies linger on scenes rendering an allegedly unattractive woman conventionally good-looking; Hollywood's use of unusually normatively beautiful actors, of course, often makes such makeovers frankly illusory. But plot points are also crucial in film versions. In *Fairy Tale and Film: Old Tales with a New Spin* (2015), Sue Short points out that "the 'Cinderella' story encapsulat[es] the standard Hollywood rom-com plot in charting a heroine's struggle to overcome specific obstacles before being united with her love" (26). Indeed, the

---

3   Sue Short (2015, 21–26) briefly summarizes feminist controversies about fairy tale. For examples of ongoing feminist disdain of the form, see, for example, Baker-Sperry and Grauerholz (2003); Barnes (2009); and Fisher and Silber (2000).

vast majority of mainstream "Cinderella" live-action, present-day-setting American features are romantic comedies.[4]

That group includes *Working Girl* (directed by Mike Nichols, 1988),[5] which, in the minority for its time, provides a second-wave feminist Cinderella.[6] Protagonist Tess (played by Melanie Griffith) is clearly an adult, not a teen or child. As an already attractive underclass woman, she has difficulty being taken seriously or having her intelligence recognized. Indeed, her prettiness more than her class location apparently makes it difficult for patriarchal women and men alike to see her as anything other than a sex object and/or destined at best for pink-collar work. Tess's makeover clothing is not a beautifying gown and glass slippers but a dress-for-success power suit and short hair. Her transformation event is not a ball but a professional (literal) elevator pitch to the head of an advertising firm, leading her to obtain her first executive position. Her love interest is supportive, but he is not her ultimate goal, and there is no concluding marriage. As Short argues, such films "question 'the male rules of the game,' with women proving they have an

---

[4] Exceptions include the "Cinderella"-themed biopic *Gia* (directed by Michael Cristofer, 1998), problematizing conventional beauty expectations. The latter theme also appears in Korean "Cinderella" films. Tellingly, both the horror *Sin-de-rel-la* (Cinderella, directed by Man-Dae Bong, 2006) and the rom-com *200 Pounds Beauty* use plastic surgery as their theme. The latter and *Cinderella Pact/Lying to Be Perfect* make weight loss their Cinderellas' transformations. Other films do little more than name a Cinderella character. Mockbuster *Avengers Grimm* (directed by Jeremy M. Inman, 2015) places Cinderella in a quartet of shit-kicking superhero fairy-tale princesses with Rapunzel, Sleeping Beauty, and Snow White, along with Red Riding Hood, fighting the likes of Rumpelstiltskin and the Wolf. (Generally low-budget mockbusters, usually released direct to video, piggyback on major films, using similar titles and/or subjects.) Another outlier, Iain Softley's (2013) thriller-drama *A Trap for Cinderella*, concerns a young woman who searches for her true identity.

[5] A colloquial term for female-identified sex workers is "working girl." The Cinderella sex worker, of course, appears in *Pretty Woman*.

[6] Though contested for oversimplification and metaphorical limitations, the concept of European and North American feminist waves distinguishes the first wave, beginning in the late eighteenth century, with woman suffrage as a crucial issue; the second wave, associated with the 1960s–1980s and the concerns surrounding the (female) body; the third wave, beginning in the 1990s, influenced by postmodern and poststructural theory, working to incorporate intersectional perspectives; and an emerging fourth wave, dealing with justice and using the Internet, in particular social media, to advance feminist causes (see Mann and Patterson 2016).

equal right (and ability) to advance themselves at college and the workplace, with love interests often sidelined" (2015, 30).[7]

Working Girl's male "Cinderella" (henceforth "Cinderfella") counterpart, *The Secret of My Succe$s* (directed by Herbert Ross, 1987), resembles millennial mainstream films in its lack of class consciousness (as I discuss below). Protagonist Brantley (played by Michael J. Fox), like Tess, is a young adult.[8] His goal is an executive position and a supportive, appropriate love interest. Representing a man as primarily interested in his job is less than socially revolutionary, but as I discuss below, cinematic Cinderfellas are not necessarily career oriented. Some films, more unconventionally, and unlike many millennial movies with female Cinderellas, paradoxically focus primarily on performing makeovers of their main character's appearance to make him more attractive to his "princess."[9]

Millennial mainstream live-action "Cinderella" films using contemporary settings present as their main topic the most blatantly prescribed hegemonic heterosexual relationships, almost always between attractive, White, middle- or upper-class female teens and their attractive, White, middle- or upper-class male counterparts. Some patterns remain from earlier films like *Pretty Woman* (directed by Garry Marshall, 1990), which, of course, insists on marriage as the happy ever after. Cinderella main

---

7 Many fairy-tale-themed rom-coms do conclude with and trenchantly explore issues around marriage, as indicated in Brook's feminist analysis (2015).
8 See deGraff (1996) on *Secret* and Labrie (1997) on both films. The millennial, thematically similar, British television *Cinderella* (directed by Peter Lydon, 2008), with Maxine Peake as Cindy Mellor and Lucy Punch as a stepsister figure, includes a woman of color fairy godmother cleaner (played by Mona Hammond). The helper as Other invokes the gay male helpers in American films discussed below—and looks relatively conservative. Hans M. Prince (played by James Nesbitt) is an erstwhile (hetero)sexist patriarchal professor. Competition between young women graduate students for a position as his research assistant ends up including competition for his sexual attention (though, as in American films, the job is crucial and there is no concluding marriage).
9 Christie Barber shows that Japanese television "Cinderfellas" use the traditional tale "to explore tensions in how masculine gender identities are deemed desirable or otherwise in contemporary Japanese society" (2014, 126). They address the protagonist men's need for an appropriate love object; their Cinderella moment is about getting the woman, not about getting work, though sometimes a better job also follows. These shows require men to transform physically; more conventional, appropriate clothing helps them attract the women they seek.

character Vivian Ward's (played by Julia Roberts) paid sex work is, by implication, replaced at the film's conclusion by the unwaged but expected sex work normally required of women in marriage. Vivian's occupation is precisely what she seeks to escape, not into another form of paid labor but into a life of leisure with a rich husband. Undermining the latter expectation, as does *Working Girl*'s Tess, the millennial cinematic Cinderella does not seek marriage as the sole or even primary aim in life. Indeed, these films take great care to ensure that their young women main characters take their high school or university studies very seriously and/or are involved in or seeking meaningful paid work and careers. Sexuality and partnering, though significant plot elements, are downplayed in comparison with their focal role in traditional versions, though work may threaten a romantic relationship, as in *The Devil Wears Prada* (directed by David Frankel, 2006).[10]

Some millennial movies render Cinderellas who are also budding entrepreneurs and/or (potential) inheritors of businesses they want to run (crucially, not just wealth and real estate) (see Short 2015, 28–32, 46–49), as Warner Brothers' (so far) four-film "Cinderella Story" franchise exemplifies. In the opening salvo, *A Cinderella Story* (directed by Mark Rosman, 2004), Sam's (played by Hilary Duff) wicked stepmother (played by Jennifer Coolidge) has (illegally) appropriated Sam's late father's estate and diner, which the mature young woman is more than capable of running. *A Cinderella Story: Once Upon a Song* (directed by Damon Santostefano, 2011) has Katie (played by Lucy Hale) seeking a recording contract and entrance into Juilliard. *A Cinderella Story: If the Shoe Fits* (directed by Michelle Johnston, 2016) makes Tessa (played by Sofia Carson) a mechanic/dancer (evoking *Flashdance* [directed by Adrian Lyne, 1983], also a "Cinderella" film with a career-oriented protagonist) who vies for the lead in a movie.

Another Cinderella Story (directed by Damon Santostefano, 2008) deviates from the inexorable main character Whiteness, with Latina teen pop singer Selena Gomez as Mary, who wins a high school contest for the opportunity to dance in a music video. *Maid in Manhattan* (directed by Wayne Wang, 2002), starring adult Latina actor and pop singer Jennifer Lopez, also has a woman of color Cinderella, a single mother seeking a professional

---

10   Short identifies *Devil* as "King Thrushbeard" (ATU 900), in which "a haughty heroine gets what's good for her" (2015, 16), and also as "Household of the Witch" (ATU 334), with another lesson-learning protagonist.

career. Yet these two films are exceptions; conventional plots and White castings are reproduced in films with apparently diverse settings and primary characters; *Jersey Girl* (directed by Kevin Smith, 2004), *Mean Girls* (directed by Mark Waters, 2004), *Miss Congeniality* (directed by Donald Petrie, 2000), *The Prince and Me* (directed by Martha Coolidge, 2004), and *The Princess Diaries* (directed by Garry Marshall, 2001) maintain the pattern. Most do not conclude with a marriage, though the ethnically identified adult Cinderella does marry in the Canadian-American coproduction *My Big Fat Greek Wedding* (directed by Joel Zwick, 2002), written by and starring Winnipeg-born Canadian Nia Vardalos.

Still, marriage is not the sole represented ambition of these millennial heroines. They get the guy, but unlike their predecessors, they also get the job. As Nabila Huq (2014) trenchantly characterized the conclusion of the pastiche fairy-tale film *Enchanted* (directed by Kevin Lima, 2007), the real-life (live-action, not animated) happy-ever-after ending is not a wedding but a career and "endless dating." Heterosexuality is implicit, but its expression takes place outside the confines of marriage. These Cinderellas don't "rely on the idea that a man is the answer to their troubles. In fact, they each provide the solution to their problems through their own resources and abilities. . . . 'Cinderella' provides an apt means of playing with [gender roles], with its emphasis on costume, disguise and transformation" (Short 2015, 32).

Winnipeg-born Canadian filmmaker Sean Garrity offers an excellent example of just that kind of gender play in *After the Ball* (2015). Asked by legendary producer Don Carmody to work on this film based on and bankrolled by Canadian clothing manufacturer Le Chateau, Garrity indicates that he

> immediately dove into research, not only on the fashion stuff and some of the weird espionage stuff that happens in the film, but on the central metaphor, or allusion, the "Cinderella" story. I became very interested in finding the common thread, and the one thing that struck me about "Cinderella" was that it was a story of female empowerment, but stuck in its historical context. But it is a story of a woman [who] doesn't like her circumstances and she finds a way, through a variety of means, to get out of it, leave the concept of what society had in store for her behind. (2017)

In *After the Ball*, fashion major Kate (played by Portia Doubleday) gets a job with the clothing manufacturing company of her distanced father, Lee

Kassell (pronounced "Castle," played by Chris Noth). Machinations by her evil stepmother (played by Lauren Holly) and wicked stepsisters (played by Natalie Krill and Anna Hopkins) lead to Kate's firing. But costumed, made up, and schooled by her fairy (implicitly queer) godfather, Richard (played by Carlo Rota), and self-described "dogmother," Bella (played by Mimi Kuzyk), this Cinderella returns in disguise, cross-dressed and with a new persona as young gay male designer Nate Ganymede.

An indispensable transformation scene has Kate trying on different outfits and walks, still looking very much like herself, until abruptly a view of the fully realized Nate, with costume, hair, contact lenses, and glasses, shows that Kate is genuinely unrecognizable (see figure 7.1). Given her radically changed appearance, viewers can believe that Bella does not know Kate until she hears the young woman's voice. (Unlike in so many "Cinderella" films, no willing suspension of disbelief is required to support the idea that the main character can't be identified at the ball just because she has on a sparkly gown and make up!)[11] Garrity comments:

> There was a lot of work to . . . get her to where she is. And in the movie, we lie that it's just a nose and a wig. But . . . she's supposed to stand half a metre away from her own father, and he can't recognize her. We have to make him somewhat unrecognizable! And I actually spent a lot of time locking the first time we see Nate. I use a film bait-and-switch in that sequence. We know he's about to come into the room, and a man comes in the back of the shot. And so I was hoping that the film audience would go "Ah, there he comes!" And then I have the actual Nate come in from the other side of the frame; he's already in the shot. So then hopefully for at least just a second, the audience is fooled. Cause I feel like if I can fool the audience for a second, then all the rest of it they'll buy. (2017)

For Garrity,

> the costume was a persona. How does that guide her? How does becoming that person show her a side of herself that she hadn't seen before? I was very focussed on trying to make Nate a Boy George sort of a

---

11 Willing suspension of disbelief is required in other filmic contexts, not only in fairy tales, as when Superman becomes unrecognizable when he puts on dark horn-rimmed glasses to become Clark Kent.

character, a little more androgynous, somebody who's got that Boy George sense of a cuteness about him. (2017)

The notion of gender as binary is underlined in Richard's instruction: "Just remember. Remember. Do the opposite of what Kate would do." However, he renders sex/gender more complex when he continues, "Just be me."

Assisted by her love interest, shoe designer Daniel (played by Marc-André Grondin), and gay design assistant Maurice (played by David Michael), whom Nate befriends, Kate outmaneuvers her stepmother and sisters, as well as rival manufacturer Frost (played by Colin Mochrie), who seeks to take over Kassell Fashion. On the way to the happy ending, there is disguise shtick (including Maurice's expression of sexual attraction to Nate) and a business/social event, in which Kate must play both herself and Nate, requiring quick changes behind the scenes (echoing *Mrs. Doubtfire* [directed by Chris Columbus, 1993]), that provide her with crucial information about Frost's plan to hijack Kassell Fashion. As one would by now expect, the closing scenes show that Kate has become the company's head designer and is dating Daniel.

The ending was one for which Garrity fought:

FIGURE 7.1. Nate/Kate.

As a guy who considers himself a feminist . . . there was a lot of focus on my part on changing elements of the story so it was driven by the protagonist and by her choices, as opposed to external elements. . . . In earlier versions of the script, a lot of the choices that she now makes were actually foisted on her by other characters. And I would say "Wouldn't it be more interesting if she made that choice? And especially later, when she has to take responsibility for it?" I had to fight off a bunch of producers who wanted it to be more traditionally "Cinderella." So there was a really strong movement among some of the producers to have her be Daniel's bride. And so, the sum of her achievement was to be the bride of the lead guy. And I was just "That's so wrong for . . . what I'm trying to do with this material, and what I'm trying to do with this story." And I helped to push it in the direction of what was—it's a silly film for teenage girls, but within that a female empowerment story. My daughter's nine now, but when we were making that movie, very much in my mind was, all my other films are restricted. And I want a film that my daughter can see and provide her with a role model that I think is at least not terrible. It's not like there's a great plethora of female role models in cinema. (2017)

Rom-coms often include a gay male sidekick, a friend and helper for the primary (female) character. The helper's sexuality means that he cannot be suspected as an interloper or rival for the affections of the female protagonist's chosen love object. The gay boy's or man's role is often, in fairy godmother style, to transform the main character either into a more conventionally palatable feminine appearance, as in *Miss Congeniality* or *The Devil Wears Prada*, or conversely into a (cross-dressed) masculinity, as in *She's the Man* (directed by Andy Fickman, 2006) as well as *After the Ball*. These gay male characters are invariably free of any sexual relationship, probably so that their sexuality cannot risk poisoning the rating of a family-oriented film with a restricted status in theaters (see, e.g., "MPAA" 2014). These men's gayness is almost invariably expressed in stereotypically affected appearance and/or mannerisms.

In *After the Ball*, god/dogparents Richard and Bella have a heterosexual alibi (it's not clear whether they are siblings, lovers, or business partners), but in creating Nate in Richard's image as explicitly *gay*, along with the admonition to "be me," the presumption cannot be avoided that Kate's godfather is at the very least bisexual. Garrity notes:

> I thought that it was important to not define it, and let people assume whatever they want to assume, but knowing that they didn't quite exactly know. And there was some pressure to define it more clearly. I think there was an explanation at some point of who they were [i.e., the precise relationship of Richard and Bella, and his sexuality], and luckily it also dramatically just didn't work, just killed the momentum of the story. (2017)

Thus, this film offers two gay male helper figures/fairy godfathers, both crucial to Kate's success, as well as the gay Nate, who, given the heterosexual Kate behind him, is appropriately sexually attracted to men. Maurice is the brains behind protecting Nate from Kate's stepmother and stepsisters, as well as from Frost. In particular, Maurice sets up a decoy fashion collection that the evil conspirators predictably steal from Kate's computer and then produce—to universal ridicule—allowing her father to finally realize that he has been duped.

Though there are no clearly identifiable primary characters of color in the film, intercultural relations appear in *After the Ball* (set in Montreal) with significant Quebecois characters—gay sidekick Maurice and love interest Daniel—who contrast with the implicitly Jewish English owners Kate and her father. Issues of class are submerged but present. The garment industries in Montreal (and elsewhere in Canada) have been decimated by neoliberal global capitalism. Signally beginning with Canada-US free trade agreements, most production is farmed to the global South and local manufacture is reduced to "producing samples and niche products" ("Winnipeg Garment Industry" 2007)—as is the case at the fictitious Kassell Fashion. The French Canadian characters are workers/employees, not owners—thus, there's also an element of Cinderfella when Daniel courts the owner/capitalist "princess" Kate. In economic terms, she's more of a catch than he is. Notably, though, he already has a rewarding, personally satisfying job, so as is often the case with Cinderfellas, as I discuss below, his film plot is about getting the woman as a romantic partner.

Similarly, the Canadian fairy-tale pastiche feature *L'odyssée d'Alice Tremblay* (Alice's Odyssey, directed by Denise Filiatrault, 2002), has a Cinderella-like main character, adult factory worker Alice (played by Filiatrault's daughter Sophie Lorain), who thinks she's seeking the conventional prince, foreperson Guillaume (played by Marc Béland). But when she enters a fantasy world, she encounters prince-in-training Ludovic (played by Martin Drainville) trying to achieve his goal of becoming charming. Alice claims she doesn't need a man, and yet manifestly that's precisely what she wants. The story she chooses to read her daughter is "Cinderella"—though the child switches the narrative to "Sleeping Beauty." In this film's doubled roles, Cinderella is also fellow worker Sandrine (played by Pascale Desrochers), dismissed by Alice and her friend Audrey (played by Myriam Poirier) as a miniskirt-wearing airhead. Sandrine/Cinderella's success in getting the attention of Guillaume/Prince Guillaume occasions Alice's jealousy.

Director Filiatrault presents this Cinderella character as shallow and interested only in male attention. Yet the man for whom, in both real and fantasy worlds, Alice and Sandrine/Cinderella vie (in one fairy-tale scene, using physical combat with staves) is equally superficial, if not more. Guillaume too is ridiculed, even vilified; Alice ultimately rejects him, in the magical realm, only when he tries to rape her. But the perspective on Sandrine implies a second-wave feminist betrayal. Women should expect nothing good from patriarchal men; Sandrine/Cinderella, as a woman who should know better, is worse than Guillaume. Why Alice is attracted to Guillaume remains a mystery; the viewer joins Audrey in evaluating him as vain and self-involved, an unfitting partner for her friend.

Filiatrault's attitude toward Sandrine seems somewhat paradoxical. She seems to condemn the woman for wearing revealing clothing, not only for apparently cultivating a persona of shallowness and stupidity. Sandrine's apparent self-sexualization per se could not be the problem. Certainly, Filiatrault allows for relatively unfettered female sexuality, for example, by representing Snow White as a middle-aged woman in sexual relationships with *all* the Dwarfs, choosing "one for each night of the week, depending on my mood." Snow White's decision seems progressive: "when [the Prince] started to court my younger cousin, I'd had enough, I decided to come back here," she says. Alice comments wryly, "Princes don't stay charming long." Snow White says, "I missed my dwarfs. As I got older, I realized that this was ideal." Ludovic explains that Snow White started to age once she left the prince, and Alice comments, "Smart move. She's the only well-adjusted person I've met here." Third- and fourth-wave feminists would applaud this representation of Snow White as a woman who celebrates her own sexuality, but they would take issue with Filiatrault's slut shaming of Sandrine, arguing that women should be able to represent themselves both sartorially and sexually as they wish.[12]

12 Feminist critiques do not differ with the idea that slut shaming is a problem, inap-

Racial representation in *Alice's Odyssey* also raises critical issues around race and intersectionality.[13] The "Snow White" segment closes with a completely unmotivated basketball game between the (White) Dwarfs and a group of tall Black players; impossibly, the Dwarfs win. The African Canadian players appear only in this sequence and only in the fantasy realm; they are bit players at best (for example, they have no names);[14] and nowhere else do people of color appear. The sole obvious role of color, Scheherazade (who also tries to seduce Ludovic and has no real-world counterpart) is Polish-born, White-identified Liliana Komorowska; she and Santa Claus (also relegated only to the magical world) have an annual sexual relationship. Tellingly, racially marked characters like Scheherazade and differently abled characters like the Dwarfs have no counterparts in Alice's real life, which is adamantly White and able/normatively embodied. Thus, though ultimately Alice makes her choice in both worlds to kiss "Prince" Ludovic/Louis and to reject Guillaume, the film is less than progressive.

The American-Canadian production, Thinderella-themed *Cinderella Pact* (directed by Gary Harvey, 2010), like the Korean *Minyeo-neun goerowo* (200 Pounds Beauty, directed by Yong-hwa Kim, 2006), uses the premise of an (allegedly) overweight woman accepted by her fat women friends but not by her employers or love interest. When she and her supportive friends lose weight together, they gain confidence to get what they want in life. Cinderella

---

propriate, and sexist, but they also note that
> slut-shaming has particular resonance for white women, whose sexuality has largely been constructed based upon middle-class, often Christian, hetero-norms of proper chaste womanhood. The positive referent about chastity against which slut becomes the negative referent has never been universally available to Black women. A Black woman who "freely enjoys hers own sexuality" has been called "jezebel, hoochie, hoodrat, ho, freak, and perhaps, slut." In other words, "slut" is merely part of a constellation of terms used to denigrate Black female sexuality; it is not at the center of how our particular sexuality has been constructed. (crunktastic 2011)

13 Tellingly, Filiatrault was one of twenty-one White Quebecois feminists who wrote an open letter supporting the proposed Quebec Charter of Values, which would have prohibited public employees from wearing "conspicuous" religious symbols like the hijab ("Charter of Quebec Values" 2013). Filiatrault subsequently apologized for some of her comments ("Filiatrault Apologizes" 2013). Nevertheless, Bill 21, Loi sur la laïcité de l'État (An Act respecting the laicity of the State), passed June 17, 2019, which affects public sector workers and public services (see, e.g., Stevenson 2019).

14 On IMDb these actors are unlisted.

Nola Devlin (played by Poppy Montgomery) wants women to be "their own fairy godmothers." Again, the career and the boyfriend (not marriage) come to self-transforming Cinderellas, in this case, those who are thin enough (see Bosc 2018).

Experimental and short films often go further with casting and thematic issues, offering more progressive, even radical, alternatives. Often self-funded or otherwise produced outside the mainstream studio system, these films avoid the constraints imposed by producers' fears that something too far beyond conventional expectation simply won't make enough money at the box office.[15] Independent filmmaker Ericka Beckman's *Cinderella* (1986) explores a contemporary working-class woman's experience of fitting and not fitting into capitalism and culture. Zipes's discussion terms the film "Brechtian" (2011, 189–91). *DysEnchanted* (directed by Terri Miller, 2004) presents a therapy support group session with disgruntled fairy-tale heroines—Alice (played by Jaime Bergman), Cinderella (played by Laura Kightlinger), Dorothy (played by Jill Small), Goldilocks (played by Alexis Bledel), Sleeping Beauty (played by Sarah Wynter), Snow White (played by Shiva Rose), and Little Red Riding Hood (played by K. D. Aubert)—complaining about their lives and relationships. New group member Clara (played by Amy Pietz), "just your average divorced single mom," says she doesn't belong, because she's "not like them." Sleeping Beauty says, "All women are like us." Clara "believed in happily ever after" but has been disillusioned. The heroines conclude that they are all "survivors," and Sleeping Beauty says, "I believe all women are heroes in their own stories." Though the other characters are White, *DysEnchanted* has an African American Little Red Riding Hood.

Canadian filmmaker Kellie Benz's short *Cinderella: Single Again* (2000) offers a drunken Prince (played by Christopher Shyer) who says he has difficulty being charming all the time. Cinderella (played by Sarah Chalke) packs her bags and leaves, heading for a singles bar, where she encounters her fairy godmother, who tells her that her happy ever after is up to her—and she

---

15   The Australian *Little Black Dress* (directed by Bramwell Noah and Dan Noah, 2009) casts part-Aboriginal actor Sandy Greenwood as Cinderella character Ebony, but the plot remains unrelentingly heterosexual. Often television can also be more experimental than feature films, which *The 10th Kingdom* (directed by David Carson and Herbert Wise, 2000) miniseries exemplifies. It presents outside-the-box fairy-tale characters, including a Cinderella who is two hundred years old (played by Ann-Margret); arguably, main character Virginia (played by Kimberly Williams-Paisley) is also a Cinderella, whose ultimate partner choice is the wolf, not the prince.

must again achieve it by midnight. Another prince appears, and Cinderella dances with him until he begins sexually assaulting her. With fifteen minutes left, Cinderella returns home, but nothing changes as the clock begins striking midnight. She kicks off her glass slippers, letting them shatter behind her, throws her ring into the night, and pitches her tiara into the sky. As the last bell sounds, she runs away laughing, freeing herself to go and find her own happy ever after. This truly independent Cinderella, unlike her mainstream counterparts, rejects being controlled by fairy-tale expectations. Benz comments:

> The fairy tale, as you age and mature and join the dating world, feels like a promise betrayed for women. Little boys don't read the same books so they don't have any notion, nor feel any responsibility to uphold their end of the fairy-tale deal, while women feel like failures for not being able to achieve this idealized fantasy. And grown men struggle with, or just plain don't get or care about, the burden they carry to achieve this goal. I like the stories like *Frozen* that little girls are being told today. Having real relationships—not competitions—with other women is a far better goal to aspire to than expecting some random man you meet to act like a prince. (email communication, December 13, 2016)

Annika Pampel's *A No Fairy Fairytale: The Cinderella Nightmare* addresses non-Disneyfied versions of the tale. The opening credits show Barbie dolls, mainly in underwear, including a foot in a shoe dripping with shiny red liquid. A woman (played by Pampel) sits beside her young sister (played by Catherine McGibbon) in bed, admonishing her not to eat chocolate or she will "get big and ugly and people won't like [her] any more." The woman tells her "the real story of Cinderella." Cut from the frame narrative: Cinderella (played by Sarah Nicole Baldwin) bleeds, staining the crotch of her long white gown. She runs through a forest, chased by the Prince (played by Dylan Marks), who has found her white shoe. He encounters the stepsisters (played by Jenny Gibson and Alana Cheshire), one of whom cuts her foot to fit into the shoe. At crucial points a female voice-over chorus intones verses, including some based on those found in traditional versions of the tale. The Prince, making out with the stepsisters, laughs at Cinderella with them, and one throws her shoe at Cinderella. She screams. An abrupt cut to the frame scene: the child reaffirms her unfamiliarity with that version of the story but also says, "I never want to go to sleep! Don't make me!" The camera pulls out to show that the two are in what appears to be a morgue. As in the Korean "Cinderella" horror film, the filmmaker condemns the deadly beauty system that constantly enjoins women to seek male attention but also points out that men are easily duped.[16]

Cinderfellas: Hyper-Gendering and Heterosex

As already indicated, on rare occasions, a Cinderella character is male. Probably the best-known film example is Frank Tashlin's *Cinderfella* (1960), which offers a vehicle for Jerry Lewis, playing Fella, the downtrodden step*son*, whose step*mother* and step*brothers* take his father's fortune, make him their servant, and mistreat him. Ed Wynn's arch *fairy* step*father* plays on the colloquial linking of fairy with gay male sexuality, echoed in some other "Cinderella" rom-coms. The presentation of an evil step*mother*, despite the gender reversal of the other roles and thus the expectation that the evil stepparent should be male, for example, bears out Zipes's (fair) accusation of the movie's misogyny (2011, 186).

One crucial scene showing Fella's transformation further witnesses the hyper-gendering of the traditional character while representing a male Cinderella. That is, in showcasing Fella's physical changes, not only his dress but also his voice and deportment, this movie directly seeks the audience's attention to a disconnect in expectations that women, not men, should transform to become more appropriate partners. The makeover reveal, as Lewis's own DVD commentary avers, "is the highlight of the movie." Introducing the sequence, a stage at the ball turns so that Count Basie and his orchestra face the diegetic and extra-diegetic audiences. The Princess (played by Anna Maria Alberghetti), with one of the stepbrothers, emerges to watch. At the close of Basie's piece, the audience claps.

Abruptly, a shot from the stair top looks down into the party. A man dressed in a red tuxedo jacket and black trousers with a red stripe down the side strolls confidently into the shot from the left. He is seen only from behind. Quick cut to the Princess looking up. The man snaps his fingers as the music starts. Another quick cut to the Princess and back and then an abrupt zoom from her perspective to the stair top, revealing that the man is Fella with some graying added to his dark hair (see figure 7.2). His bearing

---

16 See also discussions of the Rodgers and Hammerstein Broadway musical *Cinderella* and its three television versions (Sawin 2014; Rudy 2018, 558–60).

FIGURE 7.2. Fella as the Prince.

has so changed that he little resembles his hitherto goofy character. The shot returns to a view from behind as Fella begins descending the stairs. He alternately walks and stands wide-legged, confidently facing his diegetic audience, adjusting his collar, lapels, and jacket. About a quarter of the way down, Fella begins to dance. His self-assurance greatly contrasts with his usual self-presentation. At the stairway bottom, Fella dances along a receiving line, until he finally reaches the Princess. He kisses her hand and then smiles, for the first time in this sequence momentarily returning to the goofy Lewis persona. "Excuse me, our dance, Your Highness?" he says.

As in *After the Ball*, the audience sees only the startling result, the reveal, not the *process* of transformation. Once again, a willing suspension of disbelief is necessary; though his stepmother (played by Judith Anderson) recognizes Fella, his stepbrother (played by Henry Silva) says, "Don't be silly, Mother. That's a much older man." At the end of the film, the Princess literally chases Fella—she knows exactly who he is—and declares, "I love you." Her clothing transformation process is visualized; she lets down her hair and tears the sleeves off her expensive dress and the heels from her shoes to make herself a better fit for the "ordinary" Fella. Thus, although *Cinderfella* might appear to bend gender, it instead reinstalls strict gender binaries with a vengeance. The stepparent as mother, not father, underlines her illegitimacy to be in control. (In contrast, a stepfather's power, male control under patriarchy, must be valid.) Further, though Fella dresses up to attract the Princess's attention, he returns to his erstwhile clothing. In the end, she transforms herself to fit him, as in traditional versions, not the other way round, as the title suggests.

The 1936 *Mister Cinderella* (directed by Edward Sedgwick) has an improbably complex plot about a barber who substitutes for a drunken millionaire. But one must look outside North and South America to locate millennial "Cinderfella" films, and they are rare, confirming the hyper-gendering of Cinderella as almost necessarily female. Alessandro Paci's Italian *Cenerentolo* (2004) offers a fairly straightforward role-reversal "Cinderfella." Unlike in the Lewis vehicle, the wicked stepparent is male. Another Italian film, *Il professor Cenerentolo* (Professor Cenerentolo, directed by Leonardo Pieraccioni, 2015), along with the Malaysian Amad Idham's *Mr. Cinderella* (2002) and Din CJ's *Mr. Cinderella 2* (2003) focus primarily on the relationship between Cinderfella and the princess he seeks. The latter two films lack the transformation of clothing; the first relies on a mistaken identity, and the second centers on the young man's attraction to another woman, who unlike the first is not literally a princess but the capable daughter of a rich business owner. These films draw on plot points like the need to return at midnight and the lost shoe.

Perhaps the main Cinderfella in recent fairy-tale films is Harry Potter, whom several theorists have viewed as Cinderella-like (see, e.g., Lin 2010). Though none of these characters is anything but heterosexual, the Malaysian *Mr. Cinderella 2* uses homophobic shtick in which the prince figure appears to have sex with his friend/servant. However, looking beyond cinematic film, from the United States, among other fairy-tale-themed music videos he has made, Todrick Hall's "Cinderfella" (2014), which concludes with the banner "Legalize Love," has the popular media star attend a ball where he meets "Prince Charming," out former boy band member Lance Bass. Again, independent, alternative, smaller-scale works offer more choices than their mainstream counterparts.

Intersectional Cinderellas

Films that overtly render fairy-tale primary characters beyond heterosexuality are rare. Will Gould's English *The Wolves of Kromer* (1998) is an exception, a "Little Red Riding Hood"–themed work in which wolves as gay men who are persecuted by a rural community provide the film's themes. However, for a fairy-tale movie about lesbians and gay men that is not per se about their sexuality and its unhappy consequences, the "Cinderella"-themed *Celestial Clockwork* is a perhaps surprising offering. This French/Belgian/Spanish/Venezuelan film production ends with a church wedding, but that's not the fairy-tale happy ever after; rather, it's a marriage of convenience between a gay man wanting his family's approval and an immigrant seeking to stay in France. Indeed, weddings (complete with women singing Franz Schubert's "Ave Maria") bookend this film, which begins with the innocent persecuted heroine (see Bacchilega 1993), an aspiring operatic mezzo-soprano, fleeing her Venezuelan marriage ceremony to fly to Paris, still in her wedding dress. *Clockwork* further subverts the conventional "Cinderella" by offering a lesbian instead of a heterosexual main love story, with a doubled handsome prince/ss and fairy godmother Parisian psychoanalyst.

The feminist plot also includes a male prince/seeker, the producer filming Giacomo Rossini's opera *La Cenerentola* who hunts for the perfect lead. Though there's a physical transformation and a "ball," Cinderella heroine Ana (played by Ariadna Gil) eschews the traditional gown and shows up in a white pantsuit. Again against expectation, she doesn't meet producer Italo Medici (played by Lluís Homar) at the ball, prevented by roommate and wicked stepsister/mother Celeste (played by Arielle Dombasle). Celeste lies that Italo is looking for a blue-eyed blonde like herself to play Cenerentola: "Think about it. Grimm, Walt Disney . . . Nordic stuff. The dominant iconography."

In further mediations on the movie's "meta-filmic, intertextual swerve" (Soliño 2001, 68), Ana, prevented from doing a live audition, sends Italo a cassette tape of her singing. Further, Celeste is frequently represented with animations that underline her wicked role but also show her diegetic work as a video artist. In this enjoyable, satisfying movie, Torres not only "parodies and appropriates many of Disney's most memorable visual techniques" but also explores the "plight of the Latin American artist in the European world of high culture" (69; see also Lawless 2015).

Ana has a plethora of fairy godparents, male and female: her voice coach, Grigorief (played by Michel Debrane), who helps her prepare for her audition and make the tape despite his disdain for Rossini; Italo, seeking the ideal Cenerentola for his opera film; her romantic partner, Alcanie (played by Evelyne Didi), who finally admits her love when she shows up at Ana's religious marriage to her gay friend Armand (played by Frédéric Longbois), arranged so that Ana can avoid being deported and Armand can satisfy his family's wish for a church wedding; Toutou, the Afro-Caribbean witch doctor (played by Hildegarde García Madriz) who prepares a potion for Ana's and Alcanie's romance; and the young Latina women who welcome her into their apartment in Paris, her roommate helper/stepsisters Lucila (played by Alma Rosa Castellanos), Tina (played by Chantal Aimée), and Gaby (played by Dominique Abel). Evil stepsister/mother Celeste, who is White, blonde, and heterosexual, contrasts with the many gay and ethnic helpers. And yet she's clearly a significant agent of the plot—her machinations are the literal Celeste-ial clockwork that sets the events in motion. The reference is perhaps ironic because Celeste's plans don't work like clockwork; always, Ana's helpers extricate or assist their Cinderella.

Animations point to some of the magic in the film. Celeste's first appearance marks her as evil, devil-like; she gives off a puff of smoke that remains in her wake. Celeste's imagination-fueled animations show her, for example, "[taking] New York by storm" as she twirls in a sparkling gown and feather boa, with an animated lighted cityscape and fireworks behind her and in a music-video-like performance with brightly colored pop art and Andy Warhol–like stylized representations of her face. Her eyes flash orange and flame as she apparently casts a spell on Ana to make her leave. As already indicated, many of the animations associated with Celeste represent her video art, and she video-records a great deal of what goes on around her, including in crucial scenes like Ana's registry office wedding.

Armand's animated visions are less literally Technicolor, as are Italo's (he imagines Ana singing with a background of musical staff). Ana's black-and-white poster of Maria Callas is also animated to register some of her emotions, such as her shock when the police are looking for her. Callas even sings a few notes when Toutou enters Ana's bathroom to persuade her to marry Armand so she can stay in France. Alcanie's visions are brought on by her interactions with Toutou; when she confesses her lesbian passion, she imagines herself as a torch singer backed up by Vegas-style chorus girls. After Ana drinks the potion Toutou has prepared, animation represents the beginning of Ana and Alcanie's sexual relationship. The second-to-last animation is realistic; it's the commercial for Toutou, Armand, and their friend Claude's (played by Olivier Granier) company selling magical services. The last animation has Ana singing joyously, registering her delight that Alcanie has shown up for her church wedding, as has Italo, who finally locates her thanks to Toutou (see figure 7.3).

FIGURE 7.3. Ana's happy ending.

Not all the magic in the film comes via animation, however. Wonder appears in astrology, predictions, visions, spells, and potions but also in the way the brutal lives of immigrants, refugees, and migrant workers, some of them illegal, turn out to their satisfaction. Clearly, many immigrants cannot find such a happy ending. Magic also appears in the music that pervades, sometimes shading between diegetic and non-diegetic. Italo listens to Ana's tape of the aria "Una volta c'era un re" (Once upon a time there was a king) and immediately wants her as his Cenerentola; his search to locate her backgrounds a great deal of the film. Composers whose music appears include not only Rossini but also Franz Schubert, Robert Schumann, and Vincenzo Bellini (at one crucial moment Ana sings along with Callas to her signature "Casta Diva" from Bellini's *Norma*). French and Latin American popular music also enhances the mise-en-scène. The song "Mecanicas Celestes," written and sung by Alma Rosa Castellanos, performed at the ball, in effect narrates Ana's story as a common narrative of migrant experience:

> My life runs like celestial clockwork / Yes, my life runs like celestial clockwork / Let me tell you the story / of what happened to me / I left the land I love to come sing here / I quickly discovered hypocrisy and envy / but I also met / people who helped me / They became brothers / They

nurture and encourage me / When things get tough, / they're always by my side.

Of course, not all migrants encounter the success and support the lyrics imply (and that make possible Ana's happy ending). Narrating the story within the story, this song parallels the role of Cenerentola's fairy-tale song, "Una volta c'era un re" in the opera: "Once upon a time there was a king / Who was alone, / Who was bored of being alone: / So he searched and searched and found / But all three wanted to marry him, / so what does he do? / He scorns pomp and beauty, / And in the end, he chose for himself / Innocence and virtue" (Fink, n.d.). Despite its clear "Cinderella" theme, this charming film has received little attention from fairy-tale scholars but some from intersectional feminist (see Soliño 2001) and queer theorists (see Lawless 2015).

Like the American rom-coms, *Clockwork* is about the job more than the relationship. When other non-White Cinderellas appear in nonmainstream North and South American cinema, they also muck with the traditional "Cinderella" script but avoid comedy. Marcia (played by Audrey Reid) in the Jamaican drama *Dancehall Queen* (directed by Don Letts and Rick Elgood, 1997), Ye Xian (played by Vietnamese American An Nguyen) in New York's Chinatown in the romance *Year of the Fish* (directed by David Kaplan, 2007) (both discussed by Bacchilega [2013]), and Maria (played by Catalina Sandino Moreno) in the Colombian/Ecuadorian/US drama *Maria Full of Grace* (directed by Joshua Marston, 2004) (discussed by Hubner [2016]) deal with poverty, oppression, and sexual abuse and/or the threat of it. These underclass Cinderellas must rely primarily on themselves and their own capacities. Of the three, only Ye Xian ends up with a boyfriend—both Maria and Marcia seek to escape various men and unwanted male suitors.

Rotoscoped to transform live-action footage mechanically into animation, *Year of the Fish* offers the story of the motherless seventeen-year-old Ye Xian, who comes to New York from China as an illegal immigrant to make money to send home to her sick father. She works for her cousin, Mrs. Su (played by Tsai Chin), who runs a massage parlor offering sexual services; Ye Xian refuses to participate in sex work and so instead must cook and clean. She falls in love with young musician Johnny (played by Ken Leung). The mysterious Auntie Yaga (played cross-dressed by Randall Duk King, who also plays the Old Man enigmatic helper who tells Ye Xian about Auntie Yaga and where to find her, as well as the sweatshop Foreman) gives Ye Xian the magical fish who narrates the story (voiced by David Lee). With Auntie Yaga's help, the girl finally achieves her happy ending of escaping Mrs. Su's, living with Johnny and his grandmother, and contentedly working in food service.[17]

Director Kaplan uses visual techniques to emphasize the significance of particular characters and events. In particular, he places a circle around the heads of individuals who will be crucial to the plot and then fades out the rest of the background. For example, Kaplan circles Johnny's face the first time the young man and Ye Xian see one another. The director uses the same circle technique to show Auntie Yaga's *absence* after she has given the fish "for good luck" to Ye Xian, demonstrating the old woman's magical ability to appear and disappear. Kaplan marks the fish's role as observer/chorus when he repeatedly cuts to full-screen shots of its head, again to emphasize significant plot developments. The visuals are often literally painterly, such as when Kaplan uses brush strokes in his wipes.

The fish's magic as avatar of Auntie Yaga is marked when the creature grows preternaturally fast. When the evil stepmother/sisters (Mrs. Su and two of her employees) cook it, Ye Xian lovingly gathers the bones. Her transformation scene is precipitated when Mrs. Su's brother Vinnie (played by Lee Wong) indicates he wants to marry her; Ye Xian refuses, and Mrs. Su threatens to send her to a brothel. The girl escapes out her window, looking for Auntie Yaga. The Old Man tells her to find a white door, which she enters to encounter three terrifying figures, then a realistic sweatshop, and then Auntie Yaga alone in a big room, seated at a table, eating. Ye Xian brings her the fish bones, and Auntie Yaga notes that the girl has treated the fish well and that she should go to a New Year's party, but she needs a new dress.

Ye Xian's transformation scene begins with a wipe removing paint strokes to a view of the girl sitting naked in a tub, from behind, as two women, one on either side, wash her. The light music with harp and piano and the sounds of water are soothing. Shots of Ye Xian's face, and the women and their hands with washcloths cleaning her hair, arms, and back, register calm and contemplation. The women dry Ye Xian's back and work on her fingernails and hair, smiling, till a third woman moves in from the right side of the screen, carrying a blue dress.

---

17   See Yamashiro (2011), Bacchilega (2013, 121–31), and Qiu (2017) for more detailed plot synopses and discussions of the film.

Cut to Auntie Yaga, in three-quarter shot from behind, looking out one of the windows with her arm raised. The tinkling peaceful music ceases, and Ye Xian's voice says, "Auntie Yaga. There's something I like to ask about." Auntie Yaga's head turns away from the window: "Ask away but be careful." In close-up, she warns: "Not every question has a good answer." A series of reprises of the views that Ye Xian saw when she mounted the stairs to Auntie Yaga's place start with a figure in shadow at the first landing, in medium shot, as the camera moves up. Ye Xian says, "When I come in downstairs, I see man with white face." Another paint wipe to a close-up of Auntie Yaga. Ye Xian asks, "Who is he?" Auntie Yaga turns toward Ye Xian's voice: "That was the bright day." Wipe from Ye Xian's face close-up, as the camera moves further up the stairs. "Then I see man with red face." As the camera moves closer to the figure, Auntie Yaga explains, "He is my red sun." The camera continues to move up toward another figure, with a wipe to a close-up of his face. Ye Xian says: "Then I see man with no face at all, only dark." Auntie Yaga replies: "He is my dark knight. Those three are my faithful servants," and with a threatening rising tone says: "Anything else you want to ask?" Ye Xian in a close-up says, "No," as she looks down modestly, "Auntie Yaga, that's enough." Cut to Auntie Yaga's face. "You are wise, you ask only of those things you saw outside my factory, not inside." The girl's face registers apprehension as Auntie Yaga continues: "I don't like to have my dirty laundry aired in public."

Cut to Auntie Yaga, now moving from the window toward Ye Xian. Auntie Yaga says, "Well. You stand there like you were mute." Cut to Ye Xian's face in a mirror that is being wiped with a washcloth. Auntie Yaga asks, "Tell me what you see." Hands continue to move around Ye Xian, and she smiles for the first time in the scene. The women's hands adjust her dress, also reflected in the full-length mirror. "It's so beautiful, Auntie Yaga," Ye Xian says as she turns from side to side to view the outfit better. "They make blue dress with teardrops." An extreme close-up of the dress waist in the mirror, with Ye Xian's arm. "Color of sky, color of sea," the girl says. An abrupt cut to Auntie Yaga in extreme close-up, as she explains "Ahh. They have used a bolt made from their hopes and dreams."

Cut to Auntie Yaga, who turns as the sound of fireworks begins and says, "The celebration is already begun." A wider shot shows Auntie Yaga running in and taking Ye Xian's arm: "Time for you to go." They run toward the camera (see figure 7.4). Auntie Yaga says, "You must never come back here." Ye Xian looks terrified. Auntie Yaga warns: "Never. You hear?" Her voice

FIGURE 7.4. Ye Xian transformed with Auntie Yaga.

becomes louder. "You come back and I will bite your little tits off." She moves threateningly toward Ye Xian. The camera moves back slightly, and Auntie Yaga shouts at the top of her voice, "You hear me? Now go!" as the camera moves in and her face fills the screen. Her voice has a background thunderous sound like steam escaping. An abrupt cut to a shot outside marks the scene's end.

This sequence focuses on Auntie Yaga as much as on Ye Xian. Like the Baba Yaga her name recalls, she is an ambivalent figure, which the scene underlines both visually and narratively (see, e.g., Armknecht, Rudy, and Forrester 2017). Her placement above the sweatshop, with its Asian occupants, and her three "faithful servants" beneath, along with her approval of Ye Xian's avoidance of questions about her factory as "dirty laundry," suggest that she may be exploiting workers. Kaplan's choice to have her acted by a man (echoing the transgender witches/stepmothers in "Hansel and Gretel" films, discussed in chapter 5) further underscores her ambivalence, as well as invoking binaries with Ye Xian—old/young, ugly/beautiful, male/female, evil/good, disrespect/respect. Representation of the transformation process, none of which is overtly magical, explores these oppositions.

The initial sequence of calm and contemplation with Ye Xian and the women suggests that the process of change could be pleasant. It offers a calm before a storm, however, when the next sequence has the verbal exchange, initiated by Ye Xian, as she talks with Auntie Yaga about the mysterious men on the stairs. It directly associates Auntie Yaga, herself a most daunting person, with those frightening figures. Her power grows through the scene, as she initiates all the rest of the discussions. The exchange about the dress culminates in Auntie Yaga's disclosure that the cloth for Ye Xian's dress is indeed magical. Perhaps the bolt of "hopes and dreams" cloth relates to the experiences of migrants like Ye Xian herself, the women in Mrs. Su's parlor and the sweatshop, and the women who transform Ye Xian. Clearly, then, aspects of that experience can be beautiful, but like the dress, they are contained, limited, specific, and surrounded—indeed motivated—by uglier ones. Auntie Yaga shows her most dreadful side in her fireworks monologue. Not only does she simultaneously physically pull and push Ye Xian, but Auntie Yaga also shouts abuse and threats at her.

In a Chinese version of "Cinderella," the magical yellow cow (not fish) who helps the main character, and is cooked and eaten by the evil stepmother, is actually the girl's mother (Eberhard 1973, 155–60). As in the film, the girl collects the bones (recalling "The Juniper Tree" in chapter 6). This Cinderella is also helped by an old woman, but that character is more univocally positive than Auntie Yaga. The sequence of terrifying male figures on the stairs is also associated with tale type ATU 334, "Household of the Witch." Kay Turner (2012) argues that the title character in this tale is best understood as precisely the kind of transformative being who appears in Kaplan's film.

A much friendlier helper figure presides over single mother Marcia's makeover in *Dancehall Queen*. Miss Gordon (played by Pauline Stone Myrie) agrees to make Marcia's first dress design for fifteen hundred dollars, though the dressmaker usually charges eight thousand dollars, so Marcia can begin her run-up to entering a dancing contest. She wants to make some money to escape her grinding poverty and the inappropriate attentions of sugar daddy Larry (played by Carl Davis), who expects sexual services from her older daughter in recompense for his paying for Marcia's two daughters' education. As the adult single mother of two girls, whose brother lives with them, Marcia is no ingenue. But she seeks more than just to get by; education for her girls is her priority. As in *Working Girl*, this Cinderella is clearly a responsible, if downtrodden, working-class adult. Actor Reid often conveys her subjugated position in her posture and expression; but when things appear most dire, her character rescues herself and her family. Marcia's decision to enter the dancehall comes when she recognizes that current reigning dancehall queen Olivine (played by Patrice Harrison) looks "ordinary" during the day, without her makeup and outfit. The contrast between the commonplace Marcia and the extraordinary "Mystery Lady" she becomes in the dancehall offers dramatic moments and crucial transformations in the film.[18]

Directly after Marcia decides, "Boy, it look like no man can help me, so me just have to go help myself," cut to Miss Gordon's shop, as Larry steps into the room from a door on which a colorful dress hangs. He is taking off his sunglasses. "Morning," he says, and Miss Gordon responds, "Hi." Standing confidently with his hands on either side of the door frame, he says, "I'm here to pick up that dress for Jeanie Wilson." Cut to a view from inside the dressing room as Marcia looks out of the door slats, which leave bar shadows across her, as Miss Gordon replies, "Oh okay. Let me get it for you." Cut to Marcia's restricted view out from between the slats, with Miss Gordon on the left as she turns toward the dressing room and hands the dress to Larry on the right. "What's happened? You sleeping in there?" she shouts.

Marcia inside the dressing room looks out and then turns and moves into the camera. With a view toward the dressing room doors, with Larry sitting in the foreground from the back, Marcia opens the doors and sashays out in a gold outfit and a slightly askew blonde wig, swinging her hips. "What you think, Miss Gordon?" she says in a smooth, purring, disguised voice, as Larry adjusts his seat and wipes his mouth. "Look damn good if you ask me," he notes. Marcia turns to him and says, "Thank you." "Those legs, they look like they lead straight to heaven," Larry chuckles and raises his hand. Close-up of Marcia, in full-head view, who says, **"You think you could handle this angel?"** (Boldface marks Marcia's words when she is in extreme close-up.) Larry leans forward, "I will give it a damn good try." He leans back and chuckles.

Marcia chuckles. **"Hi."** Cut back to Larry: "Hi. [He gestures with both arms toward himself.] I'm Larry. Who are you?" Shot from behind Larry, Marcia opens her arms and sways from side to side: "Who you see is who I am" (see figure 7.5). Close-up of Larry, who says, "One sexy bitch." Reverse to Marcia. "Live and in living color," she says as she moves her legs seductively. Larry gestures with his hand, "I don't want to leave without you. We can link up later?" Marcia equivocates: **"I think I'll have to take a rain check 'pon**

---

18 See Bacchilega (2013, 131–38) for a detailed discussion of the plot and of Marcia as a trickster figure. See also Duvivier (2008, 1112–18) on the politics of female sexuality in the film.

FIGURE 7.5. Marcia as the "Mystery Lady."

that, you know." She lifts her arm and says, **"Tell you what. You give me your card** . . . and I'll call you one day." Larry replies, "All right. [Reverse to Marcia close-up, licking her thumb and then reaching her hand forward.] This has my home number as well. In case." He hands the card out of the shot to Marcia. Marcia flicks it with her finger: "Great." She raises her hand in farewell. "Maybe I'll see you then," she says and turns back to the change room.

Close-up of Miss Gordon, looking amused and skeptical. Larry snaps his fingers: "Wooo! Thank you, Miss Gordon." He gets up and moves out the door. Cut to Miss Gordon leaning over and looking to make sure he is gone. The doors of the change room open. Marcia asks, "He gone?" Miss Gordon, laughing, says, "Yes. You can come out now. Boy, man fool, eh?" She laughs uproariously, shaking her head.

Unlike in some other "Cinderella" films, Marcia's makeover in this scene, and the fact that Larry (who knows her well) doesn't recognize her, is somewhat believable (as in *After the Ball*). Yet though she wears a blonde wig and has some makeup on, unlike the day-to-day Marcia, the film viewer finds her identifiable. The film thus shows Larry not only as the "fool" Miss Gordon says he is but also as a man who thinks of women only in terms of sex, which makes it impossible for him to know this woman is the usually more dowdy Marcia. Since on a day-to-day basis Larry is uninterested in her, and instead goes after her daughter, he never really looks at Marcia. But Larry's inability to recognize how shrewd she is, as much as his inability to recognize her physical person, results inevitably in his comeuppance at the end of the film. Marcia finds out that he is a murderer and gangster, but since he also takes himself so seriously, and believes that everyone else does too, the fact that she mocks him publicly, and the crowd around joins in her laughter at him, demonstrates that he has more than met his match. It also shows how wrong he is in thinking that he is the Prince (not so) Charming to the "Mystery Lady."

In the nonrecognition scene described above, directors Elgood and Letts clearly demonstrate how Marcia is manipulating Larry. Her three spoken interventions indicated in boldface are presented with Marcia in full-face close-up. That is, these three verbal items—a question, a change of topic, and a refusal—are linguistically and visually marked. By this method, the film shows not only that Marcia renders herself unrecognizable to Larry but also that she controls their interaction—while cleverly allowing Larry to think *he* has the power. The extreme close-ups underline Marcia's agency when she demonstrates her most active moves.

First, she challenges Larry on his ability to "handle her," with the implication that he must concern himself with her needs as well as his (not part of his discourse hitherto, which deals only with him and his perceptions and desires). He responds not in an unequivocal affirmation of his abilities, but with an acknowledgment that he will "try"—quite an uncharacteristic position for the invariably decisive Larry within the film. Next, she changes the direction of the discussion by greeting him as if for the first time. Marcia does what Larry should have done when he began talking to her—give a polite greeting. She simultaneously implies her better social and interactional skills and puts down Larry's lack thereof. He must then introduce himself, but since Marcia has initiated the interaction, she avoids reciprocating, with the simultaneous clever and truthful retort and avoidance of Larry's question, "Who you see is who I am."

This locution cunningly combines truth with a hint for Larry—if he were perceptive enough to comprehend it—that he *already knows* who she is. But it also asserts that there are in effect two personae present, who she *looks like* ("who you see") and who she *actually* is ("who I am"). The tensions between these two discursive figures and Marcia's ongoing manipulation of those roles inform the film's main action. Finally, Marcia outright refuses Larry's invitation to go with him immediately, while leaving open the possibility of further communication (implicitly sexual as well as conversational), initiating a request for his card, and again giving herself the power to continue (or not) their flirtation.

Once again, the close-ups showing Marcia's face—a face Larry should know—remind viewers that her image is perfectly available to him; it's his failure to recognize her that provides amusement not only to Marcia and Miss Gordon but also to the audience, who shares their private joke at Larry's expense. For the first time, the audience clearly sees Marcia in control over Larry. Her sartorial transformation shifts power—as it does in so many fairy tales, including "Cinderella," wherein the physical change of the main character's appearance puts her in a (temporary) position of power with respect to the prince.

Maria Full of Grace is the story of another seventeen-year-old, Colombian Maria Álvarez.[19] She works in a flower plantation sweatshop. Seeking an escape, and pregnant, she agrees to smuggle drugs to New York. Her Cinderella makeover in order to become a drug mule is literally internal; as Laura Hubner points out, the drugs fit inside Maria rather than her foot fitting into a shoe (2016, 270). In the transformation scene, the young man who has recruited Maria takes her on the back of his motorcycle to a pharmacy. After greeting the young man, the pharmacist leaves briefly and then opens a door. Like Ye Xian in *Fish*, Maria mounts the stairs to her transformation, arriving in a room where condoms are being prepared into pellets holding powdered drugs. She sits and watches the process apprehensively. The pharmacist brings her a glass of water and some pills to slow her digestion. He sprays her throat with anesthetic. An older man enters the room and sits in front of her with a bowl of the pellets and a bowl of oil (see figure 7.6). He leans on his cane, his gold ring visible. He takes a pellet, carefully dips it in the oil, and hands it to Maria. She has difficulty swallowing it—he instructs her, "Don't stick your fingers so far inside." When she still has problems, he offers, "If you can't do this we'll stop right now." She replies, "No. I know I can do it."

---

19 See Cortés-Conde (2011) and Schultermandl (2011) for a more detailed discussion of the plot and exploration of the film's representation of the drug trade and social injustice.

FIGURE 7.6. Maria's transformation.

"Let's see," he says. "Relax. Let it slide down." When she succeeds, he says, "Very good," and dips another pellet.

There is an abrupt cut to Maria pacing. "How many is it so far?" she asks. "Twenty-three," the man replies. "Lay down," he says. He reaches to massage her stomach. "What are you doing?" she asks. "Settling them in place," he replies. She sits again and drinks some soup from a bowl put in front of her. The man places one of the pellets in the soup. Finished, she brushes her teeth. The man gives her eight hundred dollars, her ticket to New York, her passport and visa, and the name and address of the hotel where she will stay. Then comes the warning/interdiction. "If any of what you're carrying . . . gets lost along the way or doesn't show up . . . we'll go and have a little conversation . . . with your grandmother, your mother . . . your sister . . . and little Pachito. We know exactly . . . how much each one of those sixty-two pellets weighs. Understood?" Maria nods silently.

Maria is in a minority of recent "Cinderella" films because it involves a fairy-tale-like interdiction. Just as Cinderella must return from the ball at midnight, Maria must return all the drug pellets she has swallowed. Failure will clearly cost her dearly—the stakes are higher than they are for the traditional Cinderella, who only risks disgrace. Maria risks her own life—as the film shows, the pellets can rupture and the mule inevitably dies of an overdose. She would imperil both her own and her family's lives should she try to keep and sell some of the drugs. It shares, however, the unrealistic happy endings of other "Cinderella" films. Maria's choice to remain in the United States, implicitly to offer her unborn baby better opportunities than in Colombia, counters the realities for illegal Latina immigrants even in pre-Trump America. As Hubner argues, though the film's "prolonged empathy with young female drug smugglers is in itself progressive," the fairy-tale happy ending emplotment limits the film's potentially radical elements, giving a "positive spin on her new surroundings, rather than offering a direct critique of North America's complicity in the sweatshop trade [Maria] has left behind. It upholds the fantasy of an improved life in the US" (2016, 271).

A more radical alternative manifests in Samoan Dan Taulapapa McMullin's multiple adaptations of "Sinalela"—video short, poems, and short story—about (intersexual) *fa'afafine*. These works relocate "Cinderella" to "a Samoan specificity" that calls "to decolonize lands, economies, and minds" (Bacchilega 2013, 69). McMullin's work joyously counters the discrimination encountered by *fa'afafine* and intersex folks under conditions of coloniality and refuses presumptions about the impossibility of a happy ending for those who don't fit the hegemonic mainstream. It comes closest to the transformational possibilities of two non–North American film versions of the related tale "Donkeyskin" (ATU 510B), Steve Barron's *Sapsorrow* (1989) from Jim Henson's *The StoryTeller* television series and Jacques Demy's *Peau d'âne* (Donkey Skin, 1970) (see Duggan 2013). They explore roads not taken, even in independent North American film and television, involving a female character's transformation into an apparently ugly, animal-like person, as a route to her own liberation with regard to sex, gender, and sexuality.

Drudge in a Sparkly Dress?

As sedimented within popular understandings, especially given the now canonical texts of the Grimms, Perrault, and most crucially Disney, "Cinderella" is conventionally understood as the story of a young White heterosexual woman who (as in patriarchal expectation) marries "up" into royalty. Thus, the very representation of a male, a lesbian, and/or a sometimes cross-dressed/gay Cinderella undermines convention and offers realistic alternatives. The idea that Cinderella is a woman, in and of itself and regardless of the intentions of the filmmaker, renders the Tashlin *Cinderfella* a queer text—and perhaps also a trans text, in that audience members may find it difficult, as I do, not to simultaneously and constantly read Fella in terms that recall his younger female hypotextual counterparts. Similarly, the hypotextual "marriage plot" renders queer *Celestial Clockwork*'s lesbian Cinderella marrying a gay man while in a loving relationship with another woman or *After the Ball*'s "endless dating."

These films offer alternatives to the sex-, gender-, and sexuality-normative expectations for "Cinderella," but crucially they do so while also clearly rendering a recognizable version of the tale. For these films, "Cinderella" gives the filmmakers an opportunity to tell their own stories from the realm of enchantment that avoid moralizing about normative expectations (in fact, at points they *all* expressly support anti-normative positions), providing hero/ines who are clearly active agents in their own lives. Queer as strange, odd, and attractive, as well as a rendering of sexualities, and trans as the expression of plural and pluralistic embodiments hold sway over these films. And yet, as in the interests of *After the Ball* and *Celestial Clockwork* in showing women finding rewarding work and in *Cinderfella*'s transformation, these movies also solidify narratives implicating life beyond their diegesis. Fairy tales' capability of supporting queer and trans readings, as part of narratives told—at least in part—in realist mode, suggests how malleable they are. Indeed, these films' crucial transformative moments in visual encodings show the ways that gender, sex, and sexuality find multiple expression in life, as they do in stories.

Two single mothers (in *Dancehall Queen* and *Maria Full of Grace*), three illegal immigrants (in *Year of the Fish*, *Celestial Clockwork*, and *Maria*), and a lesbian opera singer (in *Celestial*) queer the conventional idea of Cinderella as a (sexually and otherwise) innocent ingenue. Perhaps Ye Xian is most like the North American expectation of virginal purity, but the fact that she is Chinese (though played by a Vietnamese actor) nevertheless undermines expectations, as *Clockwork*'s Celeste trenchantly describes it, "Grimm, Walt Disney... Nordic stuff. The dominant iconography." None of these Cinderellas follow the latter pattern, and indeed not one is as passive as some of her traditional counterparts. Each has a vision of the life she seeks, and each uses a transformational moment or moments to achieve it.

The films' visuals support those transformations as both Cinderella-like and distinctive to each character. Though all offer realistic changes and processes, not the enchantments and magic seen in the traditional story, elements of *Clockwork* and *Fish* implicate a preternatural, racialized, and implicitly queer story, and the brutal realism of *Dancehall* and *Maria* are undermined by the unexpected happy endings in both. I suggest that these films, in bringing queer and racialized primary characters to the story, don't betray or reverse more familiar versions but instead manifest how fairy tales' already anti-normative structures can be used to represent a realm of enchantment that avoids the conventional Disneyfication too often expected of well-known fairy tales.

MOVING FORWARD?

8

Final Thoughts

To Overcome the Real

"THE PRESENT IS REPLETE WITH BEASTS THAT NEED TO BE VANquished, which is to say that investing in a fairy tale need not be a retreat from reality, but can be a certain way of facing it" (Muñoz 2009, 165). I came across this wisdom from the late José Esteban Muñoz quite by chance while conducting a word search through his profound and inspiring *Cruising Utopia: The Then and There of Queer Futurity*, in quest of reflections on queer and trans theory. I don't recall being struck by that comment during my initial reading of the influential work several years ago. If this book and my life were a fairy tale, I would have found the quotation then, picked it up, and put it in my pocket on the off chance I could use it later, as so many fairy-tale heroes do. But as the films and other media I discuss in this book show, life is not always a fairy tale.

Though those who popularly affirm that life is not a fairy tale usually mean there is no happy ending, most of the films I discuss in detail here don't join in locating the intersection of life and fairy tales solely or even mainly in that concept. And, as Sara Ahmed affirms, it's probably the wrong place to look. Her *The Promise of Happiness* deconstructs what she calls the happiness duty, challenging discourses around the allegedly unhappy groups of conventional Euro–North America—feminists, queers, Black women, and migrants (2010). Not surprising, precisely those folks become topics for the addresses to reality in many of the fairy-tale films I discuss here, and intersectional theories of those identities are touch points for my analysis.

Yet fairy tales can nevertheless be positive. They can offer reflections on utopia—or the lack of it. It is no coincidence that Muñoz draws on Ernst Bloch, whose work influenced fairy-tale scholar Jack Zipes, who co-translated Bloch's works in *The Utopian Function of Art and Literature* (1988) and frequently notes the German philosopher's importance (as discussed, e.g., in Teverson 2013, 129–30). Though utopia is literally no place, the search for it as an ideal is ongoing. And again, the films I discuss in this book offer some hints. To recall just one example, utopian processes could include rendering magic a quotidian matter in everyday life or, as Fred Pellerin put it, resisting a world in which "everything is de-magiced, reasoned, calculated" (quoted in Gendron 2009, 16).

Because he's so obviously one of the most heinous current de-magicers around, I've talked about Trump in this book. He's such a caricature of a fairy-tale villain, and his name is so pun-worthy when linked with his attitude. But he comes from a long line of odious, hideous politicians, whose influences have been equally or even more villainous and abhorrent. If I had a fairy-tale wish, it would be that the mention of Trump would soon render this book so dated that it would never again be relevant. But sadly, and horribly, as fairy tales remind me, there are always more despots, more patriarchs, more evil villains even if we can vanquish the current ones.

Extended fairy tales told by Pius Power, whose words on truth and lies opened this book, often don't end when there's a wedding. And it's not only Mr. Power's tales, but many, many others, in which, time and again, the splice is only the beginning. As was one of Bengt Holbek's (1987) trenchant insights, the primary characters in this particular spot are usually female, and they must face even more hardships. In the tale "The Shift of Sex," for example, the new bridegroom's wife, mother, and father all want to get rid of her when they find out she's dressed as a man but biologically female. A magical transformation to male fixes the immediate problem. But there's no guarantee that all the new prince's problems are perpetually resolved (see Greenhill and Anderson-Grégoire 2014). Again to look to fairy tales, there are many-headed dragons with a taste for eating princesses; greedy giants who won't let starving cattle feed on their land; and tricksters with bizarre names who are profoundly uninterested in women's rights to reproductive choice. And their literal and metaphorical counterparts are everywhere.

Alas, when Trump goes, legions will take his place, in the United States and all over the world. So what might it mean to invest in a fairy tale not as a retreat from reality but as a way of facing it? Perhaps the fairy-tale film answer is to keep facing real problems head-on, gathering your community, and never forgetting to believe.

FILMOGRAPHY

A.I.: Artificial Intelligence. 2001. Directed by Steven Spielberg. United States.
After the Ball. 2015. Directed by Sean Garrity. Canada.
Another Cinderella Story. 2008. Directed by Damon Santostefano. United States, Canada.
Audition. 2005. Directed by Luc Picard. Canada.
Avengers Grimm. 2015. Directed by Jeremy M. Inman. United States.
The Babadook. 2014. Directed by Jennifer Kent. Australia, Canada.
Babine. 2008. Directed by Luc Picard. Canada.
Bad Times at the El Royale. 2018. Directed by Drew Goddard. United States.
Beauty and the Beast. 2017. Directed by Bill Condon. United States.
Black Field. 2009. Directed by Danishka Esterhazy. Canada.
The Blue Bird. 1918. Directed by Maurice Tourneur. United States.
The Boxtrolls. 2014. Directed by Graham Annable and Anthony Stacchi. United States.
Bram Stoker's Dracula. 1992. Directed by Francis Ford Coppola. United States.
The Brothers Grimm. 2005. Directed by Terry Gilliam. United States, Czech Republic, United Kingdom.
Buffy the Vampire Slayer. (TV) 1999. "Gingerbread" (episode 3.11). Directed by James Whitmore Jr. United States.
Bumblebee. 2018. Directed by Travis Knight. United States.
The Cabin in the Woods. 2012. Directed by Drew Goddard. United States.
Cannibal Holocaust. 1980. Directed by Ruggero Deodato. Italy.
Castle. (TV) 2009–16. Created by Andrew W. Marlowe. United States.
The Cell. 2000. Directed by Tarsem Singh. United States, Germany.
Cenerentolo. 2004. Directed by Alessandro Paci. Italy.
A Chairy Tale. 1957. Directed by Norman McLaren and Claude Jutra. Canada.
Chicken Run. 2000. Directed by Peter Lord and Nick Park. United Kingdom, United States, France.
Cinderella. 1899. Directed by Georges Méliès. France.
Cinderella. 1986. Directed by Ericka Beckman. United States.

Cinderella. (TV) 2008. Directed by Peter Lydon. United Kingdom.
Cinderella: Single Again. 2000. Directed by Kellie Benz. Canada.
Cinderella Pact/Lying to Be Perfect. 2010. Directed by Gary Harvey. United States, Canada.
A Cinderella Story. 2004. Directed by Mark Rosman. United States, Canada.
A Cinderella Story: If the Shoe Fits. 2016. Directed by Michelle Johnston. United States.
A Cinderella Story: Once Upon a Song. 2011. Directed by Damon Santostefano. United States.
Cinderfella. 1960. Directed by Frank Tashlin. United States.
Coraline. 2009. Directed by Henry Selick. United States.
Corpse Bride. 2005. Directed by Tim Burton and Mike Johnson. United States, United Kingdom.
Dancehall Queen. 1997. Directed by Rick Elgood and Don Letts. Jamaica.
The Devil Wears Prada. 2006. Directed by David Frankel. United States, France.
District 31. (TV) 2016–. Created by Luc Dionne. Canada.
DysEnchanted. 2004. Directed by Terri Miller. United States.
El laberinto del fauno (Pan's Labyrinth). 2006. Directed by Guillermo del Toro. Spain, Mexico, United States.
Emerald City. (TV) 2017. Directed by Tarsem Singh. United States.
Enchanted. 2007. Directed by Kevin Lima. United States.
Eréndira. 1983. Directed by Ruy Guerra. France, Mexico, West Germany.
Ésimésac. 2012. Directed by Luc Picard. Canada.
Ever After: A Cinderella Story. 1998. Directed by Andy Tennant. United States.
The Exorcist. 1973. Directed by William Friedkin. United States.
The Fall. 2006. Directed by Tarsem Singh. United States, South Africa, India.
Flashdance. 1983. Directed by Adrian Lyne. United States.
Freeway. 1996. Directed by Matthew Bright. United States, France.
Freeway 2: Confessions of a Trickbaby. 1992. Directed by Matthew Bright. United States.
The French Connection. 1971. Directed by William Friedkin. United States.
Gia. 1998. Directed by Michael Cristofer. United States.
Grimm. (TV) 2011–17. Created by Stephen Carpenter, David Greenwalt, and Jim Kouf. United States.
Grimm. 2003. Directed by Alex van Warmerdam. Netherlands.
Groundhog Day. 1993. Directed by Harold Ramis. United States.
The Guardian. 1990. Directed by William Friedkin. United States.
H & G. 2013. Directed by Danishka Esterhazy. Canada.
The Hand of the Artist. 1906. Directed by Walter R. Booth. United States. (See https://aso.gov.au/titles/shorts/the-hand-of-the-artist/.)
The Hand That Rocks the Cradle. 1992. Directed by Curtis Hanson. United States.
Hansel and Gretel. (TV) 1983. Directed by Tim Burton. United States.
Hansel and Gretel: Faerie Tale Theatre. (TV) 1983. Directed by James Frawley. United States.

Hansel & Gretel. 2002. Directed by Gary J. Tunnicliffe. United States.
Hansel & Gretel. 2013. Directed by Anthony C. Ferrante. United States.
Hansel & Gretel: An Appalachian Version. 1975. Directed by Tom Davenport. United States.
Hansel & Gretel: Warriors of Witchcraft. 2013. Directed by David DeCoteau. United States.
Hansel & Gretel: Witch Hunters. 2013. Directed by Tommy Wirkola. Germany, United States.
Hansel & Gretel Get Baked. 2013. Directed by Duane Journey. United States.
Hansel vs. Gretel. 2015. Directed by Ben Demaree. United States.
Henjel gwa Geuretel (Hansel & Gretel). 2007. Directed by Pil-sung Yim. South Korea.
The House with a Clock in Its Walls. 2018. Directed by Eli Roth. India, Canada, United States.
I, Robot. 2004. Directed by Alex Proyas. United States, Germany.
Il professor Cenerentolo (Professor Cenerentolo). 2015. Directed by Leonardo Pieraccioni. Italy.
Immortals. 2011. Directed by Tarsem Singh Dhandwar. United States.
Invisible Ink. 1921. Directed by Dave Fleischer. United States.
The IT Crowd. (TV) 2006–13. Directed by Graham Linehan. United Kingdom.
Jersey Girl. 2004. Directed by Kevin Smith. United States.
Jin-Rô (Jin-Roh: The Wolf Brigade). 1999. Directed by Hiroyuki Okiura. Japan.
The Juniper Tree. 1990. Directed by Nietzchka Keene. Iceland.
Koca Dünya (Big Big World). 2016. Directed by Reha Erdem. Turkey.
Kubo and the Two Strings. 2016. Directed by Travis Knight. United States.
Le mythe de la bonne mère (The Myth of the Good Mother). (TV) 2006. Directed by Micheline Lanctôt. Canada.
Le piège d'Issoudun (The Issoudun Exit/Trap; Juniper Tree). 2003. Directed by Micheline Lanctôt. Canada.
Les rois mongols (Cross My Heart). 2017. Directed by Luc Picard. Canada.
Lights Out. 2016. Directed by David F. Sandberg. United States.
Little Black Dress. 2009. Directed by Bramwell Noah and Dan Noah. Australia.
The Little Mermaid. 1989. Directed by John Musker and Ron Clements. United States.
L'odyssée d'Alice Tremblay (Alice's Odyssey). 2002. Directed by Denise Filiatrault. Canada.
Maid in Manhattan. 2002. Directed by Wayne Wang. United States.
Maleficent. 2014. Directed by Robert Stromberg. United States.
Mama. 2013. Directed by Andy Muschietti. Canada, Spain.
Maria Full of Grace. 2004. Directed by Joshua Marston. Colombia, United States, Ecuador.
Mean Girls. 2004. Directed by Mark Waters. United States, Canada.
Mécaniques célestes (Celestial Clockwork). 1995. Directed by Fina Torres. France, Belgium, Spain, Venezuela.
Minyeo-neun goerowo (200 Pounds Beauty). 2006. Directed by Yong-hwa Kim. South Korea.

Mirror Mirror. 2012. Directed by Tarsem Singh. United States, Canada.
Miss Congeniality. 2000. Directed by Donald Petrie. United States.
Missing Link. 2019. Directed by Chris Butler. United States.
Mister Cinderella. 1936. Directed by Edward Sedgwick. United States.
Moongirl. 2005. Directed by Henry Selick. United States.
The Moth Diaries. 2011. Directed by Mary Harron. Canada, United States, Ireland.
Mr. Cinderella. 2002. Directed by Amad Idham. Malaysia.
Mr. Cinderella 2. 2003. Directed by Din CJ. Malaysia.
Mrs. Doubtfire. 1993. Directed by Chris Columbus. United States.
My Big Fat Greek Wedding. 2002. Directed by Joel Zwick. Canada, United States.
Neighbours. 1952. Directed by Norman McLaren. Canada.
The Night of the Hunter. 1955. Directed by Charles Laughton. United States.
The Nightmare Before Christmas. 1993. Directed by Henry Selick. United States.
9. 2016. Directed by Claude Brie, Erik Canuel, Jean-Philippe Duval, Marc Labrèche, Micheline Lanctôt, Luc Picard, Stéphane E. Roy, Éric Tessier, and Ricardo Trogi. Canada.
A No Fairy Fairytale: The Cinderella Nightmare. 2008. Directed by Annika Pampel. United States.
Once Upon A Time. (TV) 2011–2018. Creators Adam Horowitz and Edward Kitsis. United States.
ParaNorman. 2012. Directed by Chris Butler. United States.
Peau d'âne (Donkey Skin). 1970. Directed by Jacques Demy. France.
Pieds nus dans l'aube (Barefoot at Dawn). 2017. Directed by Francis Leclerc. Canada.
Poslední motýl (The Last Butterfly). 1991. Directed by Karel Kachyna. Czechoslovakia, France, United Kingdom.
Pretty Woman. 1990. Directed by Garry Marshall. United States.
The Prince and Me. 2004. Directed by Martha Coolidge. United States, Czech Republic.
The Princess Diaries. 2001. Directed by Garry Marshall. United States.
Psycho. 1960. Directed by Alfred Hitchcock. United States.
Ruka (The Hand). 1965. Directed by Jiří Trnka. Czechoslovakia.
Sapsorrow (The StoryTeller). (TV) 1989. Directed by Steve Barron. United States.
The Secret of My Succe$s. 1987. Directed by Herbert Ross. United States.
Self/less. 2015. Directed by Tarsem Singh. United States.
She's the Man. 2006. Directed by Andy Fickman. United States, Canada.
The Shining. 1980. Directed by Stanley Kubrick. United Kingdom, United States.
The Silence of the Lambs. 1991. Directed by Jonathan Demme. United States.
Sin-de-rel-la (Cinderella). 2006. Directed by Man-Dae Bong. South Korea.
Snow White. 1987. Directed by Michael Berz. United States.
Snow White: A Deadly Summer. 2012. Directed by David DeCoteau. United States.
Snow White: The Fairest of Them All. 2001. Directed by Caroline Thompson. Canada, Germany, United States.
Snow White: A Tale of Terror. 1997. Directed by Michael Cohn. United States.
Snow White and the Huntsman. 2012. Directed by Rupert Sanders. United States.

Snow White and the Seven Dwarfs (Faerie Tale Theatre). (TV) 1984. Directed by Peter Medak. United States.
The Sweet Hereafter. 1997. Directed by Atom Egoyan. Canada.
The 10th Kingdom. (TV) 2000. Directed by David Carson and Herbert Wise. United Kingdom, Germany, United States.
The Thief of Bagdad. 1924. Directed by Raoul Walsh. United States.
Tideland. 2005. Directed by Terry Gilliam. United Kingdom, Canada.
A Trap for Cinderella. 2013. Directed by Iain Softley. United Kingdom.
Waltz with Bashir. 2008. Directed by Ari Folman. Israel, France, Germany, United States, Finland, Switzerland, Belgium, Australia.
West Side Story. 1961. Directed by Jerome Robbins and Robert Wise. United States.
What Lies Beneath. 2000. Directed by Robert Zemeckis. United States.
The Wizard of Oz. 1939. Directed by Victor Fleming. United States.
The Wolves of Kromer. 1998. Directed by Will Gould. United Kingdom.
The Woodsman. 2004. Directed by Nicole Kassell. United States.
Working Girl. 1988. Directed by Mike Nichols. United States.
Year of the Fish. 2007. Directed by David Kaplan. United States.
Yo ho ho. 1981. Directed by Zako Heskiya. Bulgaria.

REFERENCES CITED

"About." n.d. *LAIKA*. Accessed December 27, 2017. http://www.laika.com/about

"About Filmography." n.d. *The International Fairy-Tale Filmography*. http://iftf.uwinnipeg.ca/Home/About

"About Rotten Tomatoes." n.d. *Rotten Tomatoes*. https://www.rottentomatoes.com/about#whatisthetomatometer

Ahmed, Sara. 2010. *The Promise of Happiness*. Durham, NC: Duke University Press.

Alexander, Chris. 2015. "In Defense of William Friedkin's *The Guardian*." *Coming-Soon.net*, December 28. http://www.comingsoon.net/horror/news/748112-defense-william-friedkins-guardian

Alger, Jed. 2012. *The Art and Making of ParaNorman*. San Francisco: Chronicle Books.

Allen, Graham. 2011. *Intertextuality*. 2nd ed. Abingdon: Routledge.

Allsop, Jon. 2017. "Inside the Fairy Tale Mind of Trump." *Columbia Journalism Review*, September 27. https://www.cjr.org/special_report/trump-fairy-tale.php

Anderson, Kristin J. 2015. *Modern Misogyny: Anti-Feminism in a Post-Feminist Era*. New York: Oxford University Press.

"The Animators: The Breath of Life." 2005. *Corpse Bride*. DVD special features.

Armknecht, Megan, Jill Terry Rudy, and Sibelan Forrester. 2017. "Identifying Impressions of Baba Yaga: Navigating the Uses of Attachment and Wonder on Soviet and American Television." *Marvels & Tales* 31 (1): 62–79.

Ashe, Marie. 1997. "'Bad Mothers' and Welfare Reform in Massachusetts: The Case of Claribel Ventura." In *Feminism, Media, and the Law*, edited by Martha Fineman and Martha T. McCluskey, 203–16. New York: Oxford University Press.

Aultman, B. 2014. "Cisgender." *TSQ: Transgender Studies Quarterly* 1 (1–2): 61–62.

Auter, Philip J., and Donald M. Davis. 1991. "When Characters Speak Directly to Viewers: Breaking the Fourth Wall in Television." *Journalism Quarterly* 68 (1–2): 165–71.

Bacchilega, Cristina. 1993. "An Introduction to the 'Innocent Persecuted Heroine' Fairy Tale." *Western Folklore* 52 (1): 1–12.

———. 2013. *Fairy Tales Transformed? Twenty-First-Century Adaptations and the Politics of Wonder*. Detroit: Wayne State University Press.

Bakan, Abigail B., and Enakshi Dua, eds. 2014. *Theorizing Anti-Racism: Linkages in Marxism and Critical Race Theories.* Toronto: University of Toronto Press.

Baker-Sperry, Lori, and Liz Grauerholz. 2003. "The Pervasiveness and Persistence of the Feminine Beauty Ideal in Children's Fairy Tales." *Gender and Society* 17 (5): 711–26.

Balanzategui, Jessica. 2017. "*The Babadook* and the Haunted Space between High and Low Genres in the Australian Horror Tradition." *Studies in Australasian Cinema* 11 (1): 18–32.

Barber, Christie. 2014. "'Appearance Does Not Make the Man': Masculinities in Japanese Television Retellings of 'Cinderella.'" In *Channeling Wonder: Fairy Tales on Television*, edited by Pauline Greenhill and Jill Terry Rudy, 125–43. Detroit: Wayne State University Press.

Barnes, Sandra L. 2009. "Romantic and Familial Relationships with Black Males: Implications of the Cinderella Complex and Prince Charming Ideal." *Black Women, Gender & Families* 3 (2): 1–28.

Bauer, Stephen F. 1999. "Oedipus Again: A Critical Study of Charles Laughton's *The Night of the Hunter.*" *Psychoanalytic Quarterly* 68 (4): 611–36.

Baum, L. Frank. 1973. *The Annotated Wizard of Oz: The Wonderful Wizard of Oz.* Annotated by Michael Patrick Hearn. New York: Clarkson N. Potter.

Bédard, Annie, and Josée Bédard. 2018. Interview by Pauline Greenhill. Winnipeg, June 24.

Beeton, Sue. 2005. *Film-Induced Tourism.* Clevedon, UK: Channel View Publications.

Ben-Amos, Dan. 2010a. "Introduction: The European Fairy-Tale Tradition between Orality and Literacy." *Journal of American Folklore* 123 (490): 373–76.

———. 2010b. "Straparola: The Revolution That Was Not." *Journal of American Folklore* 123 (490): 426–46.

Bennett, Jamie. 2008. "Reel Life after Prison: Repression and Reform in Films about Release from Prison." *Probation Journal* 55 (4): 353–68.

Bergeron, Bertrand. 2014. "Autour de Fred Pellerin." *Boitatá* 17 (January–July): 13–25.

Bernini, Lorenzo. 2017. *Queer Apocalypses: Elements of Antisocial Theory.* Translated by Julia Heim. Cham, Switzerland: Palgrave Macmillan.

Best, Anita, Martin Lovelace, and Pauline Greenhill. 2019. *Clever Maids, Fearless Jacks, and a Cat: Fairy Tales from a Living Oral Tradition.* Logan: Utah State University Press.

Bignell, Jonathan. 2013. *An Introduction to Television Studies.* 3rd ed. London: Routledge.

"Biographie." 2016. *Fred Pellerin.* http://www.fredpellerin.com/biographie

Blécourt, Willem de. 2012. *Tales of Magic, Tales in Print: On the Genealogy of Fairy Tales and the Brothers Grimm.* Manchester, UK: Manchester University Press.

Bloch, Ernst. 1988. *The Utopian Function of Art and Literature: Selected Essays.* Translated by Jack Zipes and Frank Mecklenburg. Cambridge: MIT Press.

Blouin, Michael J. 2015. "Research Cluster—'A Growing Global Darkness': Dialectics of Culture in Goddard's *The Cabin in the Woods.*" *Horror Studies* 6 (1): 83–99.

Bosc, Lauren. 2018. "Fat Studies ('Where Everything Round Is Good': Exploring and Reimagining Fatness in Fairy-Tale Media)." In *The Routledge Companion to Media and Fairy-Tale Cultures*, edited by Pauline Greenhill, Jill Terry Rudy, Lauren Bosc, and Naomi Hamer, 252–62. New York: Routledge.

Bottigheimer, Ruth B. 2009. *Fairy Tales: A New History*. Albany: State University of New York Press.

"'The Boxtrolls' Trailer 2." 2014. *YouTube*. https://www.youtube.com/watch?v=HOKou-3TuVQ

Bradford, Phillips Verner, and Harvey Blume. 1992. *Ota Benga: The Pygmy in the Zoo*. New York: St. Martin's Press.

Briefel, Aviva. 2017. "Parenting through Horror: Reassurance in Jennifer Kent's *The Babadook*." *Camera Obscura* 32 (2): 1–27.

Broderick, Damien. 1995. *Reading by Starlight: Postmodern Science Fiction*. New York: Routledge.

Brook, Heather. 2015. "Engaging Marriage: Rom Coms and Fairy Tale Endings." In *The Happiness Illusion: How the Media Sold Us a Fairy Tale*, edited by Luke Hockley and Nadi Fadina, 145–61. New York: Routledge.

Brotherton, Philip. 2014. *The Art of* The Boxtrolls. San Francisco: Chronicle Books.

Brown, Noel. 2017. *British Children's Cinema: From* The Thief of Bagdad *to* Wallace and Gromit. London: I. B. Tauris.

Brown, Tom. 2012. *Breaking the Fourth Wall: Direct Address in the Cinema*. Edinburgh: Edinburgh University Press.

Buerger, Shelley. 2017. "The Beak That Grips: Maternal Indifference, Ambivalence and the Abject in *The Babadook*." *Studies in Australasian Cinema* 11 (1): 33–44.

Butler, David. 2009. *Fantasy Cinema: Impossible Worlds on Screen*. London: Wallflower.

Cailher, Diane. 2008. "Luc Picard." *The Canadian Encyclopedia*. http://thecanadianencyclopedia.com/en/article/luc-picard/

Carpenter, Ginette. 2016. "Mothers and Others." In *Women and the Gothic: An Edinburgh Companion*, edited by Avril Horner and Sue Zlosnik, 46–59. Edinburgh: Edinburgh University Press.

Carr, Kevin. 2014. "35 Things We Learned from the *Coraline* Commentary." *FSR Film School Rejects*, September 25. https://filmschoolrejects.com/35-things-we-learned-from-the-coraline-commentary-7f1ead093149/

Case, Sue-Ellen. 1991. "Tracking the Vampire." *differences: A Journal of Feminist Cultural Studies* 5 (2): 1–20.

Cavender, Gray, and Nancy Jurik. 2007. "Scene Composition and Justice for Women." *Feminist Criminology* 2 (4): 277–303.

Chanady, Amaryll. 1995. "Territorialization of the Imaginary." In *Magical Realism: Theory, History, Community*, edited by Lois Parkinson Zamora and Wendy B. Faris, 125–44. Durham, NC: Duke University Press.

Chance, Maia. 2014. *Snow White Red-Handed*. New York: Berkley Prime Crime.

———. 2015. *Cinderella Six Feet Under*. New York: Berkley Prime Crime.

———. 2016. *Beauty, Beast, and Belladonna*. New York: Berkley Prime Crime.

———. 2017. *Sleeping Beauty, Borrowed Time: A Fairy Tale Fatal Novella*. Cork: BookBaby.

Chang-Kredl, Sandra. 2015. "Coraline's Split Mothers: The Maternal Abject and the Childcare Educator." *Continuum* 29 (3): 354–64.

"Charter of Quebec Values Would Ban Religious Symbols for Public Workers." 2013. *CBC News Montreal*, September 20. http://www.cbc.ca/news/canada/montreal/charter-of-quebec-values-would-ban-religious-symbols-for-public-workers-1.1699315

Chaudhuri, Shohini. 2006. *Feminist Film Theorists: Laura Mulvey, Kaja Silverman, Teresa De Lauretis, Barbara Creed*. London: Routledge.

Chávez, Karma R., and Cindy L. Griffin, eds. 2012. *Standing in the Intersection: Feminist Voices, Feminist Practices in Communication Studies*. Ithaca: State University of New York Press.

Cheng, Susan. 2016. "Why White Actors Play Japanese Characters In 'Kubo And The Two Strings.'" *Buzzfeed*, August 18. https://www.buzzfeed.com/susancheng/kubo-and-the-two-strings

Cherry, Brigid. 2002. "Refusing to Refuse to Look: Female Viewers of the Horror Film." In *Horror, the Film Reader*, edited by Mark Jancovich, 169–82. London: Routledge.

———. 2009. *Horror*. London: Routledge.

Child, Ben. 2012. "Snow White and the Huntsman Casting Condemned by Campaigners." *The Guardian*, June 7. https://www.theguardian.com/film/2012/jun/07/snow-white-hunstman-casting-condemned

Chrupała, Aleksandra, and Joanna Warmuzińska-Rogóż. 2013. "Est-ce un royaume paisible? Image du pays à travers les contes choisis." *TransCanadiana* 6:113–30.

Chung, Hae Jean. 2012. "Media Heterotopia and Transnational Filmmaking: Mapping Real and Virtual Worlds." *Cinema Journal* 51 (4): 87–109.

Clover, Carol J. 1992. *Men, Women, and Chain Saws: Gender in the Modern Horror Film*. Princeton, NJ: Princeton University Press.

Collins, Jo, and John Jervis. 2008. "Introduction." In *Uncanny Modernity: Cultural Theories, Modern Anxieties*, edited by Jo Collins and John Jervis, 1–9. Houndmills, Hampshire: Palgrave Macmillan.

Collins, Patricia Hill. 2002. *Black Feminist Thought: Knowledge, Consciousness, and the Politics of Empowerment*. New York: Routledge.

Cook, Malcolm. 2018. *Early British Animation: From Page and Stage to Cinema Screens*. Cham, Switzerland: Palgrave Macmillan.

Cormack, Patricia, and Clare Fawcett. 2003. "Cultural Gatekeepers in the L. M. Montgomery Tourist Industry." In *Literature and Tourism: Essays in the Reading and Writing of Tourism*, edited by Mike Robinson and Hans Christian Andersen, 171–90. London: Thomson.

Cortés-Conde, Florencia. 2011. "Telling Identities: Crime Narratives for Local and International Markets in *María, Full of Grace* (Marston, 2004) and *Rosario Tijeras* (Maillé, 2005)." *Studies in Latin American Popular Culture* 29 (1): 80–101.

Coulombe, Michel. 2009. "Les films de genre dans le cinéma québécois: Transformation en tous genres." *Ciné-Bulles* 27 (4): 22–29.

Craven, Allison. 2017. *Fairy Tale Interrupted: Feminism, Masculinity, Wonder Cinema*. Bern, Switzerland: Peter Lang.

Crawford, Lucas. 2016. "Snorting the Powder of Life: Transgender Migration in the Land in Oz." In *Queering the Countryside: New Frontiers in Rural Queer Studies*, edited by Mary L. Gray, Colin R. Johnson, and Brian Joseph Gilley, 126–45. New York: New York University Press.

"Crazy Credits." n.d. *IMDb*. Accessed December 28, 2017. http://www.imdb.com/title/tt0327597/crazycredits

Creed, Barbara. 1993. *The Monstrous-Feminine: Film, Feminism, Psychoanalysis*. London: Routledge.

Crenshaw, Kimberlé Williams. 1991. "Mapping the Margins: Intersectionality, Identity Politics, and Violence against Women of Color." *Stanford Law Review* 43 (6): 1241–99.

Cruikshank, Julie. 2014. *Do Glaciers Listen? Local Knowledge, Colonial Encounters, and Social Imagination*. Vancouver: University of British Columbia Press.

crunktastic. 2011. "I Saw the Sign but Did We Really Need a Sign? SlutWalk and Feminism." *Crunk Feminist Collective*, October 6. http://www.crunkfeministcollective.com/2011/10/06/i-saw-the-sign-but-did-we-really-need-a-sign-slutwalk-and-racism/

De Vos, Gail. 2009. "Review of *Grimm Pictures*." *Journal of the Fantastic in the Arts* 20 (1): 121–25.

Dégh, Linda, and Andrew Vázsonyi. 1983. "Does the Word 'Dog' Bite? Ostensive Action: A Means of Legend Telling." *Journal of Folklore Research* 20: 5–34.

DeGraff, Amy. 1996. "From Glass Slipper to Glass Ceiling: 'Cinderella' and the Endurance of a Fairy Tale." *Merveilles & Contes* 10 (1): 69–85.

Delgado, Richard, and Jean Stefancic. 2001 *Critical Race Theory: An Introduction*. New York: New York University Press.

Dibeltulo, Silvia, and Ciara Barrett, eds. 2018. *Rethinking Genre in Contemporary Global Cinema*. Cham, Switzerland: Palgrave Macmillan.

Dillman, Joanne Clarke. 2014. *Women and Death in Film, Television, and News: Dead but Not Gone*. New York: Palgrave Macmillan.

Doherty, Thomas. 2015. "Genre, Gender, and the *Aliens* Trilogy." In *The Dread of Difference: Gender and the Horror Film*, 2nd ed., edited by Barry Keith Grant, 209–27. Austin: University of Texas Press.

Doty, Alexander. 2000. *Flaming Classics: Queering the Film Canon*. New York: Routledge.

Doxey, George V. 1975. "A Causation Theory of Visitor-Resident Irritants: Methodology and Research Inferences." *Travel and Tourism Research Association Sixth Annual Conference Proceedings*, 195–98. San Diego, CA.

Doyon, Frédérique. 2007. "Babine, ou l'ode à la folie." *Le Devoir*, October 4. https://www.ledevoir.com/culture/159351/babine-ou-l-ode-a-la-folie

Duggan, Anne E. 2013. *Queer Enchantments: Gender, Sexuality, and Class in the Fairy-Tale Cinema of Jacques Demy*. Detroit: Wayne State University Press.

Dutheil de la Rochère, Martine Hennard, Gillian Lathey, and Monika Woźniak, eds. 2016. *Cinderella across Cultures: New Directions and Interdisciplinary Perspec-*

tives. Detroit: Wayne State University Press.

Duvivier, Sandra C. 2008. "'My Body Is My Piece of Land': Female Sexuality, Family, and Capital in Caribbean Texts." *Callaloo* 31 (4): 1104–21.

Eberhard, Wolfram, ed. 1973. *Folktales of China*. New York: Pocket Books.

Ebert, Roger. 1990. "The Guardian." *RogerEbert.com*, April 27. https://www.rogerebert.com/reviews/the-guardian-1990

Edelman, Lee. 2004. *No Future: Queer Theory and the Death Drive*. Durham, NC: Duke University Press.

Elder, Glen Strauch. 2003. *Hostels, Sexuality, and the Apartheid Legacy: Malevolent Geographies*. Athens: Ohio University Press.

Ellis, Bill. 1989. "Death by Folklore: Ostension, Contemporary Legend, and Murder." *Western Folklore* 48 (3): 201–20.

———. 2001. *Aliens, Ghosts, and Cults: Legends We Live*. Jackson: University Press of Mississippi.

Ellis, John M. 1983. *One Fairy Story Too Many: The Brothers Grimm and Their Tales*. Chicago: University of Chicago Press.

Elsaesser, Thomas. 1998. "Spectacularity and Engulfment: Francis Ford Coppola and *Bram Stoker's Dracula*." In *Contemporary Hollywood Cinema*, edited by Steve Neale and Murray Smith, 191–208. London: Routledge.

Faber, Liz, and Helen Walters. 2003. *Animation Unlimited: Innovative Short Films since 1940*. London: Laurence King.

"Fairy Tale Fatal." n.d. *Maia Chance National Bestselling Mystery Author*. Accessed December 14, 2017. http://www.maiachance.com/fairy-tale-fatal/

Faludi, Susan. 1991. *Backlash: The Undeclared War against American Women*. New York: Crown.

Faradji, Helen. 2008. "*Babine* de Luc Picard." *24 images*, no. 140: 62.

Faris, Wendy B. 1995. "Scheherazade's Children: Magical Realism and Postmodern Fiction." In *Magical Realism: Theory, History, Community*, edited by Lois Parkinson Zamora and Wendy B. Faris, 163–90. Durham, NC: Duke University Press.

Fedosik, Marina. 2018. "Adoption in Ste[v]en Spielberg's *A. I. Artificial Intelligence*: Kinship in the Posthuman Context." *Adoption & Culture* 6 (1): 182–205.

"Filiatrault Apologizes for Derogatory Comments She Made about Muslim Women." 2013. *Montreal Gazette*, October 18. http://www.montrealgazette.com/life/filiatrault+apologizes+derogatory+comments+made+about+muslim+women/9050287/story.html

Fink, Katharina. n.d. "Una volta c'era un re, Cenerentola's aria from La Cenerentola." *Aria Database*. http://www.aria-database.com/translations/ceneren16_una.txt

Fisher, Jerilyn, and Ellen S. Silber. 2000. "Good and Bad Beyond Belief: Teaching Gender Lessons through Fairy Tales and Feminist Theory." *Women's Studies Quarterly* 28 (3/4): 121–36.

Fisher, Lucy. 1996. *Cinematernity: Film, Motherhood, Genre*. Princeton, NJ: Princeton University Press.

Foucault, Michel. 1980. *Language, Counter-Memory, Practice: Selected Essays and Interviews*. Ithaca, NY: Cornell University Press.

"Fred Pellerin absent de la cérémonie de l'Ordre national du Québec." 2012. *Radio-Canada*, June 7. https://ici.radio-canada.ca/nouvelle/564914/ordre-national-quebec

"Fred Pellerin reçoit l'Ordre national du Québec." 2012. *La Presse*, December 19. http://www.lapresse.ca/arts/201212/19/01-4605439-fred-pellerin-recoit-lordre-national-du-quebec.php

Friedkin, William. 2011. "Return to the Genre." *The Guardian*. DVD Extras.

Frow, John. 2006. *Genre*. London: Routledge.

Gaiman, Neil. 2002. *Coraline*. New York: HarperCollins.

Garrity, Sean. 2017. Telephone interview by Pauline Greenhill. February 10.

Gendron, Nicholas. 2009. "Fred Pellerin, scénariste de *Babine*." *Ciné-Bulles* 27 (1): 16–21.

Genette, Gérard. 1997. *Palimpsests: Literature in the Second Degree*. Lincoln: University of Nebraska Press.

Get Into Film. 2016. "All the PUPPET SECRETS from animation Kubo and the Two Strings." *YouTube*, September 9. https://www.youtube.com/watch?v=Vhpq7-c911A

Gingras, Chantale. 2008. "Pellerinage au coeur du conte: Incursion dans l'univers du conteur Fred Pellerin." *Québec français* 150:39–43.

Giovacchini, Saverio, and Robert Sklar, eds. 2012. *Global Neorealism: The Transnational History of a Film Style*. Jackson: University Press of Mississippi.

"Glossary of Terms—Transgender, Transsexual, Trans." n.d. *GLAAD Media Reference Guide—Transgender*. https://www.glaad.org/reference/transgender

Goodall, Jane. 2016. "Looking Glass Worlds: The Queen and the Mirror." *M/C Journal* 19 (4). http://journal.media-culture.org.au/index.php/mcjournal/article/view/1141

Gordon, Andrew. 2008. *Empire of Dreams: The Science Fiction and Fantasy Films of Steven Spielberg*. Lanham, MD: Rowman & Littlefield.

Gordon, Phillip. 2016. "Bullying, Suicide, and Social Ghosting in Recent LGBT Narratives." *Journal of Popular Culture* 49 (6): 1261–79.

Gothie, Sarah Conrad. 2016. "Playing 'Anne': Red Braids, Green Gables, and Literary Tourists on Prince Edward Island." *Tourist Studies* 16 (4): 405–21.

Grant, Barry Keith. 2012. "Introduction." In *Film Genre Reader IV*, edited by Barry Keith Grant, xvii–xxii. Austin: University of Texas Press.

Gray, Jonathan. 2010. *Show Sold Separately: Promos, Spoilers, and Other Media Paratexts*. New York: New York University Press.

Greenhill, Pauline. 1997. "'Who's Gonna Kiss Your Ruby Red Lips?' Sexual Scripts in Floating Verses." In *Ballads into Books: The Legacies of Francis James Child*, edited by Tom Cheesman and Sigrid Rieuwerts, 225–35. Bern, Switzerland: Peter Lang.

———. 2014. "*Le piège d'Issoudun*: Motherhood in Crisis." *Narrative Culture* 1 (1): 49–70.

———. 2015. "'The Snow Queen': Queer Coding in Male Directors' Films." *Marvels & Tales* 29 (1): 110–34.

———. 2016. "Team Snow Queen: Feminist Cinematic 'Misinterpretations' of a Fairy Tale." *Studies in European Cinema* 13 (1): 32–49.

———. 2017a. "*Le piège d'Issoudun*: Fairy-Tale Murder." In *Screening Justice: Canadian Crime Films, Culture and Society*, edited by Steven A. Kohm, Sonia Bookman, and Pauline Greenhill, 218–39. Winnipeg: Fernwood.

———. 2017b. "Fairy-Tale Films." In *Oxford Research Encyclopedia of Literature*, edited by Paula Rabinowitz. Oxford University Press. http://literature.oxfordre.com/view/10.1093/acrefore/9780190201098.001.0001/acrefore-9780190201098-e-83

———. 2018a. "Cinematic." In *The Routledge Companion to Media and Fairy-Tale Cultures*, edited by Pauline Greenhill, Jill Terry Rudy, Naomi Hamer, and Lauren Bosc, 357–66. New York: Routledge.

———. 2018b. "Sexualities/Queer and Trans Studies." In *The Routledge Companion to Media and Fairy-Tale Cultures*, edited by Pauline Greenhill, Jill Terry Rudy, Naomi Hamer, and Lauren Bosc, 290–98. New York: Routledge.

———. 2019a. "Camera Obscura and Zoetrope: Tarsem and Magic/Reality in Transcultural Fairy Tale Film." *Narrative Culture* 6 (2): 119–39.

———. 2019b. "Sexes, Sexualities, and Gender in Cinematic North and South American Fairy Tales." In *The Fairy Tale World*, edited by Andrew Teverson, 248–59. London: Routledge.

Greenhill, Pauline, and Emilie Anderson-Grégoire. 2014. "'If Thou Be Woman, Be Now Man!' 'The Shift of Sex' as Transsexual Imagination." In *Unsettling Assumptions: Tradition, Gender, Drag*, edited by Pauline Greenhill and Diane Tye, 56–73. Logan: Utah State University Press.

Greenhill, Pauline, and Anne Brydon. 2010. "Mourning Mothers and Seeing Siblings: Feminism and Place in *The Juniper Tree*." In *Fairy Tale Films: Visions of Ambiguity*, edited by Pauline Greenhill and Sidney Eve Matrix, 116–36. Logan: Utah State University Press.

Greenhill, Pauline, and Steven Kohm. 2013. "*Hoodwinked!* and *Jin-Roh: The Wolf Brigade*: Animated 'Little Red Riding Hood' Films and the Rashômon Effect." *Marvels & Tales* 27 (1): 89–108.

———. 2016. "Fairy-Tale Films in Canada/Canadian Fairy-Tale Films." In *Fairy-Tale Films Beyond Disney: International Perspectives*, edited by Jack Zipes, Pauline Greenhill, and Kendra Magnus-Johnston, 246–16. New York: Routledge.

———. Forthcoming. "Hansel and Gretel Films: Families, Crimes, and Harms to Children." *Dzieciństwo. Literatura i Kultura*.

Greenhill, Pauline, and Kay Turner. 2016. "Queer and Transgender Theory." In *Folktales and Fairy Tales: Traditions and Texts from around the World*, 2nd ed., edited by Anne E. Duggan and Donald Haase, 3:843–46. Santa Barbara, CA: Greenwood.

Grow Film Company. n.d. "Paranorman Behind The Scenes—Making Norman." *Vimeo*. https://vimeo.com/45852276

Guindon, Alex. 2007. "Face-à-face avec Fred Pellerin." *Argus* 36 (1): 43–35.

Gunning, Tom. 2008. "Uncanny Reflections, Modern Illusions: Sighting the Modern Optical Uncanny." In *Uncanny Modernity: Cultural Theories, Modern Anxieties*, edited by Jo Collins and John Jervis, 68–90. Houndmills, Hampshire: Palgrave Macmillan.

Halberstam, Jack (Judith). 1991. "Skinflick: Posthuman Gender in Jonathan Demme's *The Silence of the Lambs*." *Camera Obscura: Feminism, Culture, and Media Studies* 9 (3): 36–53.

———. 2008. "Animating Revolt/Revolting Animation: Penguin Love, Doll Sex and the Spectacle of the Queer Nonhuman." In *Queering the Non/Human*, edited by Noreen Giffney and Myra J. Hird, 265–81. Aldershot, UK: Ashgate.

———. 2011. *The Queer Art of Failure*. Durham, NC: Duke University Press.

Hancock, Joel. 1978. "Gabriel García Márquez's 'Eréndira' and the Brothers Grimm." *Studies in 20th & 21st Century Literature* 3 (1): 43–52.

"Hansel & Gretel: Witch Hunters." n.d. Wikipedia. Accessed May 18, 2018.

Haraway, Donna J. 1988. "Situated Knowledges: The Science Question in Feminism and the Privilege of Partial Perspective." *Feminist Studies* 14 (3): 575–99.

———. 1997. *Modest_Witness@Second_Millennium. FemaleMan©_Meets_OncoMouse^{TM}: Feminism and Technoscience*. New York: Routledge.

Harron, Mary. 2017. Interview with Pauline Greenhill and Allison Norris. March 9.

Haynes, Emily. 2016. *The Art of Kubo and the Two Strings*. San Francisco: Chronicle Books.

Higgins, Scott. 2012. "3d In Depth: Coraline, Hugo, and a Sustainable Aesthetic." *Film History: An International Journal* 24 (2): 196–209.

Hill, Donald R. 2007. *Caribbean Folklore: A Handbook*. Westport, CT: Greenwood.

Hines, Sara. 2010. "Collecting the Empire: Andrew Lang's Fairy Books (1889–1910)." *Marvels & Tales* 24 (1): 39–56.

Hoffmann, Kathryn A. 2005. "Of Monkey Girls and a Hog-Faced Gentlewoman: Marvel in Fairy Tales, Fairgrounds, and Cabinets of Curiosities." *Marvels & Tales* 19 (1): 67–85.

Holbek, Bengt. 1987. *Interpretation of Fairy Tales*. Helsinki: Academia Scientiarum Fennica.

Hollinger, Karen. 2012. *Feminist Film Studies*. London: Routledge.

hollywoodstreams. 2013. "'The Boxtrolls' Trailer 2." *YouTube*. https://www.youtube.com/watch?v=HOKou-3TuVQ

Holton, C. Lewis. 1995. "Once Upon a Time Served: Therapeutic Application of Fairy Tales within a Correctional Environment." *International Journal of Offender Therapy and Comparative Criminology* 39 (3): 210–21.

Horner, Avril, and Sue Zlosnik. 2014. "Gothic Configurations of Gender." In *The Cambridge Companion to the Modern Gothic*, edited by Jerrold E. Hogle, 55–70. Cambridge: Cambridge University Press.

Howell, Amanda. 2018. "The Terrible Terrace: Australian Gothic Reimagined and the (Inner) Suburban Horror of *The Babadook*." In *American-Australian Cinema: Transnational Connections*, edited by Adrian Danks, Stephen Gaunson, and Peter C. Kunze, 183–201. Cham, Switzerland: Palgrave Macmillan.

Hubner, Laura. 2016. "The Fairy-Tale Film in Latin America." In *Fairy-Tale Films Beyond Disney: International Perspectives*, edited by Jack Zipes, Pauline Greenhill, and Kendra Magnus-Johnston, 262–77. New York: Routledge.

———. 2018. *Fairytale and Gothic Horror: Uncanny Transformations in Film*. London:

Palgrave Macmillan.

Huq, Nabila. 2014. "Dating Is the New Happily-Ever-After and Other Post-Colonial Gendered Conclusions: A Transcultural Reading of *Enchanted*." Sixteenth Annual Women and Gender Studies Colloquium, University of Winnipeg, Manitoba, Canada, March.

Hurley, Nat. 2014. "The Little Transgender Mermaid: A Shape-Shifting Tale." In *Seriality and Texts for Young People: The Compulsion to Repeat*, edited by Mavis Reimer, Nyala Ali, Deanna England, and Melanie Dennis Unrau, 258–78. London: Palgrave Macmillan.

Huss, Christophe. 2015. "Fred Pellerin, 'par l'ouïe, avec l'ouïe et en l'ouïe'!" *Le Devoir*, December 10. https://www.ledevoir.com/non-classe/457599/concert-de-noel-fred-pellerin-par-l-ouie-avec-l-ouie-et-en-l-ouie

IFTF. 2014–. *The International Fairy-Tale Filmography*. University of Winnipeg. iftf.uwinnipeg.ca

Jackman, Josh. 2016. "The Hollywood Star Who Still Teaches at Cheder." *The JC*, May 26. https://www.thejc.com/lifestyle/features/the-hollywood-star-who-still-teaches-at-cheder-1.57684

Jackson, Rosemary. 2003. *Fantasy*. Abingdon, Oxon: Routledge.

Jagose, Annamarie. 1996 *Queer Theory: An Introduction*. New York: New York University Press.

Jameson, Fredric. 1986. "On Magic Realism in Film." *Critical Inquiry* 12 (2): 301–25.

Jervis, John. 2008. "Uncanny Presences." In *Uncanny Modernity: Cultural Theories, Modern Anxieties*, edited by Jo Collins and John Jervis, 10–50. Houndmills, Hampshire: Palgrave Macmillan.

Johnson, Merri Lisa. 2015. "Bad Romance: A Crip Feminist Critique of Queer Failure." *Hypatia* 30 (1): 251–67.

Johnson, Sophie Lucido. 2016. "Kubo and the Two Faces: The Complexity of a Beautiful Film With a Major Race Problem." *fnewsmagazine*, September 8. http://fnewsmagazine.com/2016/09/kubo-and-the-two-faces-the-complexity-of-a-beautiful-film-with-a-major-race-problem/

Joosen, Vanessa. 2007. "Disenchanting the Fairy Tale: Retellings of 'Snow White' between Magic and Realism." *Marvels & Tales* 21 (2): 228–39.

———. 2011. *Critical and Creative Perspectives on Fairy Tales: An Intertextual Dialogue between Fairy-Tale Scholarship and Postmodern Retellings*. Detroit: Wayne State University Press.

Jörg, Daniele. 2003. "The Good, the Bad, and the Ugly." *Public Understanding of Science* 12:297–306.

Kaplan, E. Ann. 1997. "The Politics of Surrogacy Narratives." In *Feminism, Media, and the Law*, edited by Martha Fineman and Martha T. McCluskey, 193–202. New York: Oxford University Press.

———, ed. 2000. *Feminism and Film*. Oxford: Oxford University Press.

Kérchy, Anna. 2016. *Alice in Transmedia Wonderland*. Jefferson, NC: McFarland.

Kessler, Glenn. 2018. "Meet the Bottomless Pinocchio, a New Rating for a False Claim Repeated Over and Over Again." *Washington Post*, December 10. https://

www.washingtonpost.com/politics/2018/12/10/meet-bottomless-pinocchio-new-rating-false-claim-repeated-over-over-again/?noredirect=on&utm_term=.82b0f770a1a5

Klein, Rachel. 2002. *The Moth Diaries: A Novel*. New York: Bantam Books.

Knight, Deborah. 1992. "Metafiction, Pararealism and the 'Canon' of Canadian Cinema." *Cinémas: Revue d'études cinématographiques/Cinémas: Journal of Film Studies* 3 (1): 125–46.

Knight, Travis. 2016. "Foreword." *The Art of Kubo and the Two Strings*, 6–7. San Francisco: Chronicle Books.

Kohm, Steven A., and Pauline Greenhill. 2011. "Pedophile Crime Films as Popular Criminology: A Problem of Justice?" *Theoretical Criminology* 15 (2): 195–215.

———. 2014. "Little Red Riding Hood Crime Films: Critical Variations on Criminal Themes." *Law, Culture and the Humanities* 10 (2): 257–78.

Kosonen, Heidi. 2015. "The Death of the Others and the Taboo: Suicide Represented." *Thanatos* 4 (1): 25–56.

Kristeva, Julia. 1982. *Powers of Horror: An Essay on Abjection*. Translated by Leon S. Roudiez. New York: Columbia University Press.

Kristof, Nicholas. 2017. "Lessons from 100 Days of President Trump." *New York Times*, April 29. https://www.nytimes.com/2017/04/29/opinion/sunday/lessons-from-100-days-of-president-trump.html?emc=edit_nk_20170429&nl=nickkristof&nlid=58925128&te=1&_r=0

Labrie, Vivian. 1997. "Help! Me, S/he and the Boss." In *Undisciplined Women: Tradition and Culture in Canada*, edited by Pauline Greenhill and Diane Tye, 151–66. Montreal: McGill-Queen's University Press.

Langevin, Sébastien. 2010. "Fred Pellerin, conteux et poète québécois." *Le français dans le monde* 372 (November–December): 4–5.

Lawless, Cecelia Burke. 2015. "Inside-Out: A Socio-Spatial Reading of *Mecánicas celestes*." In *Despite All Adversities: Spanish-American Queer Cinema*, edited by Andrés Lema-Hincapié and Debra A. Castillo, 111–24. Albany: State University of New York Press.

Leal, Luis. 1995. "Magical Realism in Spanish American Literature." In *Magical Realism: Theory, History, Community*, edited by Lois Parkinson Zamora and Wendy B. Faris, 119–24. Durham, NC: Duke University Press.

Leclerc, Félix. 1946. *Pieds nus dans l'aube*. Montréal: Fides.

Lin, Ming-Hsun. 2010. "Fitting the Glass Slipper: A Comparative Study of the Princess's Role in the Harry Potter Novels and Films." In *Fairy Tale Films: Visions of Ambiguity*, edited by Pauline Greenhill and Sidney Eve Matrix, 79–98. Logan: Utah State University Press.

Lindgren, Anne-Li, Anna Sparrman, Tobias Samuelsson, and David Cardell. 2015. "Enacting (Real) Fiction: Materializing Childhoods in a Theme Park." *Childhood* 22 (2): 171–86.

Linnemann, Travis. 2015. "Capote's Ghosts: Violence, Media and the Spectre of Suspicion." *British Journal of Criminology* 55 (3): 514–33.

"Looking Through the Mirror." 2012. *Mirror Mirror*. DVD Extra.

Lukasiewicz, Tracie D. 2010. "The Parallelism of the Fantastic and the Real: Guillermo Del Toro's *Pan's Labyrinth*/El Laberinto Del Fauno and Neomagical Realism." In *Fairy Tale Films: Visions of Ambiguity*, edited by Pauline Greenhill and Sidney Eve Matrix, 60–78. Logan: Utah State University Press.

Magnanini, Suzanne. 2008. *Fairy-Tale Science: Monstrous Generation in the Tales of Straparola and Basile*. Toronto: University of Toronto Press.

"The Making of the Boxtrolls." 2015. *YouTube*, February 4. https://www.youtube.com/watch?v=PAK10UAAHIY

Mann, Susan Archer, and Ashly Suzanne Patterson, eds. 2016. *Reading Feminist Theory: From Modernity to Postmodernity*. New York: Oxford University Press.

Massie, Jean-Marc. 2002. "Réenchanter le monde par le conte." *Cap-aux-Diamants* (Spring): 46–49.

Mast, Gerald, and Bruce F. Kawin. 2006. *A Short History of the Movies*. 9th ed. New York: Pearson Longman.

Mauricie 2018–19. Official Tourist Guide. Mauricie, Quebec.

Mayo, Andrea E. 2014. "Sacrificing Youth for a Fabricated Humanity: Governance, Youth, and Onto-Theology in *The Cabin in the Woods*." *International Journal of Organization Theory & Behavior* 17 (2): 236–63.

Moen, Kristian. 2012. *Film and Fairy Tales: The Birth of Modern Fantasy*. London: I. B. Tauris.

Moine, Raphaëlle. 2008. *Cinema Genre/Cinema Genre*. Malden, MA: Blackwell.

Monaco, James. 2000. *How to Read a Film: The World of Movies, Media, and Multimedia Art, Technology, Language, History, Theory*. 3rd ed. New York: Oxford University Press.

Monteiro, George. 1960a. "Histoire De Montferrand: L'Athlete Canadien and Joe Mufraw." *Journal of American Folklore* 73 (287): 24–34.

———. 1960b. "One Very Strong Man." *Midwest Folklore* 10 (1): 23–25.

"MPAA Accused of Homophobia over R-Rated Sex-Free Gay Romance." 2014. *The Guardian*, August 22. https://www.theguardian.com/film/2014/aug/22/mpaa-love-is-strange-r-rated-gay-romance-no-sex

Mulvey, Laura. 1975. "Visual Pleasure and Narrative Cinema." *Screen* 16 (4): 6–18.

Muñoz, José Esteban. 2009. *Cruising Utopia: The Then and There of Queer Futurity*. New York: New York University Press.

Murray, Noel. 2017. "10 Great Animated Documentaries." *PBS: Independent Lens*, February 14. http://www.pbs.org/independentlens/blog/great-animated-documentaries/

Myers, Lindsay. 2012. "Whose Fear Is It Anyway? Moral Panics and 'Stranger Danger' in Henry Selick's *Coraline*." *The Lion and the Unicorn* 36 (3): 245–57.

Nagib, Lúcia, and Anne Jerslev, eds. 2014. *Impure Cinema: Intermedial and Intercultural Approaches to Film*. London: I. B. Tauris.

Naithani, Sadhana. 2006. *In Quest of Indian Folktales: Pandit Ram Gharib Chaube and William Crooke*. Bloomington: Indiana University Press.

———. 2010. *The Story-Time of the British Empire: Colonial and Postcolonial Folkloristics*. Jackson: University Press of Mississippi.

Newell, Kate. 2017. "Witches, Gauntlets, and Guns . . . Oh My! *Emerald City* (2017) and the Oz Adaptation Network." *Adaptation* 10 (3): 386–89.

Noyes, Dorothy. 2015. "Fairy-Tale Economics: Scarcity, Risk, Choice." *Narrative Culture* 2 (1): 1–25.

Och, Dana. 2015. "Beyond Surveillance: Questions of the Real in the Neopostmodern Horror Film." In *Style and Form in the Hollywood Slasher Film*, edited by Wickham Clayton, 195–212. Houndmills, Hampshire: Palgrave Macmillan.

O'Connell, Sean. 2015. "Will Cabin In The Woods 2 Ever Happen? Here's What Drew Goddard Says." *CinemaBlend*, September 13. https://www.cinemablend.com/new/Cabin-Woods-2-Ever-Happen-Here-What-Drew-Goddard-Says-82387.html

Odrowaz-Coates, Anna. 2016. "Lessons on Social Justice: A Pedagogical Reflection on the Educational Message of *The Boxtrolls*." *Education as Change* 20 (2): 67–85.

Ortiz, Fernando. 1995. *Cuban Counterpoint: Tobacco and Sugar*. Trans. Harriet De Onís. Durham, NC: Duke University Press.

"Paparmane." n.d. *Je parle québécois*. http://www.je-parle-quebecois.com/lexique/definition/paparmane.html

Pedersen, Erik. 2016. "Watchdog Group Chides Laika For 'White-Washing' *Kubo and the Two Strings*." *Deadline Hollywood*, August 23. http://deadline.com/2016/08/kubo-and-two-strings-protest-white-actors-japanese-characters-manaa-1201807914/

Pellerin, Fred. 2003. *Il faut prendre le taureau par les contes! Contes de village*. Montreal: Planète rebelle.

———. 2006. *Zoom sur Saint-Élie-De-Caxton: Sur la trace du merveilleux*. Saguenay, Quebec: Éditions Groupe photo média international.

Penuel, Arnold M. 1995. "A Contemporary Fairy Tale: García Márquez' 'El Rastro De Tu Sangre En La Nieve.'" *Studies in 20th & 21st Century Literature* 19 (2): 239–55.

Petri, Alexandra. 2016. "Terrifying Trump Fairy Tales." *Washington Post*, May 19. https://www.washingtonpost.com/blogs/compost/wp/2016/05/19/and-they-all-lived-happily-ever-after-if-fairy-tales-went-like-the-megyn-kelly-trump-interview/?utm_term=.5522a7ab22

Pikkov, Ülo. 2010. *Animasophy: Theoretical Writings on the Animated Film*. Translated by Eva Näripea. Tallinn: Estonian Academy of Arts.

Price, Brian L. 2012. "Heterotemporal *Mise-en-scène* in the Films of Luis Estrada." *Arizona Journal of Hispanic Cultural Studies* 16:259–74.

Protat, Zoe. 2013. "Croire à la magie/*Ésimésac* de Luc Picard." *Ciné-Bulles* 31 (1): 57.

Provencher, Normand. 2008. "Babine: La belle histoire d'un pays d'en haut." *Le Soleil*, November 22. https://www.lesoleil.com/archives/babine-la-belle-histoire-dun-pays-den-haut-3baf29f42d32df97318fef9ecb6100fc

Pugh, Tison. 2008. "'There Lived in the Land of Oz Two Queerly Made Men': Queer Utopianism and Antisocial Eroticism in L. Frank Baum's Oz Series." *Marvels & Tales* 22 (2): 217–39.

Qiu, Xiaoqing. 2017. "Cinderella in Chinatown: Seeking Identity and Cultural Values in *Year of the Fish*." *Marvels & Tales* 31 (2): 370–85.

Quigley, Paula. 2016. "When Good Mothers Go Bad: Genre and Gender in *The Babadook*." *Irish Journal of Gothic and Horror Studies* 15:57–75.

Radner, Joan N., and Susan Lanser. 1993. "Strategies of Coding in Women's Cultures." In *Feminist Messages: Coding in Women's Folk Culture*, edited by Joan N. Radner, 1–29. Urbana: University of Illinois Press.

Rafter, Nicole Hahn, and Michelle Brown. 2011. *Criminology Goes to the Movies: Crime Theory and Popular Culture*. New York: New York University Press.

Ramanathan, Geetha. 2006. *Feminist Auteurs: Reading Women's Film*. London: Wallflower.

Rankin, Walter. 2007. *Grimm Pictures: Fairy Tale Archetypes in Eight Horror and Suspense Films*. Jefferson, NC: McFarland.

Rea, Peter W., and David K. Irving. 2001. *Producing and Directing the Short Film and Video*. 2nd ed. Boston: Focal Press.

Reijnders, Stijn. 2011. *Places of the Imagination: Media, Tourism, Culture*. Farnham, UK: Ashgate.

Reijnders, Stijn, Leonieke Bolderman, Nicky Van Es, and Abby Waysdorf. 2015. "Locating Imagination: An Interdisciplinary Perspective on Literary, Film, and Music Tourism." *Tourism Analysis* 20 (3): 333–39.

Renée, V. 2016. "A Day in the Life of a Laika Studios Animator." *No Film School*, January 28. https://nofilmschool.com/2016/01/day-life-laika-studios-animator

Renner, Eric. 2009. *Pinhole Photography: From Historic Technique to Digital Application*. Amsterdam: Focal Press.

Rieder, John. 2017. *Science Fiction and the Mass Cultural Genre System*. Middletown, CT: Wesleyan University Press.

———. 2018. "Cinema Science Fiction." In *The Routledge Companion to Media and Fairy-Tale Cultures*, edited by Pauline Greenhill, Jill Terry Rudy, Naomi Hamer, and Lauren Bosc, 460–65. New York: Routledge.

Rieti, Barbara. 2009. *Making Witches: Newfoundland Traditions of Spells and Counterspells*. Montreal: McGill-Queen's University Press.

Risker, Paul. 2017. "Confronting Uncertainty: Jennifer Kent Discusses *The Babadook*." *Quarterly Review of Film and Video* 34 (1): 13–17.

Roberts, Adam. 2006. *Science Fiction*. 2nd ed. New York: Routledge.

Robin, Patricia. 2013. "*Ésimésac*." *Séquences* 282:60.

Robinson, Mike, and Hans Christian Andersen, eds. 2003. *Literature and Tourism: Essays in the Reading and Writing of Tourism*. London: Thomson.

Roe, Annabelle Honess. 2017. "Interjections and Connections: The Critical Potential of Animated Segments in Live Action Documentary." *Animation* 12 (3): 272–86.

Röhrich Lutz. 1991. *Folktales and Reality*. Translated by Peter Tokofsky. Bloomington: Indiana University Press.

Roper, Caitlin. 2016. "How Laika Crafted Kubo and the Two Strings' Epic Opener." *Wired*, August 19. https://www.wired.com/2016/08/art-of-kubo-video/

Rose, Steve. 2017. "Paddington, Go Home: Should Our Fantasy Stories Be More Truthful?" *The Guardian*, October 30. https://www.theguardian.com/film/2017/oct/30/paddington-go-home-should-fantasy-stories-be-more-truthful

Rösing, Lilian Munk. 2016. *Pixar with Lacan: The Hysteric's Guide to Animation*. London: Bloomsbury Academic.

Roy, Bruno, Christian Rioux, Denise Ménard, and Hélène Plouffe. 2008. "Félix Leclerc." *The Canadian Encyclopedia.* http://thecanadianencyclopedia.com/en/article/felix-leclerc/

Royle, Nicholas. 2003. *The Uncanny: An Introduction.* New York: Manchester University Press.

Rubin, Gayle. 1984. "Thinking Sex: Notes for a Radical Theory of the Politics of Sexuality." In *Pleasure and Danger: Exploring Female Sexuality*, edited by Carole S. Vance, 157–210. New York: Monthly Review Press.

Rudy, Jill Terry. 2018. "Broadcast (Radio and Television)." In *The Routledge Companion to Media and Fairy-Tale Cultures*, edited by Pauline Greenhill, Jill Terry Rudy, Naomi Hamer, and Lauren Bosc, 367–75. New York: Routledge.

"Saint-Élie: Ça existe vraiment!" n.d. *Saint-Élie: Ça existe vraiment!* http://tourisme.st-elie-de-caxton.ca/

"Saint-Élie-de-Caxton." 2017. *Wikipedia*, July 27. https://en.wikipedia.org/wiki/Saint-%C3%89lie-de-Caxton

"A Samurai's Son Makes Stop-Motion Magic With Music And Origami." 2016. *NPR*, August 19. https://www.npr.org/2016/08/19/490398272/a-samurais-son-makes-stop-motion-magic-with-music-and-origami

Santos-Phillips, Eva. 2003. "Power of the Body in the Novella 'The Incredible and Sad Tale of Innocent Eréndira and of Her Heartless Grandmother' and the Film 'Erendira.'" *Literature/Film Quarterly* 31 (2): 118–23.

Sawers, Naarah. 2010. "Building the Perfect Product: The Commodification of Childhood in Contemporary Fairy Tale Film." In *Fairy Tale Films: Visions of Ambiguity*, edited by Pauline Greenhill and Sidney Eve Matrix, 42–59. Logan: Utah State University Press.

Sawin, Patricia. 2014. "Things Walt Disney Didn't Tell Us (But at Which Rodgers and Hammerstein at Least Hinted): The 1965 Made-for-TV Musical of Cinderella." In *Channeling Wonder: Fairy Tales on Television*, edited by Pauline Greenhill and Jill Terry Rudy, 103–24. Detroit: Wayne State University Press.

Sayad, Cecilia. 2014. *Performing Authorship: Self-Inscription and Corporeality in the Cinema.* London: I. B. Tauris.

Scholes, Robert. 1975. *Structural Fabulation: An Essay on Fiction of the Future.* Bloomington: Indiana University Press.

Schultermandl, Silvia. 2011. "From Drug Mule to Miss America: American Exceptionalism and the Commodification of the 'Other' Woman in *María Full of Grace*." *Journal of American Culture* 34 (3): 275–88.

Schwabe, Claudia. 2014. "Getting Real with Fairy Tales: Magic Realism in *Grimm* and *Once Upon a Time*." In *Channeling Wonder: Fairy Tales on Television*, edited by Pauline Greenhill and Jill Terry Rudy, 294–315. Detroit: Wayne State University Press.

Seidel, Linda. 2013. *Mediated Maternity: Contemporary American Portrayals of Bad Mothers in Literature and Popular Culture.* Lanham, MD: Lexington Books.

Seifert, Lewis C. 2015a. "Introduction: Queer(ing) Fairy Tales." *Marvels & Tales* 29 (1): 15–20.

———. 2015b. Special Issue, "Queer(ing) Fairy Tales." *Marvels & Tales* 29 (1).
"Semaine québécoise de la déficience intellectuelle." n.d. *Société québécoise de la déficience intellectuelle.* https://www.sqdi.ca/fr/participer/semaine-quebecoise-de-la-deficience-intellectuelle/
"Separation at the Border: Children Wait in Cages at South Texas Warehouse." 2018. *The Guardian*, June 17. https://www.theguardian.com/us-news/2018/jun/17/separation-border-children-cages-south-texas-warehouse-holding-facility
Shadbolt, Jane. 2013. "Parallel Synchronized Randomness: Stop-Motion Animation in Live Action Feature Films." *Animation Studies* 8. https://journal.animationstudies.org/jane-shadbolt-parallel-synchronized-randomness-stop-motion-animation-in-live-action-feature-films/
Short, Sue. 2015. *Fairy Tale and Film: Old Tales with a New Spin.* Houndsmills, Hampshire: Palgrave Macmillan.
Smith, Kevin Paul. 2007. *The Postmodern Fairytale: Folkloric Intertexts in Contemporary Fiction.* New York: Palgrave Macmillan.
Snow, Alan. 2005. *Here Be Monsters!* New York: Atheneum Books for Young Readers.
Sobchack, Vivian. 1987. "Bringing It All Back Home: Family Economy and Generic Exchange." In *American Horrors: Essays on the Modern American Horror Film*, edited by Gregory Albert Waller, 175–94. Austin: University of Texas Press.
Soliño, María Elena. 2001. "From Perrault through Disney to Fina Torres: Cinderella Learns Spanish and Talks Back in *Celestial Clockwork*." *Letras Femeninas* 27 (2): 68–84.
Spencer, Leland G. 2014. "Performing Transgender Identity in the Little Mermaid: From Andersen to Disney." *Communication Studies* 65 (1): 112–27.
Squire, Shelagh J. 1996. "Literary Tourism and Sustainable Tourism: Promoting 'Anne of Green Gables' in Prince Edward Island." *Journal of Sustainable Tourism* 4 (3): 119–34.
Stafford, Roy. 2014. *The Global Film Book.* London: Routledge.
Stam, Robert. 2000. *Film Theory: An Introduction.* New York: Blackwell.
Stevens, E. Charlotte. 2010. "Telling the (Wrong) Story: The Disintegration of Transcultural Communication and Narrative in *The Fall*." *Cineaction* 80: 30–37.
Stevenson, Verity. 2019 "'We Will Keep On Fighting': Muslim Women Devastated by Appeal Court Decision to Uphold Bill 21." *CBC News*, December 13. https://www.cbc.ca/news/canada/montreal/court-of-appeal-bill-21-reaction-1.5394522
Stockton, Kathryn Bond. 2009. *The Queer Child, or Growing Sideways in the Twentieth Century.* Durham, NC: Duke University Press.
Stryker, Susan, and Aren Z. Aizura, eds. 2013. *The Transgender Studies Reader 2.* New York: Routledge.
Stryker, Susan, and Stephen Whittle, eds. 2006. *The Transgender Studies Reader.* New York: Routledge.
Sullivan, Nikki. 2003 *A Critical Introduction to Queer Theory.* New York: New York University Press.
Sundmark, Björn. 2017. "(Child) Reign of Terror: Dangerous Child Régimes." In *Child Autonomy and Child Governance in Children's Literature: Where Children*

Rule, edited by Christopher Kelen and Björn Sundmark, 96–106. New York: Routledge.

Suvin, Darko. 1988. *Metamorphoses of Science Fiction: On the Poetics and History of a Literary Genre*. New Haven, CT: Yale University Press.

"Takiyasha the Witch and the Skeleton Spectre" by Utagawa Kuniyoshi (c. 1844). n.d. *Wikipedia*. Accessed February 18, 2018. https://en.wikipedia.org/wiki/Takiyasha_the_Witch_and_the_Skeleton_Spectre#/media/File:Takiyasha_the_Witch_and_the_Skeleton_Spectre.jpg

Tallerico, Brian. 2016 "Movies Inspire Us to Dream: Travis Knight on 'Kubo and the Two Strings.'" *Roger Ebert.com*, August 16. http://www.rogerebert.com/interviews/movies-inspire-us-to-dream-travis-knight-on-kubo-and-the-two-strings

Tatar, Maria. 1987. *The Hard Facts of the Grimms' Fairy Tales*. Princeton, NJ: Princeton University Press.

———. 1992. *Off with Their Heads! Fairy Tales and the Culture of Childhood*. Princeton, NJ: Princeton University Press.

———. 2004. *The Annotated Brothers Grimm*. New York: Norton.

Tedman, Alison. 2017. "A Multifaceted Emerald (City): The Reinvention of Oz." *Fantastika Journal* 1 (1): 167–72.

Telotte, J. P. 2010. *Animating Space: From Mickey to Wall-E*. Lexington: University Press of Kentucky.

Teverson, Andrew. 2013. *Fairy Tale*. Abingdon, UK: Routledge.

———, ed. 2019. *The Fairy Tale World*. London: Routledge.

Thériault, Gaétan. 2008. *Saint-Élie: L'histoire de chez nous*. Saint-Élie-de-Caxton: privately published.

Thompson, Deborah L. 2013. "Not All Cinderellas Wear Glass Slippers: A Critical Analysis of Selected Cinderella Variants from the Black Perspective." In *Fairy Tales with a Black Consciousness: Essays on Adaptations of Familiar Stories*, edited by Vivian S. Yenika-Agbaw, Ruth McKoy Lowery, and Laretta Henderson, 1–12. Jefferson, NC: McFarland.

Thomson-Jones, Katherine. 2007. "The Literary Origins of the Cinematic Narrator." *British Journal of Aesthetics* 47 (1): 76–94.

Thornham, Sue. 1999. *Feminist Film Theory: A Reader*. New York: New York University Press.

Tiffin, Jessica. 2009. *Marvelous Geometry: Narrative and Metafiction in Modern Fairy Tale*. Detroit: Wayne State University Press.

Till, Benedikt, Arno Herberth, Gernot Sonneck, Peter Vitouch, and Thomas Niederkrotenthaler. 2013. "Who Identifies with Suicidal Film Characters? Determinants of Identification with Suicidal Protagonists of Drama Films." *Psychiatria Danubina* 25 (2): 158–62.

Todorov, Tzvetan. 1970. *The Fantastic: A Structural Approach to a Literary Genre*. Ithaca, NY: Cornell University Press.

Tresca, Don. 2014. "Lost in the Woods: Adapting 'Hansel and Gretel' for Television." In *Channeling Wonder: Fairy Tales on Television*, edited by Pauline Greenhill and Jill Terry Rudy, 64–81. Detroit: Wayne State University Press.

Turner, Kay. 2012. "Playing with Fire: Transgression as Truth in Grimms' 'Frau Trude.'" In *Transgressive Tales: Queering the Grimms*, edited by Kay Turner and Pauline Greenhill, 243–74. Detroit: Wayne State University Press.

———. 2015. "At Home in the Realm of Enchantment: The Queer Enticements of the Grimms' 'Frau Holle.'" *Marvels & Tales* 29 (1): 42–63.

Turner, Kay, and Pauline Greenhill, eds. 2012. *Transgressive Tales: Queering the Grimms*. Detroit: Wayne State University Press.

Tye, Diane. 1989. "Local Character Anecdotes: A Nova Scotia Case Study." *Western Folklore* 48 (3): 181–99.

———. 1994. "Multiple Meanings Called Cavendish: The Interaction of Tourism with Traditional Culture." *Journal of Canadian Studies* 29 (1): 122–34.

Uther, Hans-Jörg. 2004. *The Types of International Folktales: A Classification and Bibliography*. 3 vols. Helsinki: Academia Scientiarum Fennica.

Van den Oever, Annie, and Suzanne Human, eds. 2015. "Gestures of Healing: Themed Issue in Honour of Laura Mulvey." *De Arte* 52 (92): 6–81.

Vaz da Silva, Francisco. 2010. "The Invention of Fairy Tales." *Journal of American Folklore* 123 (490): 398–425.

Venable, Malcolm. 2017. "Emerald City Takes on Science and Magic at a Most Opportune Moment." *TV Guide*, January 20. http://www.tvguide.com/news/emerald-city-recap-science-and-magic/

Victor, Daniel. 2017. "Trump, Calling Journalists 'Sick People,' Puts Media on Edge." *New York Times*, August 23. https://www.nytimes.com/2017/08/23/business/media/trump-rally-media-attack.html

Warner, Marina. 1998. *No Go the Bogeyman: Scaring, Lulling, and Making Mock*. New York: Farrar, Straus, and Giroux.

———. 2014. *Once Upon a Time: A Short History of Fairy Tale*. Oxford: Oxford University Press.

Watercutter, Angela. 2015. "How the Tiny Studio Behind *Coraline* Became a Powerhouse." *Wired*, December 15. https://www.wired.com/2015/12/laika-coraline-boxtrolls-10-year-anniversary/

Weber, Eugen. 1981. "Fairies and Hard Facts: The Reality of Folktales." *Journal of the History of Ideas* 42 (1): 93–113.

Wells, Paul. 1998. *Understanding Animation*. London: Routledge.

———. 2006. *The Fundamentals of Animation*. Lausanne, Switzerland: AVA.

Wells, Paul, and Johnny Hardstaff. 2008. *Re-imagining Animation: The Changing Face of the Moving Image*. Lausanne, Switzerland: AVA.

Williams, Linda. 1984. "When the Woman Looks." In *Re-vision: Essays in Feminist Film Criticism*, edited by Mary Ann Doane, Patricia Mellencamp, and Linda Williams, 83–99. Frederick, MD: University Publications of America.

Wilson, Rawdon. 1995. "The Metamorphoses of Fictional Space: Magical Realism." In *Magical Realism: Theory, History, Community*, edited by Lois Parkinson Zamora and Wendy B. Faris, 209–34. Durham, NC: Duke University Press.

"Winnipeg Garment Industry Shrinking Rapidly: Union." 2007. *CBC News*, October

23. http://www.cbc.ca/news/canada/manitoba/winnipeg-garment-industry-shrinking-rapidly-union-1.678330

Wise, Damon. 2008. "Final Fantasy." *The Guardian*, October 4. https://www.theguardian.com/film/2008/oct/04/fall.tarsem.singh

Wisker, Gina. 2016. "Female Vampirism." In *Women and the Gothic: An Edinburgh Companion*, edited by Avril Horner and Sue Zlosnik, 150–65. Edinburgh: Edinburgh University Press.

Wright, Stuart A. 2005. "Satanic Cults, Ritual Abuse, and Moral Panic: Deconstructing a Modern Witch-Hunt." In *Witchcraft and Magic: Contemporary North America*, edited by Helen A. Berger, 120–36. Philadelphia: University of Pennsylvania Press.

Yamashiro, Aiko. 2011. "Review of *Year of the Fish*." *Marvels & Tales* 25 (1): 178–81.

Yenika-Agbaw, Vivian. 2013. "Introduction: Multiculturalism and Children's Literature." In *Fairy Tales with a Black Consciousness: Essays on Adaptations of Familiar Stories*, edited by Vivian S. Yenika-Agbaw, Ruth McKoy Lowery, and Laretta Henderson, 1–12. Jefferson, NC: McFarland.

Yenika-Agbaw, Vivian S., Ruth McKoy Lowery, and Laretta Henderson, eds. 2013. *Fairy Tales with a Black Consciousness: Essays on Adaptations of Familiar Stories*. Jefferson, NC: McFarland.

York, Lorraine M. 2007. *Literary Celebrity in Canada*. Toronto: University of Toronto Press.

Young, Katharine Galloway. 1987. *Taleworlds and Storyrealms: The Phenomenology of Narrative*. Dordrecht, Netherlands: Nijhoff.

Ziolkowski, Jan M. 2010. "Straparola and the Fairy Tale: Between Literary and Oral Traditions." *Journal of American Folklore* 123 (490): 377–97.

Zipes, Jack. 1983. *Fairy Tales and the Art of Subversion: The Classical Genre for Children and the Process of Civilization*. New York: Wildman Press.

———. 1996. "Towards a Theory of the Fairy-Tale Film: The Case of *Pinocchio*." *Lion and the Unicorn* 20 (1): 1–24.

———. ed. 2003. *The Complete Fairy Tales of the Brothers Grimm*. 3rd ed. New York: Bantam Books.

———. 2006. *Why Fairy Tales Stick: The Evolution and Relevance of a Genre*. New York: Routledge

———. 2011. *The Enchanted Screen: The Unknown History of Fairy-Tale Films*. New York: Routledge.

———. 2012. *The Irresistible Fairy Tale: The Cultural and Social History of a Genre*. Princeton: Princeton University Press.

———, ed. 2013. *The Golden Age of Folk and Fairy Tales: From the Brothers Grimm to Andrew Lang*. Indianapolis: Hackett.

Zipes, Jack, Pauline Greenhill, and Kendra Magnus-Johnston, eds. 2016. *Fairy-Tale Films Beyond Disney: International Perspectives*. New York: Routledge.

INDEX

abandonment, 127–28, 130, 135–36, 140, 144–46, 152
ability, 35. *See also* disability
abuse: child, 142–44, 150, 152, 156; sexual, 135–36, 205
adoption, 146–47. *See also* family; stepmother
A.I.: Artificial Intelligence (Spielberg), 18, 144–47
After the Ball (Garrity), 198–201, 224
Ahmed, Sara, 229–30
animation, 64–65; drawn, 53; hybrid, 60–61, 210–11; stop-motion, 34–39; rotoscoped, 213–14; zoetrope, 80–81. *See also* CGI
Anne of Green Gables, 119–20, 121–22
Another Cinderella Story (Santostefano), 197
anti-racist, 15, 91
apocalypse, 28
Astrid Lindgren's World, Sweden, 122
ATU (Aarne-Thompson-Uther tale types), 14. *See also specific tale-type names*
ATU 980D, 20–21
Audition (Picard), 102
auteur, 16n5, 28, 65, 138, 155
authenticity, 27–28, 39–40, 73, 167
Avengers Grimm (Inman), 195n4
Ayoade, Richard, 53–57, 59–60, 63

Baba Yaga, 213–17
Babadook, The (Kent), 24, 163–64, 166, 170, 183–88
Babine (Picard), 28, 95, 99, 103–14
Bacchilega, Cristina, 14, 92–93, 151n7, 152, 193
Bad Times at the El Royale (Goddard), 155n9
Beauty and the Beast (Condon), 84
behavior modeling, 23
Benga, Ota, 76
Black Field (Esterhazy), 36n3
Blue Bird, The (Tourneur), 73
Bollywood, 67, 72, 83–84

book as film prop, 107, 148, 150–52, 170, 179–82, 184–88
Boxtrolls, The (Annable and Stacchi), 34, 47–58
Bram Stoker's Dracula (Coppola), 69n5
breadcrumbs (trail of), 129, 134, 148
Brothers Grimm, The (Gilliam), 20
Buffy the Vampire Slayer (TV), 128–29
Bumblebee (Knight), 34
Butler, David, 23–25

Cabin in the Woods, The (Goddard), 137, 155–58
camera obscura, 73, 92
Cannibal Holocaust (Deodato), 136
cannibalism, 127, 134–38, 178, 182
capitalism, 15, 117, 132, 202; anti- 65, 155, 158; and bodies 144. *See also* career focus; class; labor
career focus, 195–201, 204, 213, 224. *See also* capitalism; class
casting: gender-swapped, 216; multiple roles with same actor; 135, 152–53; race and, 58–60, 82–83, 85; representation in, 79, 202, 204, 211. *See also* transgender
Castle (TV), 18
Cavendish, Prince Edward Island, 121–22
Cell, The (Tarsem), 71
Cenerentolo (Paci), 209
CGI, 38–39, 47, 79, 80, 84
Chairy Tale, A (McLaren and Jutra), 44n5
Chance, Maia, 19–20
Charette, Quebec, 116, 118
Chicken Run (Lord and Park), 33–34
chronotope, 82. *See also* heterotemporality
"Cinderella" (ATU 510A), 14, 191–92, 194–207, 209. *See also specific film titles*
Cinderella (Méliès), 73
Cinderella (Beckman), 205

259

Cinderella (Lydon), 196n8
Cinderella: Single Again (Benz), 205–6
Cinderella Pact/Lying to Be Perfect (Harvey), 195n4, 204–5
Cinderella Story, A (Rosman), 197
Cinderella Story: If the Shoe Fits, A (Johnston), 197
Cinderella Story: Once Upon a Song, A (Santostefano), 197
"Cinderfella" (Hall), 209
Cinderfella (Tashlin), 207–9, 223
Cinderfellas, 195–96, 202, 207–9
cisgender, 191–92. *See also* transgender
class: hidden, 202; lower/working, 16n6, 18, 77, 153, 195, 205, 213, 217; middle, 142, 204n12; upper, 29, 90, 196. *See also* capitalism; career focus; labor
coding, 43, 132, 135
Collins, Lily, 78–79, 84
Collins, Patricia Hill, 92, 167, 193
community, 46, 65, 116–17
coping, 168, 174, 178, 182–83, 187–88
costumes, film, 81–82, 85
Coraline (Selick), 34, 39–43
Corpse Bride (Burton and Johnson), 34, 38
Crenshaw, Kimberlé Williams, 16n6, 193
critical crime films, 167–68, 188–89
critical race theory, 192–93
crime, 19–20, 16. *See also* critical crime films; murder

dance, 34, 83–84, 197, 206, 208, 217–18
Dancehall Queen (Elgood and Letts), 24, 213, 217–21, 224
Darwin, Charles, 76
deception: control and, 77; disguise and, 199–200, 208, 219–21; illusion and, 75–76; intention required for, 13–14, 91–92
decolonial, 15, 84, 193, 223
Devil Wears Prada, The (Frankel), 197, 201
disability, 15, 16n6, 75–76, 114, 204. *See also* ability
disbelief, suspension of, 51, 199, 208
disclosure (critical crime film process), 176, 182, 187–88
Disney: as canon, 27, 130, 136, 223; contrast with, 21, 84, 138, 206, 210, 224–25. *See also specific films*
District 31 (TV), 114
divorce, 174, 204
documentary, 26, 36, 111, 174
"Donkey Skin" (ATU 510B), 135, 223

DysEnchanted (Miller), 205
dystopia, 137, 155

Edelman, Lee, 131–32, 140–41, 143–44, 148
editing (film), 26, 42, 66, 75, 84
El laberinto del fauno (Pan's Labyrinth; del Toro), 18, 24, 25–26
Emerald City (Tarsem), 67–68, 84–91, 92
Enchanted (Lima), 198
equality, 16n6, 57, 131, 192, *see also* class
Eréndira (Guerra), 103
Ésimésac (Picard), 28, 95, 103–7, 114–17
etiology (critical crime film process), 174, 178, 182–83
Ever After: A Cinderella Story (Tennant), 20
Exorcist, The (Friedkin), 138, 188

fairy-tale origin studies, 19–21
Fall, The (Tarsem), 18, 67–68, 71–78, 91–92
family, 127, 131, 144–45; blended, 169, 171–73; custody, 160; nuclear hetero-, 147, 160–62, 166; queer, 149–50. *See also* father; mother; stepmother
fantasy, 23–25, 167, 183–84
fat/fatness, 204–5, 206
father, 78, 81, 134, 140; as creator, 147–48; estranged, 198–99; death of, 152, 169; neglectful, 146
feminist/feminism, 15, 92; and ATU 720, 163–64; backlash against, 139–40; motives, 201; standpoint and, 193; waves of, 195, 203
final girl, 156
First Nations, 15, 74–75. *See also* Indigenous
Flashdance (Lyne), 197
food, 116, 127–28, 134, 143–44
fourth wall, 49–50
Freeway (Bright), 141
Freeway 2: Confessions of a Trickbaby (Bright), 141–44
French Connection, The (Friedkin), 138
Frost, Nick, 53–56, 60, 63, 79
Frozen (Buck and Lee), 205

García Márquez, Gabriel, 103–4
gaze (male, female), 164–65, 194–95
gender, 200. *See also* power; gendered; sexuality
genre, 24, 35–36n3, 52, 93, 130, 138. *See also specific genres*
Gia (Cristofer), 195n4
gingerbread, 128–29, 134–35, 153–54
"Glass Axe, The" (ATU 480), 193

gnome, 95, 97, 99, 119–21, 124
"Goldener" (ATU 314), 13n1
"Goldilocks and the Three Bears" (ATU 171), 205
Grimm, Brothers, 20, 138–39, 223–24
Grimm (TV), 104
Grimm (van Warmerdam), 133n5
Groundhog Day (Ramis), 35
Guardian, The (Friedkin), 138–41

H & G (Esterhazy), 18–19, 130
Halberstam, Jack, 65, 127, 131–32, 141, 155
Hall, Todrick, 209
Hand of the Artist, The (Booth), 44n5
Hand That Rocks the Cradle, The (Hanson), 140
"Hansel and Gretel" (ATU 327A), 14, 127–31, 134–38. *See also related film titles*
Hansel and Gretel (Burton), 135
Hansel and Gretel (Faerie Tale Theatre) (Frawley), 135
Hansel & Gretel (Tunnicliffe), 135
Hansel & Gretel (Ferrante), 133
Hansel & Gretel: An Appalachian Version (Davenport), 135
Hansel & Gretel: Warriors of Witchcraft (DeCoteau), 133
Hansel & Gretel: Witch Hunters (Wirkola), 133
Hansel & Gretel Get Baked (Journey), 17, 153–55
Hansel vs. Gretel (Demaree), 133
happy ending, 69, 83, 205–6, 229–30; escapism and, 21, 77; for gay romance, 210–11; immigrant, 212–14, 223; rejecting simple, 104, 143
Hard Candy (Slade), 18
Harry Potter (character), 133, 209
helper figure: dangerous, 188, 216–17; endings for, 83; gay, 196n8, 201–2, 207; racially diverse, 211
Henjel gwa Geuretel (Hansel & Gretel; Pil-sung Yim), 150–53
heterospatiality, 67–70, 71–78, 92
heterotemporality, 67–71, 78–84, 92, 105, 109–12
Hoffman, Kathryn A., 22
Hollywood: conventions of, 25, 58, 194–95; independence from, 23, 37–38, 72, 164, 205
Holton, C. Lewis, 17
homophobia, 43, 209, 179
horror, 134–38, 139–41, 153–60, 207; elements in other genres, 39, 43, 47, 51, 63, 144; genre conventions, 52, 166, 170n11, 179, 190; positive influence of, 183–84
House with a Clock in Its Walls, The (Roth), 20
"Household of the Witch" (ATU 334), 197n10, 217
human exceptionalism, 146–47, 149
hypertext, 17n8, 39, 52
hypotext, 17, 18, 224

I, Robot (Proyas), 137, 147–50
Il professor Cenerentolo (Professor Cenerentolo; Pieraccioni), 209
Immortals (Tarsem), 71n6
immigration, 74–75, 211–14, 221–23, 229–30. *See also* transcultural
impossible, 34, 65–67. *See also* reality; uncanny
Indigenous, 70–71. *See also* First Nations
interdiction, 215–16, 222–23
intersectionality, 16n6, 192–93, 209–23
intertext, 18–19. *See also* hypertext, hypotext
Invisible Ink (Fleischer), 44n5
Ishioka, Eiko, 81–82
IT Crowd, The (TV), 55

Jackson, Rosemary, 27
Jameson, Fredric, 103
Jersey Girl (Smith), 198
Jin-Rô (Jin-Roh: The Wolf Brigade; Okiura), 130–31n2
Joosen, Vanessa, 19, 104, 128–29
"Juniper Tree, The" (ATU 720), 14, 18, 135, 147, 163–71, 177. *See also specific film titles*
Juniper Tree, The (Keene), 163, 166, 169, 171–74
justice, 28, 33, 107, 152, 190

"King Thrushbeard" (ATU 900), 197n10
Koca Dünya (Big Big World; Erdem), 130
Kubo and the Two Strings (Knight), 24, 34, 58–64
Kubrick, Stanley, 52, 144

labor, 55, 205, 216. *See also* career focus, class
LAIKA Entertainment, 14, 34, 37–39, 58–60. *See also specific titles*
legend, 94, 100
lesbian, 133, 143, 210–12, 223–24. *See also under* vampire
local character, 106–7
lutin. See gnome

Le mythe de la bonne mère (The Myth of the Good Mother; Lanctôt), 188
Le piège d'Issoudun (The Issoudun Exit/Trap; Lanctôt), 18, 163, 166, 169–70
Les rois mongols (Cross My Heart; Picard), 102
Lights Out (Sandberg), 170n12
Little Black Dress (Noah and Noah), 205n15
Little Mermaid, The (Musker and Clements), 27n14
"Little Red Riding Hood" (ATU 333), 130, 205
L'odyssée d'Alice Tremblay (Alice's Odyssey; Filiatrault), 202–4

magic: film as, 27; illusion, 45, 51; and science, 15, 84–91; removal from fairy tales, 19–20; wonder and, 211, 230. *See also* animation, mechanical magic and
magic realism, 23n10, 95–96, 103–4, 107–8, 115
Magnanini, Suzanne, 21–23
Maid in Manhattan (Wang), 197–98
Maleficent (Stromberg), 92
Mama (Muschietti), 158–60
Maria Full of Grace (Marston), 213, 221–23, 224
Marriage, 78–79, 195–98, 210–11. *See also* divorce; family
McConaughey, Matthew, 58–59
Mean Girls (Waters), 198
Mécaniques célestes (Celestial Clockwork; Torres), 193, 210–13, 224
Méliès, Georges, 187
millennial mainstream films, 196–97
Minyeo-neun goerowo (200 Pounds Beauty; Kim), 195n4, 204
Mirror Mirror (Tarsem), 67–68, 78–84, 92
Miss Congeniality (Petrie), 198, 201
Missing Link (Butler), 60
Mister Cinderella (Sedgwick), 209
Moongirl (Selick), 34
mortality, 68, 92, 108, 120, 178–79. *See also* murder; suicide
Moth Diaries, The (Harron), 163, 166, 169, 170, 178–83
Monster, 63–64, 89. *See also* witch
Mother, 95, 115, 139–40; abjection, 137; anguish of, 184, 188, 217–18; dead, 158–60, 173, 177; murderous, 164, 174–78, 185–87
Mr. Cinderella (Idham), 209
Mr. Cinderella 2 (Din CJ), 209
Mrs. Doubtfire (Columbus), 200
multimedia, 42

Mulvey, Laura, 164
Muñoz, José Esteban, 127, 132–33, 155, 229–30
murder: by children, 135, 150–52; of children, 18, 164, 169–70; mystery, 19; ostension and, 94; types of, 141–43; of women, 34, 146
music: diegetic, 47–49, 78, 83–84, 207, 212; non-diegetic, 42, 70, 72, 109–14, 180, 185–86; as story element, 58
My Big Fat Greek Wedding (Zwick), 198

Neighbours (McLaren), 44n5
Night of the Hunter, The (Laughton), 130
Nightmare Before Christmas, The (Selick), 34
9 (Brie, Canuel, Duval, Labrèche, Lanctôt, Picard, Roy, Tessier, and Trogi), 102
No Fairy Fairytale: The Cinderella Nightmare, A (Pampel), 206–7
Noyes, Dorothy, 23

"Old Woman in the Forest, The" (ATU 442), 181n14
Once Upon A Time (TV), 104
oral tradition, 16–17, 19, 69, 99–101
ostension, 14n2, 94–97, 99, 102, 122–23

paparmane, 95–96, 105, 120
ParaNorman (Butler), 34, 43–46
pastiche, 69n5, 198, 202–3, 205
Path, The (Tale of Tales), 17–18
patriarchy, 127–28, 137–38, 189, 196n8, 203. *See* power, gendered
Peau d'âne (Donkey Skin; Demy), 223
Pellerin, Fred, 16, 97–101, 230; as source for tales, 28, 95
Picard, Luc, 28, 102
Pieds nus dans l'aube (Barefoot at Dawn; Leclerc), 100
"Pinocchio," 144–46
pluralism, 91
Poslední motýl (The Last Butterfly; Kachyna), 130
postmodern: meta-awareness and, 39, 55, 155, 210; open-endedness, 168; skepticism and, 15, 70
power: audience, 166; control and 51–52, 63, 77, 92; gendered, 140, 141, 189, 208–9, 219–21
Power, Pius, 13, 230
preternatural, 163–64, 165–66, 170–71; control over, 189–90; vision, 175–78, 179–82, 185–87
Pretty Woman (Marshall), 195n4, 196–97
Prince and Me, The (Coolidge), 198

Princess Diaries, The (Marshall), 198
Psycho (Hitchcock), 143

queer failure, 28, 127, 132, 140–41, 155, 157–58
queer theory, 192, 223–24, 229
realist drama, 95, 104, 166, 169–70, 189–90
reality: compatibility with magic, 17; defamiliarized, 44, 57, 61–63, 73; of fairy tales, 21–23, 128; film, 23–29; hybrid, 122; in metaphor, 15, 20–21, 229. *See also* magic realism; ostension; preternatural; uncanny
Rieti, Barbara, 163, 164, 189, 190
Roberts, Julia, 78–80
Röhrich, Lutz: reality and, 15
Ruka (The Hand; Trnka), 44n5
"Rumpelstiltskin" (ATU 500), 181n14

Saint-Élie-de-Caxton, Quebec, 94–99. *See also Babine* (Picard); *Ésimésac* (Picard)
Sapsorrow (*The StoryTeller*; Barron), 223
science: and magic, 15, 84–91; shifting knowledge and, 22–23
science fiction, 63–64, 131, 136–38, 144–50
Scheherazade, 204
Schwabe, Claudia, 23n10, 104
Secret of My Succe$s, The (Ross), 196
Self/less (Tarsem), 71n6
sex work, 145, 161, 195n5, 196–97, 213
sexuality/sexual orientation, 201–2; bi-, 201; female, 203, 223; intersex, 223. *See also* helper figure, gay; homophobia; lesbian; power, gendered; queer theory; transgender
She's the Man (Fickman), 201
"Shift of Sex, The" (ATU 514), 230
Shining, The (Kubrick), 52
Silence of the Lambs, The (Demme), 143
Sin-de-rel-la (Cinderella; Bong), 195n4
"Sinalela" (McMullin), 223
"Sleeping Beauty" (ATU 410), 34, 43, 104, 122, 195n4, 205. *See also specific titles*
slut shaming, 203–4n12
Smith, Kevin Paul: hypotext interactions and, 17–18
"Snow White" (ATU 709), 78–79, 203–4, 205
Snow White (Berz), 79
Snow White: A Deadly Summer (DeCoteau), 133n6
Snow White: The Fairest of Them All (Thompson), 79
Snow White: A Tale of Terror (Cohn), 79

Snow White and the Huntsman (Sanders), 79–80, 92
Snow White and the Seven Dwarfs (*Faerie Tale Theatre*) (Medak), 79
social change, 91–93
sound 174. *See also* music
special effects (in film), 36, 43. *See also* animation; CGI; editing
stepmother: beloved, 146–47; evil, 78–79, 127, 168–69, 134–35, 197–99, 207; protective, 160; transgender, 143; witch, 130, 140, 141, 161
StoryTeller, The (TV), 223
subversion, 25
stop-motion, 34–39, 42–43, 44–45, 57
Storyrealm, 70, 77, 82, 86
suicide: attempted, 174; ideation and, 71, 76, 182–83, 184, 188; paternal, 170, 178–80; suspected, 148
"Suit the Colour of the Clouds, The" (Pius Power), 13
Sweet Hereafter, The (Egoyan), 52

Takei, George, 59
Taleworld, 69–70, 75–77, 82, 86
Tarsem, 16, 66–67, 71–73. *See also Emerald City*; *The Fall*; *Mirror Mirror*
Tatar, Maria, 128, 168–69, 177
10th Kingdom, The (Carson and Wise), 205n15
Theron, Charlize, 58–59, 79–80
Thief of Bagdad, The (Walsh), 73
"Three Stolen Princesses, The" (ATU 301), 13n1
Tideland (Gilliam), 24, 25–26
Tiffin, Jessica, 27, 66–67
Todorov, Tzvetan, 25–26, 165
"Tom Thumb" (ATU 700), 135
tourism, 95, 97, 117–24
trailers (for films), 47–52
transcultural, 67–68, 70–72, 76, 169. *See also* immigration
transformation: internal, 221–22; makeover, 194–95, 207, 214–17; physical, 199, 218–20
transgender, 27n14, 85, 141; parent, 135, 143–44; theory, 192; in traditional tales, 22, 230
translation, 101, 119
Trap for Cinderella, A (Softley), 195n4
Turner, Kay, 133
Tye, Diane, 106, 122
typecasting, 114. *See also* casting

uncanny, 25–26, 35–36, 166, 176n13, 189. *See also* reality, defamiliarized
utopia, 65, 132–33, 137, 229–31

vampire, 170; lesbian vampire, 178–80, 182–83
video game, 17
vision. *See under* preternatural

Wallace, Alfred Russel, 76
Waltz with Bashir (Folman), 36
Warner, Marina, 19, 21, 168–69
Weber, Eugen, 128
Wells, Paul, 34
West Side Story (Robbins and Wise), 52
What Lies Beneath (Zemeckis), 133
whitewashing. *See* casting, race and
witch, 20, 28–29, 43, 140; audience as, 176, 182, 188–90; science and, 89–91; Newfoundland, 101, 104, 109, 112–16, 163–64; queer, 154–55; sisterhood and, 85–86; transgender, 141–43, 160, 216; vision, 164, 166, 171–73

witnessing (critical crime film process), 173, 176, 182, 186
Wizard of Oz, The (Fleming), 84–85, 143, 205
Wolves of Kromer, The (Gould), 201–10
wonder: animation and, 67; the ordinary and, 29, 73, 76, 99, 124, 212; politics of, 14, 93; science and, 84–85; stories, 15–16, 34, 103, 105
Woodsman, The (Kassell), 16
Working Girl (Nichols), 195–96

Year of the Fish (Kaplan), 213–17, 224
Yo ho ho (Heskiya), 71

Zipes, Jack, 14, 17, 127–28, 133–135, 205, 230
zoetrope, 80–81, 92

ABOUT THE AUTHOR

Pauline Greenhill is professor of women's and gender studies at the University of Winnipeg, Manitoba, Canada. Her most recent books are *Clever Maids, Fearless Jacks, and a Cat: Fairy Tales from a Living Oral Tradition* (with Anita Best and Martin Lovelace) and *The Routledge Companion to Media and Fairy-Tale Studies* (with Jill Terry Rudy, Naomi Hamer, and Lauren Bosc). Her fairy-tale research has been published in *Feral Feminisms*; *Law, Culture, and the Humanities*; *Marvels & Tales*; *Narrative Culture*; *Studies in European Cinema*; and *Theoretical Criminology*, among others.

www.ingramcontent.com/pod-product-compliance
Lightning Source LLC
Chambersburg PA
CBHW051538230426
43669CB00015B/2645